Western Society and Culture

西方社会与文化

◎主 编 王小海

南京大学出版社

图书在版编目(CIP)数据

西方社会与文化:英文/王小海主编. -- 南京:
南京大学出版社,2021.7
　ISBN 978-7-305-24576-3

Ⅰ. ①西… Ⅱ. ①王… Ⅲ. ①西方国家－概况－英文
Ⅳ. ①D75

中国版本图书馆 CIP 数据核字(2021)第 113867 号

出版发行	南京大学出版社
社　　址	南京市汉口路 22 号　　邮　编　210093
出 版 人	金鑫荣

书　　名　西方社会与文化
主　　编　王小海
责任编辑　裴维维　　　　　　　编辑热线　025-83592123

照　　排	南京南琳图文制作有限公司
印　　刷	南京玉河印刷厂
开　　本	787×1092　1/16　印张 15.75　字数 430 千
版　　次	2021 年 7 月第 1 版　2021 年 7 月第 1 次印刷

ISBN 978-7-305-24576-3
定　　价　45.00 元

网址:http://www.njupco.com
官方微博:http://weibo.com/njupco
官方微信号:njupress
销售咨询热线:(025) 83594756

* 版权所有,侵权必究
* 凡购买南大版图书,如有印装质量问题,请与所购
　图书销售部门联系调换

前 言

本教材以文化研究理论成果以及课程思政理念为指导,以问题为导向,章节结构编排合理,内容与时俱进,有助于促进和提升外语学习者的语言学习以及专业课程的学习,可为将来的个人发展等打下坚实的文化基础。本教材的特色主要体现在以下几个方面:

一、基于文化理论研究成果的文化课教材

首先,选择英美两个讲英语的国家,与使用本教材学生所学的外语一致。学习一门外语,须对讲该语言的国家的社会与文化有一定程度的认识和了解。对文化的了解反过来也会促进语言的学习,两者是相辅相成的关系。其次,英国是一个历史悠久的欧洲国家,美国是一个历史短暂的北美国家,一长一短,但它们在当今世界舞台上都发挥着举足轻重的作用,可以视为欧洲和北美的代表,通过解剖这两个国家能够让学生对西方世界的社会和文化有一个总体的认识与了解。再次,英美两国普遍存在的种族歧视、枪支暴力以及其他社会不公平等问题也是整个西方世界的一个缩影。透过对这些社会问题的剖析,本教材能够帮助我们更加客观、全面地看待真实的西方世界。

贯穿文化课教学的主线是以对西方世界的认识和了解为出发点,但以加深对中国文化的深入了解和自信为落脚点和归宿,为实现学贯中西的目标奠定基础。

二、以融入课程思政元素为亮点,集知识性、趣味性和思辨性于一体的文化课教材

把中国文化融入西方文化教材编写和课程教学是我们重点考虑的一个因素,这是本教材的一大亮点,也是与其他同类教材的不同之处,具有一定的创新性。融入中国文化在一定程度上可解决中国学生常出现的"中国文化失语症"的问题,至少这样做是一次积极的尝试。

进入新时代,培养什么人、怎样培养人、为谁培养人成为中国高等教育必须回答的根本问题。为贯彻落实习近平总书记在学校思想政治理论课教师座谈会上提出的指示精神,课程思政需要在传授课程知识的基础上引导学生将所学到的知识和技能转化为内在的德性和素养,注重将学生个人发展与社会发展、国家发展结合起来,帮助学生解答思想困惑、价值困惑,激发其为国家学习、为民族学习的热情和动力,帮助其在创造社会价值过程中明确自身

价值和社会定位。在此背景下，文化课的教学责无旁贷，因为它站在西方文化与中国文化的交汇点上，直面的是与中国文化不同的西方文化，更应该积极主动发挥课程思政的引领和示范作用，帮助我们的学生夯实中国文化的根基，树立正确看待西方文化的态度，坚定中国文化价值观的立场，自觉肩负起向世界讲好中国故事的重任。

三、以扩大学生知识结构和提升阅读能力为目标的百科全书式文化课教材

社会与文化，是两个内涵均极其丰富的概念。人类的生产、消费、娱乐、教育等，都属于社会活动的范畴。而学术界给文化所下的定义有数百种之多，对它的分类也存在着若干不同的标准。我国著名语言与文化研究专家胡文仲教授认为："从语言教学和应用的需要来考察，文化可分为知识文化和交际文化两大类。属前者的有语言国家的历史、地理、经济……而属于后者的，则有词语文化及其他广泛的内容：小到能见可闻的衣食住行、家庭起居、婚丧生礼、节日喜庆、禁忌讳语、风俗习惯、生活方式、通讯办法、信息传媒；大至抽象的行为规范、伦理标准、人生信仰、价值观念等等。"(1994:45)

本教材涵盖了上述两国地理、历史、文学、节假日、饮食、体育、住房、传媒、建筑、艺术、电影、教育、经济、外交等主题的内容，可谓一部小型的百科全书，在帮助学生了解西方文化的同时又有利于其知识结构的扩展和完善。特别是，教材各单元提供的关于中国文化介绍的短文可以作为学生的课后补充阅读材料，既能从中了解更多的关于中国的社会与文化方面的内容，又能促进阅读能力的提升。

四、体例结构设计独特，内容适中

本教材采用了"总—分—合、比"的体例结构。这是本教材在结构设计方面的创新之处，也是与其他教材的不同之处。其他教材一般采用"先英后美"的体例结构，但往往在实际操作中会出现多种问题，譬如：讲完英国部分全部章节后，一个学期所剩授课时间已经不多，导致美国部分章节内容的讲解不足，出现"一边倒"的问题。经过几年对教材试用版的运行与检验，本教材克服了上述弊病，新颖的体例结构既保证了英美两国的相关内容得到均衡介绍，又能异中求同，并为融入中国文化的内容提供切入点，更加方便教与学。此外，每个单元的学习内容适中，便于教师的课堂教学和学生在课后开展探究式等学习。

五、实现与学生个人发展以及自我价值等的无缝对接

本教材中讨论的话题涉及地理、历史等基本国情信息以及饮食、艺术、电影等热门话题，可全面提升学生的文化素养，为学生将来的个人发展打下基础。

使用说明

一、教材总体结构、涵盖的主题以及提炼出的课程思政元素说明

本教材共编写了18个单元。正常情况下,每一周学习一个单元,足够供一个学期使用。

为了让英美两个国家得到均衡介绍并且体现英国和美国文化的共性与特殊性,并方便与中国文化展开对比,本教材采用了"总—分—合、比"的体例结构。这是本教材在结构设计方面的创新之处,也是与其他教材的不同之处。

第一单元"Introduction: Language, Culture and Communication"为"总"——从总体上介绍什么是文化及其分类与功能,什么是西方文化,什么是中国文化,语言与文化的紧密关系,并以中、英语言中独特的"文化内涵词汇"为例加以说明,让学生对文化、语言与文化学习的关系有一个初步的认识和了解,调动学生学习本门课程的积极性。

接下来是"分"——英、美各安排4个单元,共8个单元,分别介绍两国各自独特的国情信息、历史和文学等主题。

紧随其后的9个单元,是"合、比"——英美两国共有且可以相互比较的主题,包括节假日、饮食、体育运动、电影、艺术、博物馆、建筑、习俗与传统、教育体制、大众传媒、经济、社会万象等主题。教师既可引导学生展开英美两国间的对比,加深对两国的了解,又可以把英美两国与中国展开对比,揭示中国社会与文化的特色及优越性。

本教材涵盖的主题、单元框架结构及提炼出的课程思政元素图示如下:

	Introduction: Language, Culture and Communication		
The UK (英国)	1. Country Profile	5. Country Profile	The US (美国)
	课程思政元素:中国的基本国情信息——壮美的河山、勤劳勇敢的中国人民、和谐团结的多民族大家庭等		
	2. British History (1)	6. American History (1)	
	3. British History (2)	7. American History (2)	
	课程思政元素:中国悠久的历史		
	4. British Literature	8. American Literature	
	课程思政元素:中国的唐诗宋词、当代文学成就等		

9. Holidays and Festivals	课程思政元素:中国节假日的由来、意义等
10. Food and Drink	课程思政元素:中国独具特色的饮食文化
11. Sports and Films	课程思政元素:中国的体育运动及电影发展等
12. Houses, Arts, Museums and Architecture	课程思政元素:博物馆及中国特色的建筑(例如:中国园林等),中国的艺术
13. Customs and Traditions	课程思政元素:独具中国特色的习俗与传统
14. Educational System	课程思政元素:中国的教育体制
15. Mass Media	课程思政元素:大众传媒,如何提升中国的传媒力量
16. Economy	课程思政因素:中国经济发展成就等
17. Social Kaleidoscope	课程思政元素:"一带一路"倡议、构建和谐社会、人类命运共同体

二、各单元结构说明

本教材每一个单元都涵盖了如下部分,各个部分的设计用意说明如下:

❑ **In this unit you will learn about**

"从本单元中你将学习到以下主要内容"——这个部分提醒教师和学生,该单元将回答几个核心问题,后续的教学与学习可围绕这些问题展开。

❑ **Vocabulary**

"要词"——提供单元正文阅读材料部分以及补充阅读资料"更多地了解中国"(Understanding more about China)部分一些超过一二年级学生词汇量范围的生词的简要中文释义,帮助学生清除阅读中的文字障碍。本部分所列单词以字母顺序排列,方便学生快速查找。当然,每个学生应根据自己的词汇量等实际情况,自觉动手查阅相关生词的释义,积极提升自己的阅读能力和水平。

❑ **Key Sentences**

"精句"——一些从单元正文以及补充阅读材料部分提取出来的佳句,并配有中文翻译。一方面,方便学生在课前的"热身练习"环节使用,另一方面供学生在课后及日常学习、生活中模仿使用。既能加深学生对中西文化的认识和理解,又能学会一些英语表达方式,便于在对外交流中向对方传播中国文化时参考使用。当然,这只能起一个抛砖引玉的作用,建议学生们根据自己的实际情况,利用各种渠道搜集更多的类似的表达方式,提升自己用英语讲述中国文化的能力。

❑ Warm-up Exercise

"热身练习"——在正式学习某单元前,由教师组织学生开展热身练习,为下一步的教学与学习发现问题,打好基础。

❑ Introduce China in English

"用英语讲述中国"——学生可围绕教材提供的问题,结合单元补充资料"Understanding more about China"部分的素材,尝试用英语来讲述中国文化,锻炼自己的词汇、口语表达及跨文化交际能力。

📄 Text   📄 ICT

"单元正文"和"文化术语解释"——"Text",即是该单元的阅读材料正文部分,供学生在课前、课中及课后认真阅读。"ICT",为"Interpretation of Cultural Terms"的简写,其意思为"文化术语解释",为正文部分出现的一些文化术语提供进一步的解释说明,扩大学生的文化知识面。正文中以下画线的形式标示这些文化术语。

❑ Understanding More about China

"更多地了解中国"——该部分提供若干篇与中国社会与文化相关的短文,供学生在进行"Introduce China in English"时参考使用,也可供学生在课后进一步阅读使用。希望学生在此基础上能扩大范围,搜集更多的介绍中国文化的内容,藉此提升对中国文化的了解与认知水平。

◆ Exercises

"课后练习"——该部分为单元正文部分以及补充阅读资料部分的练习题目,共有三种类型,一为"选择题",二为"对错判断题",三为"简答题"。通过练习,了解学生对单元内容的掌握情况及存在的问题。

三、致学生

与其他课程比较起来,文化课具有它自身的一些特点。概括起来,可以用"knowledge-based course"(基于知识的课程)来描述,该课程主要以了解西方的社会与文化知识为目标。因此,文化课教材涵盖的主题较广泛——包括目的语国家的地理、历史、文学、衣食住行、教育、艺术、电影、大众传媒、对外关系、经济等;时间跨度大——既有目的语国家的历史回顾又有当代现状的描述;信息量丰富,知识点多。但每个主题单元的学习时间有限,教师不可能在有限的课堂时间内把每一个章节的所有知识点都讲解到。这就需要你们改变自己的学习方法,除了在课堂上认真听讲、积极参与各项课堂教学活动外,还需要在课前和课后花一定时间和精力进行延伸阅读,了解更多相关的知识点。建议把本门课程的学习视为"以扩展西方文化知识为目的的阅读课程",同时提升自身阅读水平。

如果要进行课堂讲演(presentation),建议选择每个单元"In this unit you will learn about"部分的关键问题作为题目,通过搜集更多的资料,加深对单元内容的理解。当然,每个单元正文中也有许多文化知识点可以作为很好的题目。

四、致教师

对于语言及相关专业来说,语言教学与文化教学应相互融合,在介绍西方文化的教学中应融入中国文化的内容,采取语言、西方文化介绍、与中国文化比较相结合的教学模式,这样既能让文化促进学生的语言学习,又能让学生通晓中西文化,把学生打造成"学贯中西"、能用外语讲好中国故事、推动中国文化走向世界的生力军。

在教授各章节内容前,我们特意设置了两项课前活动:一个是"Warm-up Exercise",该活动旨在要求学生针对英国、美国或者英美两国之间的共享主题展开讨论,为即将开展的教学活动做好铺垫;另一个是"Introduce China in English"(用英语讲述中国),要求学生按照教材提供的问题(教师根据实际可以自行添加问题)开展讨论,相互分享,尝试用英语来讲述中国的相关主题,在中西比较的基础上既可以扩展学生对中国文化的了解,又可以借助文化议题来提升学生的英语水平及表达能力,全面提升学生的跨文化交际能力,为将来在世界上传播中国文化奠定坚实的基础。当然,为了方便讨论,在每个单元章节后面,我们还特别设置了"Understanding More about China"板块,在此提供介绍中国文化的小短文,可供学生在讨论和分享中国文化时参考,也可作为学生课后阅读内容以及作为学生课后开展进一步的探究式学习的指引。

总之,要想教好本门课程,教师首先应提高自身对中西文化的了解,并树立坚定的中国文化主体意识,这样才能发挥好引领和塑造学生价值观的作用。任务艰巨,但使命光荣,责无旁贷!

Table of Contents

前言 ·· 1

使用说明 ··· 1

Introduction: Language, Culture and Communication ·························· 1

    What Is Culture ·· 5
    Western Culture ··· 6
    Chinese Culture ·· 7
    Language，Culture and Communication ··· 8
    Conclusion ··· 9

   * **Quick Look at Britain** * ·· 11

Unit 1   Country Profile ·· 12

    Names ·· 17
    Countries within a Country ·· 17
    Capital Cities ·· 20
    Climate ··· 22

Unit 2   British History (1) ··· 26

    Emergence of the Nation ··· 32
    Prehistoric Britain ·· 33
    The History of Invasions on the British Isles ··· 33
    The Middle Ages ·· 36

Unit 3   British History (2) ··· 40

    Tudor Renaissance ·· 43
    Stuart Britain ··· 43
    The Eighteenth Century ·· 44

Victorian Britain ······ 46
Britain from 1900 to 1950 ······ 46
Britain Today ······ 46

Unit 4　British Literature ······ 50

Old English Period (450—1066) ······ 55
Middle English Period (1066—1500) ······ 55
The Renaissance (1500—1660) ······ 56
The Neoclassical Period (1600—1785) ······ 58
The Romantic Period (1785—1832) ······ 58
The Victorian Period (1832—1901) ······ 60
The Edwardian Period (1901—1914) ······ 60
The Georgian Period (1910—1936) ······ 61
The Modern Period (1914—?) ······ 61
The Postmodern Period (1945—?) ······ 62

* **Quick Look at USA** * ······ 66

Unit 5　Country Profile ······ 67

The Addition of Two More States ······ 72
Geographic Diversity ······ 73
Climate ······ 73
Washington D.C. ······ 74
Major Cities ······ 75
A Nation of Immigrants ······ 78
America: A Melting Pot of Cultures ······ 79

Unit 6　American History (1) ······ 82

The First Americans ······ 85
Early Native Cultures ······ 86
The Arrival of Europeans ······ 86
American Revolutionary War (1775—1783) ······ 89

Unit 7　American History (2) ······ 93

American Civil War ······ 96
The Industrial Revolution ······ 98
World Wars I and II ······ 100

    Cold War and Civil Rights Movement ······ 101
    September 11, 2001 and the War on Terrorism ······ 101

Unit 8 American Literature ······ 104

    The Colonial Period (1607—1775) ······ 108
    The Revolutionary Age (1765—1790) ······ 108
    The Early National Period (1775—1828) ······ 108
    The American Renaissance (1828—1865) ······ 109
    The Realistic Period (1865—1900) ······ 110
    The Naturalist Period (1900—1914) ······ 111
    The Modern Period (1914—1939) ······ 111
    The Beat Generation (1944—1962) ······ 113
    The Contemporary Period (1939—Present) ······ 113

Unit 9 Holidays and Festivals ······ 117

    British Holidays and Festivals ······ 122
    American Holidays and Festivals ······ 125

Unit 10 Food and Drink ······ 132

    British Food ······ 137
    Tea, the National Drink ······ 138
    American Food ······ 140

Unit 11 Sports and Films ······ 143

    Sports in Britain ······ 148
    Sports in America ······ 149
    British Film Industry ······ 151
    American Movie Industry ······ 153

Unit 12 Houses, Arts, Museums and Architecture ······ 158

    Houses in England ······ 163
    Houses in America ······ 163
    British Arts ······ 164
    British Museums and Libraries ······ 164
    British Architecture ······ 165
    American Performing Arts ······ 166
    American Libraries and Museums ······ 167

Unit 13　Customs and Traditions ······································· 172

　　British Customs ·· 176
　　British Weddings ··· 179
　　American Wedding ·· 182

Unit 14　Educational System ··· 186

　　Education in England ··· 190
　　Types of Schools and Exams ·· 191
　　British Higher Education ··· 192
　　American Education System ··· 193
　　American Higher Education ··· 196

Unit 15　Mass Media ··· 200

　　Media of the United Kingdom ··· 204
　　Media of the United States ··· 207

Unit 16　Economy ··· 213

　　The UK Economy ·· 218
　　British Creative Industries ··· 222
　　The US Economy ·· 223

Unit 17　Social Kaleidoscope ··· 227

　　Gun Violence in the USA ··· 231
　　Foreign Relations of the UK ··· 232
　　Tourist Attractions in the UK ·· 234
　　Tourist Attractions in the USA ·· 235

References ··· 239

Introduction

Language, Culture and Communication

❏ **In this unit you will learn about**
1. Definitions of culture
2. Classification of culture
3. Features of culture
4. Functions of language
5. Influence of culture on language system
6. Relationship between language and culture

✓参考答案
✓更多资源

Vocabulary

- anthropologist 人类学家
- artifact 人工制品
- Australasia 澳大拉西亚（澳大利亚、新西兰及附近南太平洋诸岛的总称）
- biological 生物学的
- Celtic 凯尔特人的，凯尔特族的，凯尔特语的
- Christianity 基督教
- Christianization 基督教化
- circumference 圆周
- Confucianism 儒家
- constant adj. 经常的，不断发生的 / n. 常量，恒量
- contemporary 当代的，现代的
- cross-cultural communication 跨文化交际
- derogatory 贬低的，毁损的
- dilemma 进退两难的窘境，进退维谷的困境
- domestic （指动物）驯养的，作宠物饲养的，非野生的
- dynasty 朝代
- encompass 包含，包括
- Enlightenment 启蒙运动
- equate 认为某事物（与另一事物）相等或相仿
- ethical 伦理的
- ethnic 民族的，种族的
- euphemism 委婉说法，委婉语
- Forbidden City 紫禁城
- Four Great Classical Novels 四大名著
- Germanic 德意志的，德国的，德国人的，德语的 / 日耳曼人的，日耳曼语的，日耳曼民族的，条顿民族的
- grandeur 伟大，壮丽，壮观
- Hellenic 希腊的，希腊人的
- heritage 遗产，继承物
- humanism 人文主义，人本主义
- *I Ching*《易经》
- immigration 移居，移民
- immortality 不朽，永生
- inheritance 遗产，继承物
- instinct 本能
- integral 作为整体的一部分的
- interrelationship 相互关系
- Jewish 犹太人的
- lackey 卑躬屈膝的人
- Latin 拉丁的
- Legalism （中国古代的）法家学说，法家思想
- linear 线性的，线状的
- obsequious 逢迎的，巴结的
- overt 公开的
- Palaeolithic 旧石器时代的
- peculiarity 特点，特征，特色，特质
- pertaining to 与……有关系的，为……固有的
- porcelain 瓷器
- preservation 保留，保存
- primitive 原始的
- rationalism 理性主义
- Renaissance 文艺复兴
- reserve 保留
- revolutionary 革命性的
- ritual （宗教等仪式的）程序，仪式
- Scholasticism 经院哲学
- shelter 遮蔽物，庇护物
- Slavic 斯拉夫人的，斯拉夫语的
- superficially 表面上
- sway 摇晃，摇摆，摆动 / 影响或改变（某人）的观点或行动
- symmetry 对称

- taboo（某些文化的）禁忌，忌讳
- taichi 太极
- Taoism（中国的）道教，道家学说
- transformation 转变，转化，变形
- Warring States period 战国时期
- *yang* 阳
- *yin* 阴

Key Sentences

1. Culture is the total way of life of the human being.
   文化是人类的全部生活方式。

2. Culture can be divided into three broad categories, or three levels.
   文化可以分为三大类，或三个层次。

3. Culture is classified by some scholars into cultural knowledge information and cultural communication information.
   一些学者将文化分为文化知识信息和文化交际信息。

4. Culture exists through constant development or change.
   文化是通过不断发展或变化而存在的。

5. Culture is characterized by the following basic features.
   文化具有以下基本特征。

6. Chinese culture is one of the world's oldest cultures.
   中国文化是世界上最古老的文化之一。

7. Most of Chinese social values are derived from Confucianism and Taoism.
   中国的社会价值观大多来源于儒家和道家。

8. Language is a part of culture and a part of human behavior.
   语言是文化的一部分，也是人类行为的一部分。

9. Language is the primary tool of communication.
   语言是交际的主要工具。

10. Each culture has its own peculiarities and throws special influence on the language system.
    每一种文化都有自己的特点，并对语言系统产生特殊的影响。

11. Learning a second language also involves learning a second culture to varying degrees.
    学习一门外语也包括不同程度地学习一种外国文化。

12. Cultural differences are the most serious areas causing misunderstanding, unpleasantness and even conflict in inter cultural communication.
    在跨文化交际中，文化差异是造成误解、不愉快甚至冲突的最严重的因素。

13. Culture ... is that complex whole which includes knowledge, beliefs, arts, morals, law, custom and any other capacities and habits acquired by man as a member of society.

文化……是一个复杂的整体,包括知识、信仰、艺术、道德、法律、习俗以及人类作为社会成员所获得的任何其他能力和习惯。

Warm-up Exercise

1. What are the major functions of language?

2. What is the interrelationship between language and culture?

Introduce China in English

"Culturally-loaded words"(文化内涵词) refer to those words or phrases which convey a certain kind of cultural connotations or associations which may or may not be found in other languages or cultures. Here are some examples.

In Chinese: 秀才、炕、叩头、中秋节、刀削面、风水、八卦

In English: Punk, hippie, Achilles' heel, Trojan horse

Following this line of thought, can you find more examples of "culturally-loaded words" in both English and Chinese?

Text

ICT

Culture is a very broad subject, and the word culture has had and retains a number of meanings. Generally speaking, all activities not resulting solely from animal instinct, all activities belonging specifically to people, are a part of culture. Thus, human beings are animals with culture.

This unit mainly discusses the following questions: What is

culture? What is language? What is the interrelationship between language and culture?

■ What Is Culture

In 1871, in his classic book *Primitive Culture*, British anthropologist Edward Burnett Tylor first gave the definition of culture which is widely quoted: "Culture ... is that complex whole which includes knowledge, beliefs, arts, morals, law, custom and any other capacities and habits acquired by man as a member of society." After that, various definitions on culture are given by scholars from different points of view.

Edward Burnett Tylor 爱德华·伯内特·泰勒(1832—1917),英国文化人类学的奠基人、古典进化论的主要代表人物。《原始文化》为其代表作品之一。

Culture is the total way of life of the human being. Culture, therefore, varies with every group or society, depending on what its historical experience has been; it represents the distinctive way of life of a group of people, their complete design for living. A particular culture—one developed by a particular society—would consist of the patterns of learned behavior shared by the members of that society. This would include attitudes, ideas, values, knowledge, skills, and material objects. We can identify as many cultures as there are societies.

Some treated culture superficially as a set of specific artifacts, man-made environments, patterns of social organization and overt forms of behavior. Others treated culture in a more abstract way as the shared knowledge of members of social communities like world views, value orientations, norms, manners, customs, preferred styles of thinking and arguing, etc.

Culture can be divided into three broad categories, or three levels.

1) The first level of culture: the aspect pertaining to material goods, or people in relation to things.

2) The second level of culture: the aspect pertaining to society, or people in relation to people.

3) The third level of culture: the aspect pertaining to spirit, or people's hearts in relation to people's hearts.

The first level deals with the basic necessities of survival such as food, clothing and shelter. The second level of culture deals with the dynamics of social interaction. The third level of culture deals with the human heart.

Keep in mind that the three aspects are not linear; cultures include all three levels simultaneously. In terms of the taichi philosophy, we could call the first and second levels of culture *yin* and *yang*, and the third level the taichi circle. The third level, like the circumference of the circle, combines and transcends the relative factors, *yin* and *yang*, or the lower levels of culture.

Culture is classified by some scholars into cultural knowledge information and cultural communication information. The former refers to the factual information which does not exert a direct influence on the cross-cultural communication, including a nation's geography, history and so on. The latter points to the socio-pragmatic rules in daily communication which entail not only ways of greeting, thanking, apologizing and addressing, but also attention to taboos, euphemisms, modesty and polite formula in use, etc. The factual information provides the non-native speakers with no direct dilemmas.

Culture exists through constant development or change rather than mere preservation of tradition. In Chinese, the two characters making up the word for culture are *wen* and *hua*. *Wen* means civilization, and *hua* means change or transformation.

There is an ancient Chinese saying which states: "Immortality governs change." Change is the only constant. The transformations of culture may involve barely noticeable departures or revolutionary changes.

■ *Western Culture*

Western culture, sometimes equated with Western civilization, Western lifestyle or European civilization, is a term used very broadly to refer to a heritage of social norms, ethical values, traditional customs, belief systems, political systems, and specific artifacts and technologies that have some origin in or association with Europe.

The term has come to apply to countries whose history is strongly marked by European immigration, such as the countries of the Americas and Australasia, and is not restricted to the continent of Europe.

Western culture is characterized by a host of artistic, philosophic, literary, and legal themes and traditions; the heritage of Celtic, Germanic, Hellenic, Jewish, Slavic, Latin, and other ethnic and linguistic groups, as well as Christianity, which played an important part in the shaping of Western civilization since at least the 4th century.

Also contributing to Western thought, in ancient times and then in the Middle Ages and the Renaissance onwards, a tradition of rationalism in various spheres of life, developed by Hellenistic philosophy, Scholasticism, humanism, the Scientific Revolution and the Enlightenment.

Historical records of Western culture in Europe begin with Ancient Greece and Ancient Rome. Western culture continued to develop with Christianization during the Middle Ages, the reform and modernization triggered by the Renaissance, and with globalization by successive European empires, that spread European ways of life and European educational methods around the world between the 16th and 20th centuries.

With its global connection, European culture grew with an all-inclusive urge to adopt, adapt, and ultimately influence other cultural trends around the world.

Renaissance 文艺复兴。开始于13世纪晚期的意大利,15世纪扩展到整个欧洲,于16世纪末、17世纪初结束。

Enlightenment 启蒙运动。17~18世纪欧洲的思想运动。

■ *Chinese Culture*

Chinese culture is one of the world's oldest cultures. Here, let's take a brief look at a few important components of Chinese culture including values, literature, architecture, music, cuisine, arts and so on.

Most of Chinese social values are derived from Confucianism and Taoism. Confucianism was the official philosophy throughout most of Imperial China's history, and mastery of Confucian texts was the primary criterion for entry into the imperial bureaucracy. A number of more authoritarian strains of thought have also been influential, such as Legalism.

Chinese literature has a long past; the earliest classic work in Chinese, the *I Ching* or *Book of Changes* dates to around 1,000 BC. A flourishing of philosophy during the Warring

Confucianism 儒家。中国春秋末期孔子创立的学派。在先秦,儒家为诸子百家之一。汉武帝罢黜百家,独尊儒术,儒家文化逐渐成为中国传统文化的核心。

States period produced such noteworthy works as *the Analects of Confucius* and Laozi's *Tao Te Ching*. Dynastic histories were often written, beginning with Sima Qian's seminal *Records of the Grand Historian*, which was written from 109 BC to 91 BC.

The Tang Dynasty witnessed a poetic flowering, while the Four Great Classical Novels of Chinese literature were written during the Ming and Qing Dynasties.

Music and dance were closely associated in the very early periods of China. The music of China dated back to the dawn of Chinese civilization with documents and artifacts providing evidence of a well-developed musical culture as early as in the Zhou Dynasty. The earliest music of the Zhou Dynasty recorded in ancient Chinese texts includes the ritual music called *yayue* and each piece may be associated with a dance.

yayue 雅乐,即典雅纯正的音乐,雅,正也,是一种传统的宫廷音乐,举行帝王朝贺、祭祀天地等大典时所用。

Different forms of art have swayed under the influence of great philosophers, teachers, religious figures and even political figures. Chinese art encompasses all facets of fine art, folk art and performance art. Porcelain pottery was one of the first forms of art in the Palaeolithic period.

China is one of the main birth places of Eastern martial arts. Chinese martial arts are collectively given the name *kung fu*.

Different social classes in different eras boast different fashion trends, the color yellow or red was usually reserved for the emperor during China's Imperial era. China's fashion history covers hundreds of years with some of the most colorful and diverse arrangements.

Chinese architecture, examples for which can be found from over 2,000 years ago, has long been a hallmark of the culture. There are certain features common to Chinese architecture, regardless of specific region or use. The most important is its emphasis on width, as the wide halls of the Forbidden City serve as an example. Another important feature is symmetry, which connotes a sense of grandeur as it applies to everything from palaces to farmhouses.

■ *Language, Culture and Communication*

Language is a part of culture and a part of human behavior.

It is often held that the function of language is to express thought and to communicate information. Language also fulfills many other tasks such as greeting people, conducting religious service, etc.

Krech described the major functions of language from the following three aspects:

1) Language is the primary tool of communication.

2) Language reflects both the personality of the individual and the culture of his history. In turn, it helps shape both personality and culture.

3) Language makes possible the growth and transmission of culture, the continuity of societies, and the effective functioning and control of social group.

Each culture has its own peculiarities and throws special influence on the language system. For example, referring to the same common domestic animal, English chooses the word "dog," while Chinese has its own character "狗;" Chinese has the phrase "走狗" while English has the expression "running dog," but the meanings attributed to the two expressions are completely different according to Chinese culture and Western culture respectively.

We can obviously see that the meaning attributed to language is cultural-specific. A great deal of intercultural misunderstanding occurs when the "meanings" of words in two languages are assumed to be the same, but actually reflect different cultural patterns.

■ Conclusion

We can summarize the relationship between language and culture as the following: language is a key component of culture. It is the primary medium for transmitting much of culture. Without language, culture would not be possible. Children learning their native language are learning their own culture; learning a second language also involves learning a second culture to varying degrees. On the other hand, language is influenced and shaped by culture. It reflects culture. Cultural differences are the most serious areas causing misunderstanding, unpleasantness and even conflict in inter cultural communication. So both foreign language learners and teachers should pay more attention to cultural communication information.

Exercises

Ⅰ. Choose the answer that best completes the statement.
1. In 1871, in his classic book *Primitive Culture*, _____ anthropologist Edward Tylor first gave the definition of culture.
   A. French   B. German   C. British   D. American
2. Historical records of Western culture in Europe begin with Ancient Greece and Ancient _____.
   A. Latin   B. Celtic   C. Slavic   D. Rome

Ⅱ. Read the following statements and decide whether they are true (T) or false (F).
1. Language is a key component of culture. _____
2. Culture is classified by some scholars into cultural knowledge information and cultural communication information. The former exerts a direct influence on the cross-cultural communication. _____
3. The meaning attributed to language is cultural-specific. _____
4. Without language, culture would still be possible. _____
5. Human beings are animals with culture. _____
6. Culture can be divided into three broad categories, or three levels. And the three aspects are in a linear relationship. _____
7. Culture varies with every group or society, depending on what its historical experience has been. _____
8. Culture exists through constant development or change rather than mere preservation of tradition. _____
9. Western culture is characterized by a host of artistic, philosophic, literary, and legal themes and traditions. _____

Ⅲ. Short-answer questions.
1. What are the differences between cultural knowledge information and cultural communication information?
2. What is culture? What is Western culture?
3. According to the text, culture can be divided into three broad categories, or three levels. What are they and what are their relationships?

The United Kingdom of Great Britain and Northern Ireland
* Quick Look at Britain *

Total Area	242,495 km²
Capital and largest city	London
Official language and national language	English
Recognised regional languages	• Scots • Ulster Scots • Welsh • Cornish • Scottish Gaelic • Irish
Currency	Pound sterling (£) (GBP)
History • Acts of Union of England and Scotland • Acts of Union of Great Britain and Ireland • Irish Free State Constitution Act • EEC accession	➢1 May 1707 ➢1 January 1801 ➢5 December 1922 ➢1 January 1973
Calling code	+44

Unit 1

Country Profile

❏ **In this unit you will learn about**
  1. Different names of the country
  2. Different countries within the country
  3. Major cities
  4. Characters of English, Scottish, Welsh and Northern Irish
  5. Climate
  6. British national flag and its meaning

 ✓参考答案 ✓更多资源

Vocabulary

- altitude 海拔
- ancillary 附属的
- archipelago 群岛
- basalt 玄武岩
- bascule bridge 可开启的吊桥
- borough 享有自治权的市镇
- bound 形成(某事物)的界线;限制
- capsule 胶囊;航天舱,太空舱
- cathedral 大教堂
- column 柱子
- composite (由不同的成分或材料)组成的(事物);混合的;合成的;混合物
- coronation 加冕
- current (水、气等的)流,流动
- dome 穹顶,圆屋顶
- equator 赤道
- estuary 港湾,河口湾
- firth (尤指苏格兰的)狭窄的海湾
- generosity 慷慨,大方,宽容
- highland 高地
- Hogmanay 元旦前夕(尤指苏格兰的)
- incorporate 将某事物包括进去;包含
- incursion (对某地的)袭击,侵犯(通常指非永久性的侵占)
- influx (人或物)涌入,汇集
- latitude 纬度
- loch 湖。例如:Loch Ness 尼斯湖
- lowland 低地
- metropolis 大城市
- monarch 最高统治者;国王;女王;皇帝;女皇
- observation 观察
- outdated 过时的
- parliament 议会
- peninsula 半岛
- pretentious 自负的;自命不凡的
- proclaim 宣告,公布,声明
- sentimental 情感的,情绪的(非理智的)
- sovereign 主权的
- sovereignty 主权
- summit 最高点;顶点;(尤指)山顶
- suspension 悬挂,悬浮
- tattoo 归营鼓,归营号;文身
- temperate 温和的
- terrain 地形,地貌
- territory 领土
- transnational 跨国的
- uniqueness 独特性
- unitary 单一的,一个的

Key Sentences

1. Its territory and population are primarily situated on the island of Great Britain and in Northern Ireland on the island of Ireland, as well as numerous smaller islands in the surrounding seas.
   它的领土和人口主要分布在大不列颠岛和爱尔兰岛上的北爱尔兰,以及周围海域的许多小岛上。

2. People often confuse the names for this country, and frequently make mistakes in using them.

人们经常混淆这个国家的名称,并且经常在使用时出错。

3. The United Kingdom is a political union made up of four constituent countries: England, Scotland, Wales and Northern Ireland.
联合王国是一个由四个部分组成的政治联盟:英格兰、苏格兰、威尔士和北爱尔兰。

4. Most of England consists of rolling lowland terrain. The main rivers and estuaries are the Thames, Severn and the Humber Estuary.
英格兰大部分地区由起伏的低地组成。主要河流和河口有泰晤士河、塞文河和亨伯河口。

5. Scotland's geography is varied, with lowlands in the south and east and highlands in the north and west.
苏格兰的地理环境多种多样,南部和东部有低地,北部和西部有高地。

6. Wales is mostly mountainous.
威尔士大部分是山区。

7. London is situated in southeastern England along the Thames River.
伦敦位于英格兰东南部泰晤士河沿岸。

8. Now home to the British Crown Jewels, the Tower of London was built by William the Conqueror in 1078.
伦敦塔现在是英国皇冠珠宝的安放地,由征服者威廉于1078年建造。

9. Edinburgh is situated on the east coast of the central lowlands, on the south shore of the Firth of Forth, on the North Sea.
爱丁堡位于中部低地的东海岸,北海福斯湾的南岸。

10. They talk about the weather because it changes so often. Wind, rain, sun, cloud, snow—they can all happen in a British winter or a British summer.
他们谈论天气是因为天气经常变化。风、雨、太阳、云、雪——它们可能都会发生在英国的冬天或夏天。

11. The prevailing wind is from the southwest, bringing mild and wet weather to England regularly, from the Atlantic Ocean.
盛行风来自西南,定期从大西洋给英格兰带来温和潮湿的天气。

12. The climate of Scotland is temperate and oceanic, and tends to be very changeable.
苏格兰的气候温和,属海洋性气候,而且往往多变。

13. The People's Republic of China is located in the eastern part of the Asian continent.
中华人民共和国位于亚洲大陆东部。

14. China stretches from its westernmost point on the Pamir Plateau to the confluence of the Heilongjiang and Wusuli Rivers, to the east.
中国的最西端从帕米尔高原开始一直朝东延伸到黑龙江和乌苏里江的交汇处。

15. When inhabitants of eastern China are greeting the dawn, people in western China still face four more hours of darkness.
    当中国东部的居民在迎接黎明的时候,西部的人们还要经历四个多小时的黑夜。

16. When northern China is still gripped in a world of ice and snow, flowers are already blooming in the balmy south.
    当中国北方还沉浸在冰雪世界的时候,鲜花已经在温暖的南方盛开。

Warm-up Exercise

1. Use an appropriate term to describe the following maps.

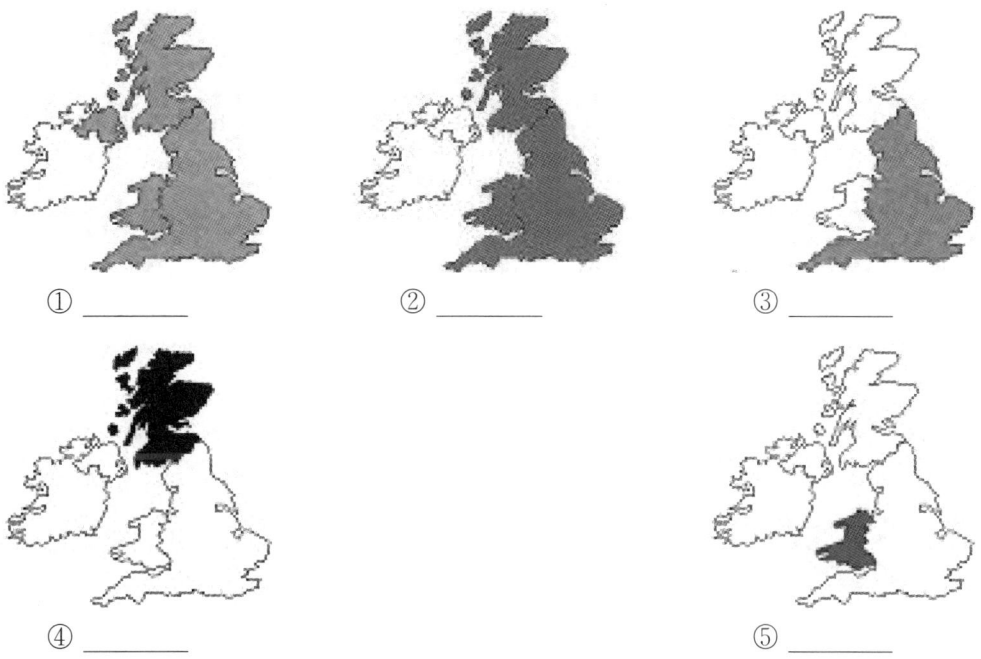

① _____   ② _____   ③ _____

④ _____   ⑤ _____

2. Put the terms in the appropriate blanks of the following diagram.

① England   ② Great Britain   ③ Ireland   ④ Northern Ireland
⑤ Republic of Ireland   ⑥ Scotland   ⑦ Wales

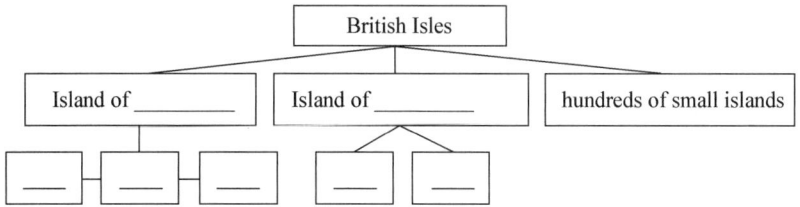

3. What is the difference between the United Kingdom and Great Britain?

4. What is the full name of the UK?

Introduce China in English

1. How do you describe China's geography?

2. Why October 1 is regarded as the National Day of the Chinese people?

📄 Text   📰 ICT

The United Kingdom of Great Britain and Northern Ireland (usually shortened to the United Kingdom, the UK, or Britain) is a country and sovereign state that is situated in west Northern Europe. Its territory and population are primarily situated on the island of Great Britain and in Northern Ireland on the island of Ireland, as well as numerous smaller islands in the surrounding seas.

The United Kingdom is bounded by the Atlantic Ocean, and its ancillary bodies of water, including the North Sea, the English Channel, the Celtic Sea, and the Irish Sea. The mainland is linked to France by the Channel Tunnel and Northern Ireland shares a land border with the Republic of Ireland.

English Channel 英吉利海峡
Channel Tunnel 英—法海底隧道

■ *Names*

People often confuse the names for this country, and frequently make mistakes in using them. The United Kingdom, the UK, and Britain are all proper terms for the entire nation, although the term Britain is also often used when talking about the island of Great Britain. The use of the term Great Britain to refer to the entire nation is now outdated; the term Great Britain, properly used, refers only to the island of Great Britain, which does not include Northern Ireland.

The term England should never be used to describe Britain, because England is only one part of the island. It is always correct to call people from England, Scotland, or Wales British, although people from England may also properly be called English, people from Scotland Scottish, and people from Wales Welsh.

the British 英国人民

■ *Countries within a Country*

The United Kingdom is a political union made up of four constituent countries: England, Scotland, Wales and Northern Ireland.

Great Britain is the largest island in the cluster of islands, or archipelago, known as the British Isles. England is the

British Isles 不列颠群岛。包括大不列颠岛和爱尔兰岛两个主要岛屿以及周边许多小岛，东南以英吉利海峡、多佛尔海峡与欧洲大陆相望。

Unit 1 Country Profile   17

largest and most populous division of the island of Great Britain, making up the south and east. It makes up 130,410 km² of the United Kingdom's total area. Wales is on the west and Scotland is to the north. Northern Ireland is located in the northeast corner of Ireland, the second largest island in the British Isles. The area of Scotland is 78,790 km², the area of Wales is 20,760 km², and the area of Northern Ireland is 14,160 km². This means that England makes up 53.4 percent of the area of the United Kingdom, Scotland 32.3 percent, Wales 8.5 percent, and Northern Ireland 5.8 percent.

the island of Great Britain 大不列颠岛

What is the difference between the United Kingdom and Great Britain?

The United Kingdom is made up of England, Scotland, Wales and Northern Ireland. Its full name is the United Kingdom of Great Britain and Northern Ireland. Great Britain, on the other hand, comprises only England, Scotland and Wales. It is the largest island of the British Isles. Northern Ireland and the Irish Republic form the second largest island.

The Isle of Man and the Channel Islands are not part of the United Kingdom. They are largely self-governing with their own legislative assemblies and systems of law. The British Government is, however, responsible for their defence and international relations.

Isle of Man 马恩岛,位于英格兰与爱尔兰间的海上岛屿。
Channel Islands 海峡群岛,在英吉利海峡内,靠近法国的诺曼底。
Thames 泰晤士河

■ England and the English

Most of England consists of rolling lowland terrain. The main rivers and estuaries are the Thames, Severn and the Humber Estuary. The largest urban area is Greater London. Near Dover, the Channel Tunnel links the United Kingdom with France.

The English are courteous, and are very proud of their long and rich history. In England, politeness and restraint are admired.

■ Scotland and the Scots

Scotland's geography is varied, with lowlands in the south

Greater London 大伦敦。范围大致包含英国首都伦敦与其周围的卫星城镇所组成的都会区。行政上,该区域在1965年设置,其下包含了伦敦市(City of London)与32个伦敦自治市(London boroughs),共33个次级行政区。

and east and highlands in the north and west, including Ben Nevis, the highest mountain in the British Isles at 1,343 metres. There are many long and deep-sea firths and lochs. Scotland has nearly 800 islands, mainly west and north of the mainland. The capital city is Edinburgh, while the largest city is Glasgow.

Scots are passionate about their country, guarding its uniqueness and refusing to go along with English ideas. While cool and aloof externally, they are extremely sentimental about their family and their country. Overall Scots are free of class consciousness. Scots have a keen, subtle sense of humor as well as value generosity and respectability.

- **Wales and the Welsh**

As a country, Wales began with Henry VIII's Act of Union in 1536. Before that time Wales had been a loose collection of independent kingdoms and lordships with influxes and incursions from Europe. It's believed that Wales, as an area of land, has been inhabited since 250,000 BC.

Wales is mostly mountainous, the highest peak being Snowdon at 1,085 metres above sea level. The greatest concentration of people lives in the south, in the cities of Swansea and Newport, as well as Cardiff, and the South Wales Valleys.

Wales has been part of the United Kingdom for more than 400 years, but has kept its own language, literature and traditions. Most residents of Wales are of Welsh or English heritage. The Welsh take great pride in their country and their heritage. They love to sing and talk.

- **Northern Ireland and the Northern Irish**

Northern Ireland, making up the north-eastern part of Ireland, is mostly hilly. The capital is Belfast, with other major cities being Derry and Armagh. Northern Ireland is home to one of the UK's World Heritage Sites, the Giant's Causeway, which consists of more than 40,000 six-sided basalt columns up to 40 feet (12 m) high. Lough Neagh, the largest body of water in the British Isles, by surface area (388 km^2), can be found in Northern Ireland. The highest peak is Slieve Donard at 849 metres in the province's Mourne Mountains.

Two-thirds of the Northern Irish have Scottish or English

roots. The others are of Irish descent. Irish value friendliness, sincerity and nature. They dislike pretentious behavior. Family ties are very important in Northern Ireland.

■ *Capital Cities*

The capitals of the United Kingdom's four countries are London, Edinburgh, Cardiff and Belfast.

■ London

London is situated in southeastern England along the Thames River. With an estimated population by July of 2021 as much as 9.12 million, this vast metropolis is by far the largest city in Europe. Although it no longer ranks among the world's most populous cities, London is still one of the world's major financial and cultural capitals.

London's metropolitan area extends for more than 30 miles at its widest point, covering some 1,610 km². This vast urban territory is divided into 33 political units—32 boroughs and the City of London.

Ten top tourist attractions in London include:

❶ Westminster Abbey

It is one of the most notable religious buildings in the United Kingdom and is the traditional place of coronation and burial site for English and, later, British monarchs.

❷ Palace of Westminster

More widely known as the Houses of Parliament, it is the seat of Parliament in the United Kingdom. The present building largely dates from the 19th century.

❸ St. Paul's Cathedral

Built in the 17th century, St. Paul's Cathedral is one of London's most famous and most recognizable sights. Its impressive dome was inspired by St. Peter's Basilica in Rome and rises 118 metres to the cross at its summit.

❹ Trafalgar Square

It is a large city square commemorating Lord Horatio Nelson's victory against Napoleon's navy at the Battle of Trafalgar in 1805. The central monument within the square is a

---

City of London 首都伦敦的市中心

Westminster Abbey 威斯敏斯特教堂。自威廉一世往后,除两位未加冕的英王爱德华五世及爱德华八世外,历代英王均在此加冕。

Palace of Westminster 威斯敏斯特宫,又称议会大厦(Houses of Parliament),是英国议会(上、下议院)的所在地。

St. Paul's Cathedral 圣保罗大教堂

Trafalgar Square 特拉法加广场

single tall column on which the figure of Nelson stands gazing over London.

❺ Tower of London

Now home to the British Crown Jewels, the Tower of London was built by William the Conqueror in 1078. It served as a prison from 1100 to the mid twentieth century.

❻ London Eye

Situated on the banks of the River Thames, the London Eye is an enormous, 135-metre high observation wheel carrying 32 exterior glass-walled capsules.

❼ Buckingham Palace

Buckingham Palace is the main residence of Queen Elizabeth Ⅱ although it is owned by the British state and is not the monarch's personal property.

Buckingham Palace 白金汉宫

❽ British Museum

Established in 1753, the British Museum in London is a museum of human history and culture.

❾ Tower Bridge

Tower Bridge is a combined bascule and suspension bridge in London, over the Thames River.

British Museum 大英博物馆，又名不列颠博物馆，位于伦敦新牛津大街北面的罗素广场。该馆成立于1753年，于1759年1月15日起正式对公众开放。

❿ Big Ben

The name Big Ben actually refers not to the clock tower itself, but to the 13-ton bell housed within the tower and takes its name from the man who first ordered the bell, Sir Benjamin Hall.

■ Edinburgh

Edinburgh is the capital of Scotland and its second-largest city. It is situated on the east coast of the central lowlands, on the south shore of the Firth of Forth, on the North Sea. Edinburgh has been the capital of Scotland since 1437 and is the seat of the country's parliament. The city was one of the major centres of the Enlightenment, led by the University of Edinburgh. The Old Town and New Town districts of Edinburgh were listed as a UNESCO World Heritage Site in 1995.

Edinburgh is well-known for the annual Edinburgh Festival a collection of official and independent festivals held annually

Firth of Forth 福斯湾

UNESCO World Heritage Site 联合国教科文组织世界遗产

Edinburgh Festival 爱丁堡音乐节

over about four weeks from early August. During this time, the population of the city is said to increase dramatically. The most famous of these events are the Edinburgh Fringe (the largest performing arts festival in the world), the Edinburgh International Festival, the Royal Edinburgh Military Tattoo, and the Edinburgh International Film Festival. Other famous events are the Hogmanay street party and the Beltane celebrations.

Edinburgh Fringe 爱丁堡边缘艺术节
Royal Edinburgh Military Tattoo 爱丁堡军乐节
Beltane 贝尔坦节（凯尔特族的节日，5月1日）

■ Cardiff

Cardiff is the capital of Wales and its largest city. Located on the south coast of Wales it is administered as a unitary authority. It was a small town until the early nineteenth century and came to prominence following the arrival of industry in the region and the use of Cardiff as a major port for the transport of coal. It eventually grew to become the largest city in Wales and a major centre of culture, sport and history in the UK. Cardiff was made a city in 1905 and proclaimed capital of Wales in 1955.

■ Belfast

Belfast is the capital of Northern Ireland. It is the largest city in Northern Ireland and the province of Ulster, and after Dublin, is the second-largest city on the island of Ireland. The city is situated near the mouth of the River Lagan at the south-western end of Belfast Lough.

Ulster 阿尔斯特（原为爱尔兰一地区，今为北爱尔兰及爱尔兰共和国所分割）
River Lagan 拉根河（根河）

■ *Climate*

The British talk about the weather a lot. For example, "Isn't it a beautiful morning?" or, "Very cold day, isn't it?" They talk about the weather because it changes so often. Wind, rain, sun, cloud, snow—they can all happen in a British winter or a British summer.

England has a temperate climate, with plentiful rainfall all year round, though the seasons are quite variable in temperature. However, temperatures rarely fall below −5 ℃ or rise above 32 ℃. The prevailing wind is from the southwest, bringing mild and wet weather to England regularly, from the Atlantic Ocean. It is driest in the east and warmest in the southeast, which is closest to the European mainland. Snowfall can occur in winter and early spring, though it is not that common away from high ground. Wales' climate is much like that of England.

The climate of Scotland is temperate and oceanic, and tends to be very changeable. It is warmed by the <u>Gulf Stream</u> from the Atlantic, and as such is much warmer than areas on similar latitudes, for example Oslo, Norway. Generally, western Scotland is warmer than the east because of the influence of the Atlantic Ocean currents and the colder surface temperatures of the North Sea. Rainfall varies widely across Scotland. Heavy snowfall is not common in the lowlands, but becomes more common with altitude.

Gulf Stream 湾流

The whole of Northern Ireland has a temperate <u>maritime climate</u>, rather wetter in the west than the east, although cloud cover is persistent across the region. The weather is unpredictable at all times of the year.

maritime climate 海洋性气候

Understanding More about China

1. Landscape of China

The People's Republic of China is located in the eastern part of the Asian continent, on the western Pacific rim. It is approximately seventeen times the size of France, 1 million square kilometres smaller than all of Europe, and 600,000 square kilometres smaller than Oceania (Australia, New Zealand, and the islands of the south and central Pacific).

When inhabitants of eastern China are greeting the dawn, people in western China still face four more hours of darkness. The northernmost point in China is located at the midpoint of the Heilongjiang River, north of Mohe in Heilongjiang Province. The southernmost point is located at Zengmu'ansha in the Nansha Islands, approximately 5500 kilometers away. When northern China is still gripped in a world of ice and snow, flowers are already blooming in the balmy south. The Bohai Sea, Yellow Sea, East China Sea, and South China Sea border China to the east and south, together forming a vast maritime area. The Yellow Sea, East China Sea, and South China Sea connect directly with the Pacific Ocean, while the Bohai Sea, embraced between the two "arms" of the Liaodong and Shandong peninsulas, forms an inland sea. China's maritime territory includes 5,400 islands, which have a total area of 80,000 square kilometres.

China possesses 20,000 kilometres of land border, plus 18,000 kilometres of coastline. Setting out from any point on China's border and making a complete circuit back to the starting point, the distance traveled would be equivalent to circling the globe at the equator.

2. National Flag

The National Flag of the PRC is a red rectangle emblazoned with five stars. The proportion of its length and height is 3 to 2. The upper left of the face of the Flag is studded with five yellow five-pointed stars. One of the stars is bigger than the others, with its circumcircle's diameter being three-tenth of the height of the Flag, and is placed in the left; the other four stars are smaller, with their circumcircle's diameter being one-tenth of the height of the Flag, encircling the big star on its right in the shape of an arch.

3. National Anthem

The National Anthem was written in 1935, with lyrics by the noted poet Tian Han and music by the famous composer Nie Er.

This song, originally named "March of the Volunteers," was the theme song of the film, *Sons and Daughters in a Time of Storm*. The film tells the story of those who went to the front to fight the Japanese invaders in Northeast China in the 1930s.

Moving and powerful, the "March of the Volunteers" gave voice to the Chinese people's determination to sacrifice themselves for national liberation, and expressed China's admirable tradition of courage, resolution and unity in fighting foreign aggression.

4. National Day

The National Day of the People's Republic of China is celebrated every year on October 1.

The Central People's Government passed the Resolution on the National Day of the People's Republic of China on December 2, 1949 and declared that October 1 is the National Day.

The PRC was founded on October 1, 1949 with a ceremony at the Tiananmen Square.

It is a public holiday in the People's Republic of China to celebrate the national day. Public places, such as Tiananmen Square in Beijing, are decorated in a festive theme during the holiday.

Exercises

Ⅰ. Choose the answer that best completes the statement.

1. In terms of area, which is the smallest country? _____
   A. England   B. Scotland   C. Wales   D. Northern Ireland
2. The highest peak Snowdon is located in _____.

A. England   B. Scotland   C. Wales   D. Northern Ireland

3. One of the UK's World Heritage Sites, the Giant's Causeway is located in _____.
   A. England   B. Scotland   C. Wales   D. Northern Ireland

4. Edinburgh Festival is a collection of official and independent festivals held annually over about four weeks from early _____.
   A. August   B. February   C. April   D. December

5. The United Kingdom is made up of _____ constituent countries.
   A. two   B. three   C. four   D. five

6. How many parts are there on the Island of Great Britain? _____
   A. Two: England and Scotland
   B. Two: England and Wales
   C. Three: England, Scotland and Wales
   D. Four: England, Scotland, Wales and Northern Ireland

7. The following are tourist attractions in London EXCEPT _____.
   A. Westminster Abbey   B. Trafalgar Square
   C. London Eye   D. Arch of Triumph

8. The capital city of Wales is _____.
   A. Edinburgh   B. Cardiff   C. Belfast   D. Glasgow

II. Read the following statements and decide whether they are true (T) or false (F).

1. The term England can be used to describe Britain. _____
2. Great Britain is the largest island in the cluster of islands, known as the British Isles. England is the largest and most populous division of the island of Great Britain. _____
3. Ben Nevis is the highest mountain in the British Isles. _____
4. The largest city in Scotland is also its capital. _____
5. Wales has been part of the United Kingdom for more than 400 years, but has kept its own language, literature and traditions. _____
6. Buckingham Palace is the official residence of British Prime Minister. _____
7. Lough Neagh is the largest body of water in the British Isles. _____
8. Tower of London was built by William the Conqueror in 1078. _____
9. London is situated in northeastern England along the Thames River. _____
10. Northern Ireland shares a land border with the Republic of Ireland. _____

III. Short-answer questions.

1. What is the difference between the United Kingdom and Great Britain?
2. What are the characters of the English, Scottish, Welsh and Northern Irish people respectively?
3. What is the climate like in England, Scotland, Wales and Northern Ireland?

Unit 2

British History (1)

❑ **In this unit you will learn about**
  1. Emergence of the nation
  2. Foreign invasions of the British Isles
  3. English Civil War

✓参考答案
✓更多资源

Vocabulary

- alien 外国的；不熟悉的，陌生的
- aristocracy 贵族阶层
- armour（旧时）甲胄；盔甲；铁甲
- cavalry 骑兵
- dependency 附属国
- dissolution 破裂；瓦解；解体；分解
- enslave 使某人成为奴隶
- flint 燧石，火石
- grace 给……荣耀，光彩
- halt 停顿
- helmet 头盔
- jurisdiction 司法权
- legendary 传奇的
- limestone 石灰石
- masterwork 杰作
- monarchy 君主制
- mound 土堆
- pirate 海盗
- puppet 傀儡
- rout 彻底打败（某人）；使（某人）溃退
- serf 农奴
- testimony 见证，证明

Key Sentences

1. It may be a small island on the edge of Europe. For centuries, invaders and incomers have made their mark.
   它是位于欧洲边缘的一个小岛。几个世纪以来，入侵者和外来者都留下了他们的痕迹。

2. Northern Ireland and Scotland have separate legal and educational systems and issue their own currency; Wales is fully incorporated within the English legal, educational, and banking systems.
   北爱尔兰和苏格兰有各自的法律和教育制度，并发行自己的货币；威尔士则完全纳入英格兰的法律、教育和银行体系中。

3. Stonehenge is the best known and probably the most remarkable of prehistoric remains in the UK.
   巨石阵是英国最著名的，也是最引人注目的史前遗迹。

4. The British Isles were the object of different foreign invasions for many times.
   不列颠群岛多次成为不同国家的入侵的对象。

5. In the middle of the first century BC Julius Caesar landed the British Isles.
   公元前一世纪中叶，恺撒登陆不列颠群岛。

6. The Roman legions occupied England and Wales. They preferred to settle down in England as it was more suitable for human settlements compared with mountainous Wales and wild and warlike Scotland.
   罗马军团占领了英格兰和威尔士。他们更喜欢在英格兰定居，因为比起多山的威尔士和

荒凉而好战的苏格兰来说，这儿更适合人类居住。

7. Hadrian's Wall is probably the most spectacular memorial to the Roman Empire in England. Much of it still exists today and its smaller sites—turrets, mile castles, signal towers and stretches of wall are worth a visit.
哈德良城墙可能是罗马帝国在英格兰留下的最壮观的纪念物。今天，它的大部分仍然存在，它的一些较小的遗址——塔楼、城堡、信号塔和城墙都值得一游。

8. Very few Romans settled down in Britain but the native language absorbed many Latin words.
很少有罗马人定居在英国，但英语吸收了许多拉丁语词。

9. The Romans introduced a lot of elements of their civilisation：they built villas adorned with frescoes.
罗马人引入了许多他们自己的文明元素：他们建造了用壁画装饰的别墅。

10. At the beginning of the 5th century the Romans were forced to withdraw from England. Many of the Romanized Britons went west into Wales and Cornwall.
在5世纪初，罗马人被迫从英格兰撤军。许多罗马化的英国人朝西来到威尔士和康沃尔。

11. The beginning of the Anglo-Saxon invasion was in the 5th century when the Teutonic tribes started enslaving England. Their names were the Angles, the Saxons and the Jutes.
盎格鲁-撒克逊的入侵开始于公元5世纪，当时条顿部落开始奴役英格兰。他们的名字分别是盎格鲁人、撒克逊人和朱特人。

12. They destroyed almost every trace of the civilization of the Romans and established their kingdoms.
他们几乎摧毁了罗马文明的每一个痕迹，建立了自己的王国。

13. The Battle of Hastings in 1066 decided the history of England and marked the beginning of the Norman invasion.
1066年黑斯廷斯战役决定了英格兰的历史，标志着诺曼入侵的开始。

14. The battle ended with Harold's death from an arrow in the eye and the English were routed.
战争以哈罗德的眼睛被箭插入致死而告终，英格兰人被击溃。

15. The English lost the battle because England was united only in name and there was no immediate resistance.
英格兰人输掉了这场战役，因为英格兰只是名义上的统一，没有立即进行抵抗。

16. Prehistoric cultures of different types have been found in all parts of China, among which Yangshao Culture, Dawenkou Culture, Hemudu Culture, Banpo Culture, Longshan Culture, and Majiayao Culture are of the greatest importance.

中国各地都有不同类型的史前文化，其中仰韶文化、大汶口文化、河姆渡文化、半坡文化、龙山文化、马家窑文化最为重要。

17. The Yangshao Culture was a Neolithic culture that existed extensively along the central Yellow River in China. The Yangshao people lived in round or rectangular houses in the mountainous regions that were below ground level and surrounded by little walls of earth. They cultivated millet extensively; some villages also cultivated wheat or rice.

仰韶文化是中国黄河中游广泛存在的新石器时代文化。仰韶人居住在山区地平面以下的圆形或长方形的屋中，四周围着小土墙。他们广泛种植小米，一些村庄还种植小麦或水稻。

Warm-up Exercise

Read the following "Timeline of British History" and discuss with your partners on the following questions:

1. Which do you think are the most significant historical events in British history?
2. Who are the Romans? Who are the Anglo-Saxons? And who are the Vikings and Normans?

Timeline of British History

3500 BC	First period of construction at **Stonehenge** begins.
AD 43	• Emperor Claudius ordered the **Roman** invasion of the province of Britannia. • Many English words are derived from the **Latin language** of the Romans.
410	The Roman army left Britain about AD 410. When they had gone there was no strong army to defend Britain.
5th—7th centuries	**Anglo-Saxons** migrated to England and expanded across the country.
829	King Egbert's grandson, Alfred, initiated the creation of the single **kingdom of England**.
843	**Kingdom of Scotland** formed.
850	**Vikings** from today's Denmark invaded northern England.
1066	• Norman French armies defeated the English at the **Battle of Hastings**. • **The Norman Conquest** of England—invasion and occupation of England by an army of Norman, Breton, Flemish, and French soldiers led by the Duke of Normandy, later styled **William the Conqueror**. • The Normans operated a feudal system, creating an aristocracy that treated native Anglo-Saxons as serfs. • The ruling class spoke **French** until the 13th century, when it mixed with the Old English used by the peasants.

(Continue)

1272	Edward Ⅰ invaded Wales and made his own son **Prince of Wales**.
1314	English army were defeated by the Scots at the Battle of Bannockburn.
1400	<u>Owain Glyndŵr</u> led Welsh rebels against the English army. ➢Owain Glyndŵr,欧文·格兰道尔(1359—1416),最后一代独立的威尔士王。
1415	The English army under Henry Ⅴ defeated the French at the <u>Battle of Agincourt</u>. ➢Battle of Agincourt（阿让库尔战役：百年战争中期,英国战胜法国的关键性战役）
1459—1487	The Wars of the Roses between the Houses of Lancaster and York.
1536 & 1543	Henry Ⅷ signed the Acts of Union, formally uniting England and Wales.
1588	The Spanish fleet, the **Armada**(无敌舰队), tried to invade England.
1603	Elizabeth Ⅰ (1533—1603), sometimes called **The Virgin Queen**, died; the last of the five monarchs of the House of Tudor.
1603	James Ⅰ (and Ⅵ of Scotland) **united the English and Scottish crowns**.
1606	The origins of the earlier **Union Flag** of Great Britain dated back to 1606.
1642—1649	**English Civil War** resulted in the **execution** of Charles Ⅰ, and exile of Charles Ⅱ.
1666	**Great Fire of London** burned much of the city to the ground.
1688—1689	The **Glorious Revolution**, also called the Revolution of 1688 • Overthrow of King James Ⅱ of England (James Ⅶ of Scotland) by a union of English Parliamentarians with the Dutch stadtholder William Ⅲ, Prince of Orange, who was James' nephew and son-in-law. William's successful invasion of England with a Dutch fleet and army led to his ascension to the throne as William Ⅲ of England jointly with his wife, Mary Ⅱ, James' daughter, after the Declaration of Right, leading to the **Bill of Rights 1689**.
1707	**The Act of Union links England, Wales and Scotland under one parliament**, forming a single, united kingdom named "Great Britain."
About 1760 to sometime between 1820 and 1840	**The Industrial Revolution**, the transition to new manufacturing processes
1800	**The Acts of Union 1800** united the **Kingdom of Great Britain** and the **Kingdom of Ireland** (previously in personal union) to create **the United Kingdom of Great Britain and Ireland** with effect from 1 January 1801.
1799—1815	Napoleon threatened invasion but was defeated at Trafalgar and Waterloo.
1837—1901	Under the reign of Queen Victoria, the British Empire expanded its influence across the globe.
1914	The assassination of Archduke Franz Ferdinand of Austria led to the outbreak of WWⅠ.
1920	• A separatist movement led to the dissolution of the Union of Great Britain and Ireland in 1920; • 26 of Ireland's 32 counties became the independent **Irish Free State** (later the Republic of Ireland), with 6 of the nine counties of Ulster remaining within the United Kingdom, thus the name "the United Kingdom of Great Britain and **Northern** Ireland."

(Continue)

1939—1945	WW II
1953	The **coronation** of Queen Elizabeth II took place in Westminster Abbey.
1960s	Many former colonies in Africa and the Caribbean declared independence from Britain.
1979	**Margaret Thatcher**'s Conservative Party won the general election.
1997	The Labour Party won the general election with a record-breaking majority.
1999	Devolution led to the formation of the Scottish Parliament and Welsh Assembly.
2003—2004	Britain joined the US-led invasion of Iraq.
2005	The Labour Party was reelected for a third term with Tony Blair still in control.
2007	Tony Blair resigned, and Gordon Brown took over as Britain's prime minister.
2010	A **coalition** between Conservatives and Liberal-Democrats won the election.
2016	An in-out **referendum** on its EU membership, also called Brexit, was held on June 23.

Introduce China in English

1. How many dynasties do you know about China? What are they?

2. What are the most important prehistoric cultures in China?

Text

It may be a small island on the edge of Europe, but Britain was never on the sidelines of history. For centuries, invaders and incomers have made their mark: <u>Neolithic</u> peoples about 5,000 years ago followed by <u>Celts</u> around 500 BC, then the Romans, the Anglo-Saxons, the Vikings, and Normans. The result is a fascinating mix of culture and language—a dynamic pattern that shaped the nation and continues to evolve today.

■ *Emergence of the Nation*

The United Kingdom was formed by <u>Acts of Union</u> between England and Wales (1536) and England, Wales, and Scotland (1707), uniting the three nations under a single monarchy and legislative council (Parliament in London).

After 1169, the island of Ireland came under British influence, and it became a colonial <u>dependency</u> in 1690. The British and Irish parliaments were united in 1801. A separatist movement led to the dissolution of the Union of Great Britain and Ireland in 1920; twenty-six of Ireland's thirty-two counties became the independent <u>Irish Free State</u> (later the Republic of Ireland), with six of the nine counties of <u>Ulster</u> remaining within the United Kingdom. The present-day nation also includes the <u>Channel Islands</u> off the coast of France and the <u>Isle of Man</u> between Britain and Ireland, which are substantially self-governing.

How did the UK come into existence?
1536: **Act of Union** joined England and Wales.
1707: **Act of Union** united Scotland and England, together with Wales to form the Kingdom of Great Britain.
1801: The Irish Parliament voted to join the Union. The then Kingdom of Great Britain became the United Kingdom of Great Britain and Ireland.
1922: Name changed to the United Kingdom of Great Britain and Northern Ireland, when most of the Southern counties in Ireland chose independence.

Northern Ireland and Scotland have separate legal and

ICT

Neolithic 新石器时代的
Celt 凯尔特人（古代西欧人，其中有些人在罗马人来到之前已定居于不列颠）

Act of Union《联合法案》

dependency 附属国；附属地

Irish Free State 爱尔兰自由邦
Ulster 阿尔斯特，爱尔兰北部的历史省份。现在成为北爱尔兰以及爱尔兰的阿尔斯特省。
Channel Islands 海峡群岛，在行政上独立于英国政府。
Isle of Man 马恩岛，爱尔兰海上的岛屿，有自己的立法机构。

educational systems and issue their own currency; Wales is fully incorporated within the English legal, educational, and banking systems. Referendums in 1990s in Scotland and Wales resulted in the establishment of a Scottish Parliament which is still under the general jurisdiction of London but has limited local tax-raising powers, and the Welsh Assembly, which does not have tax-raising powers.

Welsh Assembly 威尔士议会,成立于1999年。

■ Prehistoric Britain

Britain was part of the European landmass until the end of the last Ice Age, around 6000 BC, when the English Channel was formed by melting ice. The earliest inhabitants lived in limestone caves; settlements and farming skills developed gradually through the Stone Age. The magnificent wooden and stonehenges and circles are masterworks from around 3000 BC, but their significance is a mystery, e.g. the Stonehenge. Stonehenge is the best known and probably the most remarkable of prehistoric remains in the UK. It has stood on Salisbury Plain for about 4,000 years. There have been many different theories about its original use but no one is certain why it was built. Flint mines and ancient pathways are evidence of early trading and many burial mounds survive from the Stone and Bronze Ages.

Ice Age 冰河时代

Stone Age 石器时代

Stonehenge 巨石阵

Bronze Age 青铜器时代

■ The History of Invasions on the British Isles

Britain is an island and this fact is more important than any other in understanding its history. The British Isles were the object of different foreign invasions for many times.

■ The Roman Invasion

In the middle of the first century BC Julius Caesar landed the British Isles. On the 26th of August, 55 BC some 10,000 men and 500 cavalry landed somewhere between Dover and Deal. The highly efficient Roman army had little difficulty in routing the local Celtic chieftains. Caesar carefully noted the way they fought and determined to return the following year. On the 6th of July 54 BC an ever larger army landed in the same area.

Roman soldiers looked very differently from the Celts they

Julius Caesar 恺撒,著名的罗马将军、政治家和独裁官。

chieftain (部落或氏族的)首领,领袖;酋长

defeated. They wore metal helmets and plate armour and carried shields of wood and leather with a sword. Their life was one of discipline and drilled twice a day.

The Roman legions occupied England and Wales. They preferred to settle down in England as it was more suitable for human settlements compared with mountainous Wales and wild and warlike Scotland. Their invasion was not peaceful. The Romans tried to defend themselves against the Celtic tribes by building forts such as Caerleon, Chester and York and a great defensive wall across the north of England which was constructed by the order of the Roman Emperor Hadrian. Hadrian's Wall is probably the most spectacular memorial to the Roman Empire in England. Much of it still exists today and its smaller sites—turrets, mile castles, signal towers and stretches of wall are worth a visit. The wild landscape still evokes the spirit of the past.

Roman civilisation brought straight paved roads to England which led to garrison towns from London.

Very few Romans settled down in Britain but the native language absorbed many Latin words. Many of the towns that the Romans built still have in their names the Latin word "castra," meaning a camp or a fortified town: Lancaster, Chester, and Leicester.

The Romans introduced a lot of elements of their civilisation: they built villas adorned with frescoes, mosaics which were warmed by central heating; they constructed granaries with the ingenious system of ventilation and famous baths with underfloor heating system.

In 367 the wild Celts of the North, the Picts and Scots overran the Wall, Saxon pirates landed in the East. They were called "barbarians" by the civilized unwarlike Britons of the Roman England. At the beginning of the 5th century the Romans were forced to withdraw from England. Many of the Romanized Britons went west into Wales and Cornwall.

■ **The Anglo-Saxon Invasion**

The beginning of the Anglo-Saxon invasion was in the 5th century when the Teutonic tribes started enslaving England. Their names were the Angles, the Saxons and the Jutes. At that

legion 罗马军团

Emperor Hadrian 哈德良皇帝
Hadrian's Wall 哈德良长城

Pict 居住在现在的苏格兰东部和东北部的古代民族
barbarian 野蛮人

Teutonic 条顿人的,条顿语的(即盎格鲁-撒克逊人、荷兰人、德国人及斯堪的那维亚人的)

time Celtic countries were a centre of light, especially Ireland where its monks and saints, when not fighting, were involved in treasuring the knowledge of Latin literature and lovingly illuminating the manuscripts of the Gospel. The Angles and the Saxons advanced from east to west along the Roman roads, slaughtering and enslaving the Britons, sacking and burning Roman towns and villas. They destroyed almost every trace of the civilization of the Romans and established their kingdoms.

By the middle of the 7th century all England was converted to Christianity and it was <u>Arthur</u>, the half legendary King who was the British champion of Christianity against the heathen barbaric English.

Arthur 亚瑟王,传说中古不列颠最富有传奇色彩的伟大国王。

One of the most powerful Anglo-Saxon kingdoms was <u>Northumbria</u>, when king Edwin advanced the frontier to the north and built his stronghold of Edinburgh. It was in this kingdom that English art and letters flowered for the first time.

Northumbria 诺森布里亚,盎格鲁-撒克逊时期英格兰王国。

■ The Viking Invasion

The <u>Vikings</u> terrified the Anglo-Saxons as much as they themselves had terrified the Britons centuries before. They were people from Scandinavia whose life was working the land and fishing and who went on to attack and later settle in Britain. Each year bands of Vikings put out to sea, seeking out richer lands, bringing home gold, silver and jewels. Their leaders, kings or "<u>jarls</u>" began to divide and in the main it was Norwegians who settled in Scotland while in England it was the Danes. At first they put in puppet Anglo-Saxon kings but gradually they began to replace them with kings of their own.

Vikings（8 至 10 世纪的）北欧海盗(斯堪的纳维亚武士,活动于北欧与西欧部分地区,包括英国)

jarl（中古时代北欧的首领;贵族）

■ The Norman Invasion

England was submitted to a Danish King Conute in 1016 and became a part of the Great Danish Empire which included Denmark and Norway. After the Danish invasion King Edward Ⅰ（the <u>Confessor</u>）was restored to the throne. Previously he was brought up to Normandy during the years of Danish rule and came to England with Norman friends and clergy.

Monkish in his ideas, his main interest was the church and it was he who founded the Westminster Abbey. During his reign there was a certain opposition to the Norman rule and Edward's brother-

Confessor 忏悔者爱德华（约 1001 年—1066 年 1 月 5 日)是英国的盎格鲁-撒克逊王朝君主(1042 年至 1066 年在位),因为对基督教无比信仰,被称作"忏悔者"。

in-law named Harold, the Earl of Wessex, became the leader of anti-Norman party. So Harold Ⅱ was the last Anglo-Saxon king before the Norman Conquest of England and it was he who headed the Battle of Hastings in 1066, which decided the history of England and marked the beginning of the Norman invasion.

  14th October 1066 is the most celebrated date in English history. On that day the crucial engagement between the English army under King Harold and the invading troops of William, Duke of Normandy took place. In preparation for the great confrontation two Norman castles were put up on English soil—at Pevensey and at Hastings.

  William's well-trained army met the defending English forces. The battle ended with Harold's death from an arrow in the eye and the English were routed.

  The English lost the battle because England was united only in name and there was no immediate resistance. Had it been a united country the battle of Hastings would not have decided its history. In just one day the invasion of England had succeeded but the crown was secured, fulfilling the promise made to William by King Edward the Confessor some 15 years earlier. The Normans imposed unity and linked it permanently with the culture of Southern Europe.

Battle of Hastings 黑斯廷斯战役

Duke of Normandy 诺曼公爵；诺曼底公爵

■ *The Middle Ages*

  Remains of Norman castles on English hill tops bore testimony to the military might used by the invaders to sustain their conquest—although Wales and Scotland resisted for centuries. The Normans operated a feudal system, creating an aristocracy that treated native Anglo-Saxons as serfs. The ruling class spoke French until the 13th century, when it mixed with the Old English used by the peasants. The medieval church's power is shown in the cathedrals that grace British cities today.

feudal system 封建制度

Understanding More about China

1. Chinese Chronology

夏	Xia Dynasty	C2070—C1600 BC
商	Shang Dynasty	C1600—C1046 BC

周	Zhou Dynasty	
西周	Western Zhou Dynasty	C1046—771 BC
东周	Eastern Zhou Dynasty	770—256 BC
春秋	Spring and Autumn Period	770—476 BC
战国	Warring States	475—221 BC
秦	Qin Dynasty	221—207 BC
汉	Han Dynasty	
西汉	Western Han	202 BC—28 AD
东汉	Eastern Han	25 AD—220 AD
三国	Three Kingdoms	
魏	Wei	220—265
蜀	Shu	221—263
吴	Wu	222—280
晋	Jin Dynasty	
西晋	Western Jin Dynasty	265—316
东晋	Eastern Jin Dynasty	317—420
南北朝	Northern and Southern Dynasty	
北朝	Northern Dynasty	386—581
南朝	Southern Dynasty	420—589
隋	Sui Dynasty	581—618
唐	Tang Dynasty	618—907
五代十国	Five Dynasties and Ten States	907—979
宋	Song Dynasty	
北宋	Northern Song Dynasty	960—1127
南宋	Southern Song Dynasty	1127—1276
辽	Liao Dynasty	916—1125
西夏	Western Xia	1038—1227
金	Jin Dynasty	1115—1234
元	Yuan Dynasty	1271—1368
明	Ming Dynasty	1368—1644
清	Qing Dynasty	1644—1911
中华民国	Republic of China	1912—1949
中华人民共和国	People's Republic of China	1949—

2. Prehistoric Cultures of China
—The Yangshao Culture（仰韶文化）

Prehistoric cultures of different types have been found in all parts of China, among which Yangshao Culture, Dawenkou Culture, Hemudu Culture, Banpo Culture, Longshan Culture, and Majiayao Culture are of the greatest importance.

The Yangshao Culture was a Neolithic culture that existed extensively along the central Yellow River in China. The Yangshao people lived in round or rectangular houses in the mountainous regions that were below ground level and surrounded by little walls of earth. They cultivated millet extensively; some villages also cultivated wheat or rice. They kept such animals as pigs and dogs, as well as sheep, goats, and cattle, but much of their meat came from hunting and fishing. Their stone tools were polished and highly specialized. The Yangshao people may also have practiced a nearly form of silkworm cultivation. Especially noteworthy was their gray or red pottery, so the Yangshao Culture, also referred to as the "Painted Pottery" Culture.

Exercises

I. Choose the answer that best completes the statement.
1. For centuries, invaders and incomers have made their mark in Great Britain. The last of the foreign invasions of the British Isles is _____.
   A. the Normans   B. the Vikings
   C. the Romans   D. the Anglo-Saxons
2. Hadrian's Wall is probably the most spectacular memorial left by the _____ in England.
   A. Vikings   B. Anglo-Saxons   C. Jutes   D. Romans
3. The beginning of the Anglo-Saxon invasion was in the _____ century.
   A. 5th   B. 7th   C. 8th   D. 10th
4. The Westminster Abbey was founded by _____.
   A. King Arthur   B. King Edward I
   C. King Alfred the Great   D. King Harold

II. Read the following statements and decide whether they are true (T) or false (F).
1. The Act of Union of 1536 joined England and Scotland. _____
2. The island of Ireland came under British influence, and it became a colonial dependency in 1690. _____
3. Stonehenge is the best known and probably the most remarkable of prehistoric remains in the UK. _____
4. In the middle of the first century BC Julius Caesar landed the British Isles. _____
5. Roman soldiers looked very similar to the Celts they defeated. _____
6. The Roman legions occupied England and Scotland. _____
7. The Romans preferred to settle down in England as people there were very friendly. _____
8. Very few Romans settled down in Britain but the native language absorbed many

Latin words. _____

9. At the beginning of the 5th century the Romans were forced to withdraw from England. Many of the Romanized Britons went north to Scotland and Northern Ireland. _____

10. The Anglo-Saxons maintained almost every trace of the civilization of the Romans. _____

11. The Vikings were people from Scandinavia whose life was working the land and fishing. _____

12. During the Battle of Hastings, the Saxons were defeated, and William became king of England. _____

13. The Normans operated a feudal system, creating an aristocracy that treated native Anglo-Saxons as serfs. _____

14. The Norman ruling class only spoke English and Latin. _____

III. Short-answer questions.
1. How did the UK come into existence?
2. What elements of Roman civilization were introduced into England?
3. Why did the English lose the Battle of Hastings?

Unit 3

British History (2)

❏ **In this unit you will learn about**
1. Industrial Revolution
2. Britain today

✓参考答案
✓更多资源

Vocabulary

- behead 砍头，斩首
- cholera 霍乱
- culminate 终于获得某种结局或结果
- dearth 缺乏，稀少
- deplorable 可悲的，可怜的
- deprivation 剥夺
- ensue 继而发生
- monastery 修道院
- provoke 产生，引起
- throes 剧痛
- treason 叛国（如战时通敌）；背叛，叛逆
- typhoid 伤寒

Key Sentences

1. The Renaissance in arts and learning spread from Europe to Britain, with playwright William Shakespeare adding his own unique contribution.
   文艺复兴从欧洲传到英国，剧作家莎士比亚也做出了自己独特的贡献。

2. In the 18th century, Britain was free from the revolutionary atmosphere that prevailed in the 17th century.
   18世纪，英国摆脱了17世纪盛行的革命氛围。

3. The country became more and more wealthy through trade; the middle-class and landowners lived in a mood of complacency. The power of the king continued to decline.
   这个国家通过贸易变得越来越富裕；中产阶级和地主生活在一种自满的情绪中。国王的权力继续下降。

4. The most outstanding political leader of this time was Sir Robert Walpole (1676—1745), the first "Prime Minister," who developed the idea of the Cabinet.
   当时最杰出的政治领袖是罗伯特·沃波尔爵士(1676—1745)，他是第一位提出内阁构想的"首相"。

5. The Tories were supported by the gentry, the landed aristocracy, and the Anglican Church.
   托利党得到了贵族、地主贵族和英国国教会的支持。

6. During the reign of George III Britain lost 13 of the American colonies, which formed the United States of America.
   乔治三世统治期间，英国失去了13个美洲殖民地，这13个州成立了美利坚合众国。

7. In 1800, Parliament passed the Act of Union, which united Great Britain and Ireland into a single political unit, known as the United Kingdom of Great Britain and Ireland.

1800年,议会通过了《联合法案》,将大不列颠和爱尔兰统一为一个单一的政治单位,即大不列颠及爱尔兰联合王国。

8. At the end of the 18th century Britain entered the period known as the Industrial Revolution.
18世纪末,英国进入了工业革命时期。

9. Small children were also made to work in the factories. The working hours were long, salaries were very less and there were no holidays.
孩童也被迫在工厂里工作。工作时间长,工资低,没有假期。

10. Huang Di, or the Yellow Emperor, one of the most renowned legendary figures in Chinese mythology and culture said to have lived in the prehistoric period.
黄帝是中国神话和文化中最著名的传奇人物之一,据说生活在史前时期。

11. Chi You was a Chinese god of war and the inventor of metal weapons in Chinese mythology. In some legends he was with Huang Di; in others he was said to be defeated by him.
蚩尤是中国的战神,是中国神话中金属武器的发明者。在一些传说中他和黄帝并肩作战;也有另一种传说是他被黄帝打败了。

12. Huang Di was credited with many inventions that made life better for his people, including writing, the pottery wheel, and a method of breeding silkworms.
黄帝的许多发明让他的人民生活得更好,其中包括书写、制作陶轮和养蚕的方法。

13. Lei Zu was the first wife of Huang Di. She started sericulture, and was worshiped as the Sericulture Goddess after she died.
嫘祖是黄帝的第一任妻子。她开启了养蚕业,死后被奉为蚕神。

Warm-up Exercise

1. What was the root of English Civil War? What was the result of the Civil War?

2. What is the "divine right of kings"?

3. Why was the revolution of 1688 called the "Glorious Revolution"?

Introduce China in English

1. Who is Huang Di (黄帝)?

2. Who is Lei Zu (嫘祖)?

Text

iCT

This unit introduces the major historical events in British history after the 16th century.

■ Tudor Renaissance

After years of civil war, the Tudor monarchs established peace and national self-confidence, reflected in the split from the church of Rome—due to Henry Ⅷ's divorce from Catherine of Aragon—and the consequent closure of the monasteries. Henry's daughter, Mary Ⅰ, tried to reestablish Catholicism but under her half-sister, Elizabeth Ⅰ or the Virgin Queen, the Protestant church secured its position.

Overseas exploration began, provoking clashes with other European powers seeking to exploit the New World.

The Renaissance in arts and learning spread from Europe to Britain, with playwright William Shakespeare adding his own unique contribution.

Tudor 都铎王朝(1485—1603)
Henry Ⅷ 亨利八世
Catherine of Aragon 西班牙阿拉贡的凯瑟琳公主，血腥玛丽（Bloody Mary）的母亲。
Virgin Queen 童贞女王

Renaissance 文艺复兴

■ Stuart Britain

After the death of Queen Elizabeth Ⅰ in 1603, her nephew James Ⅰ (1603—1625), the son of Mary Queen of Scots (beheaded for treason on the order of Elizabeth), succeeded to the English throne. He then became the ruler of the two kingdoms. James believed in the mediaeval idea of the "divine right" and absolute authority of the king.

divine right 君权神授

His son Charles I (1625—1649) was a weak monarch. He had Catholic sympathies and was unpopular among the Puritans who wanted a radical reform of the Church of England. Charles attempted to reduce the power of Parliament and as a result of this a bloody civil war followed in 1642 between the king's supporters (Cavaliers) and the Parliamentary forces (Roundheads) recruited mostly from London and other towns, led by the military genius Oliver Cromwell (1599—1658). It ended with victory for the Roundheads, the king executed, and England declared a republic—with Cromwell hailed as "Protector."

Cavalier（英国内战中）拥护查理一世的人,保皇党人
Roundheads 圆颅党人（英国内战时期的议会派人士）
Protector 护国公

However, Cromwell behaved like a dictator. He dissolved Parliament and ruled with the help of his army. Soon after his death the monarchy was restored. Charles II (1660—1685) resumed the throne taken from his father. However, the king's authority was reduced significantly in favour of Parliament.

James II (1685—1688) was an ardent Catholic and wanted to reimpose Catholicism in England. He had to flee the country when Parliament invited William of Orange and his wife Mary to take the English throne. The deposition of King James II in 1688 was called by its supporters the "Glorious Revolution," achieved without bloodshed.

William of Orange 威廉三世,奥兰治国王
Glorious Revolution 光荣革命

■ *The Eighteenth Century*

In the 18th century, Britain was free from the revolutionary atmosphere that prevailed in the 17th century. The country became more and more wealthy through trade; the middle-class and landowners lived in a mood of complacency. The power of the king continued to decline. For the first time the king's ministers became real policy-makers. In 1707 the Act of Union formally united England and Scotland. In 1714, when Queen Anne, the last of the Stuarts died, Parliament chose the German-speaking elector of Hanover who was crowned as George I. He was succeeded by his son, George II, who, like his father, had little interest in British internal affairs.

The most outstanding political leader of this time was Sir Robert Walpole (1676—1745), the first "Prime Minister," who developed the idea of the Cabinet, i.e. a group of ministers who took the actual control of administration from the Crown. In Parliament a two-party system began to evolve. Those who chiefly represented the financial and mercantile interests of the cities and towns, and the progressive element in the aristocracy opposed to any interference in politics by the monarchy, were called Whigs. Those who were strongly attached to tradition and the monarchy were called Tories. The Tories were supported by the gentry, the landed aristocracy, and the Anglican Church.

During the reign of George Ⅲ Britain lost 13 of the American colonies, which formed the United States of America. In 1800, Parliament passed the Act of Union, which united Great Britain and Ireland into a single political unit, known as the United Kingdom of Great Britain and Ireland.

In the late 18th century there were the beginnings of a movement of population away from the countryside into the towns, partly as a result of enclosures. This meant that the old common land used by peasants for grazing was taken over by private landowners for more intensive agriculture and enclosed by hedgerows.

At the end of the 18th century Britain entered the period known as the Industrial Revolution. Steam engines, canals and railways announced the approach of it. Thriving commercial banks provided financing for investments in industrial plants and machinery. Advances in agriculture also contributed to the industrialization process.

The first phase of industrialization centered on the production of cotton clothing. One of the new machines was known as the spinning jenny. The operation of machinery became more efficient and profitable with the addition of waterpower and later the perfection of the steam engine by Scottish inventor James Watt. Cotton production soared. Industrialization transformed nearly every aspect of British life.

However, the labourers who actually produced goods were living in deplorable conditions. As more and more people were flocking to the cities from villages in search of job opportunities, there was a gross dearth of accommodation. The workers were forced to live in small, dingy houses which also led to the spread of communicable diseases. Many people died

Whig 辉格党党员
Tory 托利党

enclosure 圈地运动，英国新兴的资产阶级和新贵族通过暴力把农民从土地上赶走，把强占的土地圈占起来，变成私有的大牧场、大农场。
Industrial Revolution 工业革命

spinning jenny 珍妮纺纱机

James Watt 瓦特，苏格兰机器制造家和发明家。

because of fatal diseases like cholera, plague and typhoid. Small children were also made to work in the factories. The working hours were long, salaries were very low and there were no holidays. The air was filled with black smoke from the factory chimneys and the pollution was at its peak causing huge damage to the environment.

■ *Victorian Britain*

Queen Victoria ruled Britain from 1837 to 1901. Her reign was the longest of any monarch in British history and came to be known as the Victorian era. When Victoria became Queen in 1837, Britain was in the throes of its transformation from an agricultural country to the world's most powerful industrial nation. The growth of the Empire fuelled the country's confidence and opened up markets for Britain's manufactured goods. The accelerating growth of cities created problems of health and housing and a powerful labour movement began to emerge. But by the end of Victoria's long reign in 1901, conditions had begun to improve as more people got the vote and universal education was introduced.

■ *Britain from 1900 to 1950*

When Queen Victoria's reign ended in 1901, British society threw off many of its 19th-century inhibitions, and an era of gaiety and excitement began. This was interrupted by World War Ⅰ. The economic troubles that ensued, which culminated in the Depression of the 1930s, brought misery to millions. In 1939 the ambitions of Germany provoked World War Ⅱ. After emerging victorious from this conflict, Britain embarked on an ambitious programme of social, educational and health reform.

Depression 经济大萧条

■ *Britain Today*

With the deprivations of war receding, Britain entered the Swinging Sixties, an explosion of youth culture characterized by the mini-skirt and the emergence of pop groups. The Age of Empire came to an end as most colonies gained independence by

Swinging Sixties 摇摆的六十年代

the 1970s—although Britain went to war with Argentina in 1982.

People were on the move; immigration from the former colonies enriched British culture—though it also gave rise to social problems—and increasing prosperity allowed millions of people to travel abroad. Britain joined the European Community in 1973, and forged a more tangible link when the Channel Tunnel opened in 1994.

European Community 欧共体
Channel Tunnel 英法海底隧道

Scottish independence referendum took place on 18 September 2014.

An in-out referendum on its EU membership, also called Brexit, was held on June 23, 2016. Now Britain has withdrew from the European Union.

What is the future of the United Kingdom?

Understanding More about China

1. Huang Di (黄帝)

Huang Di, or the Yellow Emperor, one of the most renowned legendary figures in Chinese mythology and culture is said to have lived in the prehistoric period. He appears in a variety of myths and legends. The earliest stories portray Huang Di as a mythological ruler, a hero who fought other emperors. He defeated Yan Di (the Flame Emperor), Chi You (蚩尤), the Four Emperors, and a variety of others.

The Yellow Emperor and the Flame Emperor (炎帝) were said to be brothers, each lord of half of the world. Their battles can be thought of as wars between the elements of water and fire. Bears, wolves, and an assortment of other ferocious animals fought as part of Huang Di's army. It took three years and much blood for Huang Di finally to defeat his brother.

Chi You was a Chinese god of war and the inventor of metal weapons in Chinese mythology. In some legends he was with Huang Di; in others he was said to be defeated by him. Chi You commanded the wind and rain, but Huang Di prevailed because he had power over Ying Long, the Responding Dragon, and Ying's daughter, Drought Fury. He ordered them to prevent the rain from falling and gained the upper hand.

A later story holds that the Yellow Emperor was helped in his battles by a Daoist goddess called the Dark Lady. The Dark Lady instructed him in the art of war and helped him win. Huang Di was also said to have learned alchemy from Zao Jun, a god of the stove and kitchen in Daoism.

The Han Dynasty considered Huang Di the third of the legendary emperors, after

Fu Xi and Shen Nong. He was said to have lived from 2698 BC to 2598 BC. Huang Di was credited with many inventions that made life better for his people, including writing, the pottery wheel, and a method of breeding silkworms.

2. Lei Zu (嫘祖)

According to a text from *Shiji* (Chapter 1), Huang Di married a girl from the Xiling clan. Her name was Lei Zu. As the first wife of Huang Di, she gave birth to two sons. In many other ancient writings, Lei Zu was commonly said to have started sericulture, so she was worshiped as Xiancan, the ancestress of sericulture.

When she saw Xuan Yuan turning a waterwheel, she had an idea. She had a small wooden spinning wheel made with a handle fixed on it. When she turned the handle and reeled the silk, the threads orderly rolled onto the wheel. From then on, the silk threads were never tangled.

Then Lei Zu began to weave. At first, she tried to imitate the spider's weaving but failed, because the silk was not as sticky as the spider's thread. One day when she went out to fish, she saw a big fish swimming back and forth freely between the reeds. She then thought that she could weave by using a shuttle shaped like fish to weave back and forth between the silk threads. Her method proved effective. She quickly wove a piece of fabric and formerly named it "silk." She then taught all the women of her clan the skill of weaving. Because of her great contribution to human life, Lei Zu won considerable respect.

Exercises

Ⅰ. Choose the answer that best completes the statement.
1. Who is awarded the title of the Virgin Queen? _____
   A. Elizabeth Ⅱ   B. Mary
   C. Catherine of Aragon   D. Elizabeth Ⅰ
2. During the English Civil War, the king's supporters were called _____.
   A. Roundheads   B. Tories   C. Cavaliers   D. Whigs
3. The idea of the Cabinet was developed by the first "Prime Minister" _____.
   A. William of Orange   B. Oliver Cromwell
   C. Sir Robert Walpole   D. Queen Anne
4. The perfection of the steam engine was made by _____ inventor James Watt.
   A. English   B. Scottish   C. Welsh   D. Irish
5. Britain joined the European Community in _____.
   A. 1953   B. 1963   C. 1973   D. 1983

6. The Channel Tunnel opened in _____.
   A. 1974　　　　B. 1979　　　　C. 1985　　　　D. 1994

Ⅱ. **Read the following statements and decide whether they are true (T) or false (F).**
   1. The Renaissance started in Britain and spread to Italy. _____
   2. In the 18th century, Britain was free from the revolutionary atmosphere, and the country became more and more wealthy through trade. _____
   3. After the queen died in 1603, her nephew succeeded to the English throne. He then became the ruler of the kingdom of England and Wales. _____
   4. Soon after the death of Cromwell the monarchy was restored. _____
   5. In the 18th century, the power of the king continued to decline. For the first time the king's ministers became real policy-makers. _____
   6. Those who were strongly attached to tradition and the monarchy were called Whigs. _____
   7. In the late 18th century there were the beginnings of a movement of population away from the countryside into the towns, partly as a result of enclosures. _____
   8. The first phase of industrialization centered on the production of steel. _____

Ⅲ. **Short-answer questions.**
   1. What are the causes of the English Civil War? What are the two sides of the war? What are the final results of the war?
   2. Why did the Industrial Revolution take place in Britain? What is the process and impact of the Industrial Revolution?

Unit 4

British Literature

❑ **In this unit you will learn about**
1. Historical development of British literature
2. Famous writers and their masterpieces

✓参考答案
✓更多资源

Vocabulary

- archetypal 典型的
- aristocratic 贵族的
- artificial 人造的，人工的
- auspices / under the auspices of sb/sth 在某人/某事物的帮助或支持下；有某人/某事物赞助的
- avenge 为［某人（自己）的冤屈］报仇，伸冤，雪耻
- ballad 歌谣；诗歌；（尤指）叙事歌谣
- baronet 准男爵（英国世袭爵位中最低等级的受勋者，地位在男爵之下爵士之上）
- blank verse 无韵诗
- blossom 开花；繁荣，兴旺
- brawl 大声争吵，打架
- calf 小牛；犊
- clergy 神职人员；（尤指基督教的）教士或牧师
- comedy 喜剧
- court 宫廷，朝廷
- Dane 丹麦人
- Danish 丹麦的，丹麦人的
- deputy 副手
- dialect 方言
- diplomatic 外交的
- discard 扔掉，丢弃
- dramatist 剧作家，编剧
- drown 淹死，溺死
- dwarf 使（某人/某物）相比之下显得小
- epic 史诗
- essay （尤指）短文，小品文，散文
- experimentation 实验，试验
- flexional 词尾可变化的
- foreshadow 预示，预兆
- forester 林务员
- fugitive 逃跑者，逃亡者
- gentry 绅士，上等人

- governess （尤指旧时）家庭女教师
- hostelry 客栈，旅店
- knight （中古时代的）骑士
- lament 为（某人/某事物）感到悲痛；哀悼；痛惜
- materialism 物质享乐主义（迷恋于占有财富、肉体享受等，而轻视精神价值）
- monumental 极大的
- mystic 神秘主义者
- neoclassicism 新古典主义
- noteworthy 值得注意的，显著的
- novelist 小说家
- ode （通常为长篇的）颂诗
- pamphlet 小册子
- pastoral 乡村生活的，田园风光的，牧人的，田园式的（尤指理想化描述的）
- pilgrim 朝圣者；香客
- pit 使某人/某事物与他人/他事物较量
- playwright 剧作家
- posthumous 死后发生的，死后获得的
- preacher 传教士，讲道者
- prose 散文（区别于韵文）
- Puritan 清教徒（16世纪和17世纪英国基督教新教徒派之一，主张简化宗教仪式）
- pyre （火葬用的）大堆供燃烧之木材等
- ravage 严重损坏（某物）；毁坏
- restoration 重新采用，恢复
- satire 讽刺作品
- secular 世俗的
- *Shijing*《诗经》
- slay 杀，残杀（尤指敌人）
- Song *ci*（verse）宋词
- sonnet 十四行诗
- stab 戳（某物）；刺伤（某人）；用（刀等）捅某人
- stable-keeper 马厩看守人

- subject 臣民;国民
- swine 猪
- Tang Poetry 唐诗
- tempestuous 狂暴的
- tinker（走街串巷的）小炉匠儿
- tragedy 悲剧
- veal（食用的）小牛肉
- verse 韵文;诗;诗句;诗体
- versification 作诗法,诗学;韵律
- wicked（指人或人的行为）不道德的,缺德的,邪恶的

Key Sentences

1. Literature makes a very important part of culture.
   文学是文化的一个重要组成部分。

2. There are many ways that literary historians choose to categorize English literature.
   文学史学家对英国文学的分类方法有很多种。

3. In each period, Great Britain has produced many world famous writers.
   在每一个时期,英国都产生了许多世界知名的作家。

4. The poem provides a vivid picture of life and the way of thinking of the Anglo-Saxons.
   这首诗生动地描绘了盎格鲁-撒克逊人的生活和思维方式。

5. The Duke of Normandy's victory over King Harold in 1066 meant radical and painful changes for Anglo-Saxon culture and customs.
   1066 年,诺曼底公爵战胜哈罗德国王意味着盎格鲁-撒克逊文化和习俗发生了彻底而痛苦的变化。

6. The Normans not only forced their French language upon the English but also introduced the feudal system and martial rule.
   诺曼人不仅把法语强加给英国人,而且还引入了封建制度和军事统治。

7. However, from about 1350 onward, secular literature began to rise.
   然而,大约从 1350 年开始,世俗文学开始兴起。

8. This period witnessed Geoffrey Chaucer, known as the Father of English Literature.
   这一时期见证了被誉为英国文学之父的杰弗里·乔叟。

9. The Elizabethan Age was the golden age of English drama.
   伊丽莎白时代是英国戏剧的黄金时代。

10. It was a time of great social, religious, intellectual, and economic issues.
    那是一个社会、宗教、知识和经济问题严重的时代。

11. Dickens lived through the Industrial Revolution. He wrote about how life was changing, especially for poor people.

狄更斯经历了工业革命。他的作品描写了生活是如何改变的，尤其是穷人的生活。

12. The Brontes produced a cast of unforgettable characters.
    勃朗特三姐妹创造了一批令人难忘的人物形象。

13. George Bernard Shaw wrote a great many other plays that exposed illusions and false values.
    萧伯纳还写了许多揭露幻想和错误价值观的剧本。

14. The themes and subject matter of this period tended to be rural or pastoral in nature.
    这一时期的主题和题材倾向于乡村或田园性质。

15. Traditional Chinese poetry and music are inseparably intertwined.
    中国传统诗歌与音乐密不可分。

16. After the end of the Zhou Dynasty, Chinese poetry continued to develop over a period of more than 800 years, coming to full blossom during the Tang Dynasty.
    周代结束后，中国诗歌在800多年的时间里不断发展，到唐代达到了全盛时期。

17. The themes are mostly about specific events or persons and are often sad.
    主题大多是关于特定的事件或人，往往是悲伤的。

18. Li Bai, dubbed "The God of Poetry," was often drunk but produced the best works with flair in the intoxicated state.
    被誉为"诗仙"的李白，常常醉酒，却在醉酒的状态下写出了最富才华的作品。

19. Du Fu, dubbed "The Saint of Poetry," lived an impoverished life and moved from place to place because of war. Most of his poems are sad.
    被誉为"诗圣"的杜甫生活贫寒，因战乱辗转各地。他的诗大多是悲伤的。

20. It entered its golden period during the Song Dynasty.
    在宋代进入了黄金时代。

Warm-up Exercise

1. Can you name a few of William Shakespeare's comedies and tragedies?

2. Who are Bronte sisters and what are their representative works?

3. Who is the author of *Pride and Prejudice*? What are the other masterpieces of this author?

Introduce China in English

1. Can you recite any poems written by any poets of the Tang Dynasty?

2. When was *Shijing* (《诗经》) compiled?

Text

Literature makes a very important part of culture. There are many ways that literary historians choose to categorize English literature, but for convenience and for discussion, they tend to divide it into "periods." In each period, Great Britain has produced many world famous writers.

■ *Old English Period (450—1066)*

This period of literature dates back to Anglo-Saxon invasion (along with the Jutes) of Celtic England around 450 and ends in 1066. Much of the first half of this period, prior to the seventh-century, at least, was oral literature; however, some works, such as the bloody Anglo-Saxon epic *Beowulf*, written sometime between the 8th century and the late 10th century, is the oldest surviving epic poem in the English language.

The poem relates the deeds of Beowulf, a Danish hero, who sails from Sweden to Denmark to come to the help of his brother Hrothgar, king of the Danes. Hrothgar's castle and land are ravaged by a monster of human shape called Grendel. Beowulf fights the monster and tears away his arm. Grendel, although mortally wounded, escapes, leaving tracks of blood that lead to a cave in the sea. Hrothgar's court is overjoyed at Beowulf's victory, but Grendel's mother, determined to avenge her son, appears and carries off a Danish knight. Beowulf follows Grendel's mother into the sea-cave, kills her and returns to the court with the head of Grendel he has cut off. At Hrothgar's death, Beowulf is proclaimed king. Many years later, another fight takes place, this time involving an aged Beowulf and a fire-breathing dragon. The old hero slays the dragon but eventually dies of its fiery breath. Beowulf is then burned on a pyre, and his people lament his death.

The poem provides a vivid picture of life and the way of thinking of the Anglo-Saxons.

■ *Middle English Period (1066—1500)*

The Duke of Normandy's victory over King Harold in 1066

ICT

Beowulf《贝奥武夫》，被认为是古英语文学的最高成就和最早用欧洲地方语言写成的英雄史诗。

Grendel 格伦德尔。《贝奥武夫》中的巨人怪物，最终被贝奥武夫杀死。

Duke of Normandy "征服者威廉"（William the Conquer）。他从法国西部海岸横渡英吉利海峡并征服了英格兰。

meant radical and painful changes for Anglo-Saxon culture and customs. The new masters, the Normans, did not trouble to learn the language of their subjects. Therefore, until the fourteenth century, three languages (and many dialects) were spoken in England: French among the nobility and at court, Latin among the learned clergy, and English among the ordinary people (nine tenths of the population). The mixed character of the English language as spoken today, with its Latin and Germanic bases, goes back to this period.

This period witnessed Geoffrey Chaucer, known as the Father of English Literature. Chaucer (c. 1340—1400), the son of a London wine merchant, had an interesting career that included positions at court in the service of King Edward Ⅲ. He was buried in the Poet's Corner of Westminster Abbey.

Chaucer was initially very interested in French poetry. During the last period of his poetic career Chaucer turned to English themes, and in 1386 he began The Canterbury Tales which he left unfinished at his death. The Canterbury Tales is a collection of stories told by pilgrims who have met at a hostelry in Southwark. In order to pass the time as they travel from this part of London to the shrine of Saint Thomas à Becket at Canterbury and back, the accompanying host convinces them to tell four stories each, two on the way and two on the return trip. But the work is incomplete: instead of c. 120 tales (by the 29 pilgrims), there are only 24 stories told altogether. This work displayed not only the vigor and vitality of the English language, but also shaped the future of the language for centuries to come.

Geoffrey Chaucer 杰弗里·乔叟,英国诗人,被后人誉为"英国诗歌之父"。

Poet's Corner of Westminster Abbey 威斯敏斯特大教堂诗人角

The Canterbury Tales 《坎特伯雷故事集》

Saint Thomas à Becket 圣托马斯·贝克特,英格兰国王亨利二世的大法官兼上议院议长(Lord Chancellor),坎特伯雷大主教。

■ *The Renaissance (1500—1660)*

Recently, critics and literary historians have begun to call this the "Early Modern" period, but here we retain the historically familiar term "Renaissance." This period is often subdivided into four parts, including the Elizabethan Age (1558—1603), the Jacobean Age (1603—1625), the Caroline Age (1625—1649), and the Commonwealth Period (1649—1660).

The Elizabethan Age was the golden age of English drama.

Some of its noteworthy figures include Christopher Marlowe, Francis Bacon, Edmund Spenser, and, of course, William Shakespeare.

Shakespeare was born in Stratford-upon-Avon in 1564. He wrote 38 plays and 154 sonnets. He wrote sad stories called tragedies (like *Romeo and Juliet*, *Hamlet*, *Othello*, *King Lear*, *Macbeth*), funny stories or comedies (like *All's Well That Ends Well*, *As You Like It*, *Love's Labour's Lost*, *Measure for Measure*, *The Merchant of Venice*, *The Merry Wives of Windsor*, *A Midsummer Night's Dream*, *Much Ado About Nothing*, *The Tempest*, *Twelfth Night*) and stories about historical figures such as *Julius Caesar*. Shakespeare died on his birthday in 1616.

Stratford-upon-Avon 埃文河畔的斯特拉特福镇。

The Jacobean Age is named for the reign of James Ⅰ. The King James translation of the Bible appeared during this period.

Jacobean 英王詹姆斯一世时期的

The Caroline Age covers the reign of Charles Ⅰ. John Milton, Robert Burton, and George Herbert are some of the notable figures.

John Milton (1608—1674) was a Puritan. About the middle of 1652 he became completely blind. Blind, half-fugitive, and disillusioned, he composed some of the most powerful poetic works in the English language, *Paradise Lost* and *Paradise Regained*. Milton created a new kind of English for this poem, a blank verse which was highly artificial and removed from everyday speech.

John Milton 约翰·弥尔顿，英国诗人。代表作品有长诗《失乐园》《复乐园》等。

George Herbert (1593—1633), one of the better known Anglican metaphysical poets, poured forth his quiet and sincere verse in *The Temple* which was published posthumously and contains 160 poems. Herbert is also known for his so-called pattern poems.

metaphysical poetry 玄学派诗歌。于17世纪在英国发展出的一种高度理性的诗歌。

Finally, there is the Commonwealth Age, so named for the period between the end of the English Civil War and the restoration of the Stuart monarchy—this is the time when Oliver Cromwell ruled the nation. At this time, public theatres were closed for nearly two decades to prevent public assembly. John Milton and Thomas Hobbes' political writings appeared.

restoration 王政复辟时期。克伦威尔执政的共和时期结束后，查理二世重登王位（1660—1685年在位）时期。

■ The Neoclassical Period (1660—1785)

The Neoclassical period is also subdivided into ages, including the Restoration (1660—1700), the Augustan Age (1700—1745), and the Age of Sensibility (1745—1785).

During the Age of Restoration, Restoration Comedies developed. Satire, too, became quite popular. Notable writers of the age include John Bunyan, and John Locke.

John Bunyan (1628—1688) received little education and knew only one book really well—the Bible. Both his style and imagery depend heavily on it. Of his several works it is *The Pilgrim's Progress*, begun in Bedfordshire jail and fully published in two parts in 1684, which has left a lasting impression.

The Augustan Age was the time of Jonathan Swift (1667—1745), who is remembered for works such as *Gulliver's Travels*. Daniel Defoe (1660—1731), an English trader, writer, journalist, and spy, most famous for his novel *Robinson Crusoe*, was also popular at this time.

During the Age of Sensibility, ideas such as neoclassicism, a critical and literary mode, and the Enlightenment, a particular worldview shared by many intellectuals, were defended vigorously. Famous novelists include Henry Fielding, Samuel Richardson, as well as the poets William Cowper and Thomas Percy.

William Cowper (1731—1800) was the poet of nature and is mainly remembered for *The Task* (1785), a poem of more than 5,000 lines of blank verse pitting friendly nature against the wicked town in rural scenes foreshadowing the work of Wordsworth.

■ The Romantic Period (1785—1832)

The beginning date for this period is often debated. Some claim it is 1785, immediately following the Age of Sensibility. Others say it began in 1789 with the start of the French Revolution, and still others believe 1798, the publication year for William Wordsworth & Samuel Taylor Coleridge's *Lyrical Ballads*, is its true beginning. It ends with the passage of the

---

Neoclassical period 新古典主义时期

John Bunyan 约翰·班扬,英国著名作家,代表作有《天路历程》。

Jonathan Swift 乔纳森·斯威夫特,代表作《格列佛游记》。

Robinson Crusoe《鲁滨孙漂流记》

Enlightenment 启蒙运动。17—18世纪欧洲的思想运动,它把上帝、理性、自然、人类等各种概念综合为一种世界观,得到广泛赞同,由此引起艺术、哲学和政治诸方面的各种革命性的发展变化。

Lyrical Ballads《抒情歌谣集》,是浪漫时期华兹华斯和柯勒律治的心血结晶。

Reform Bill and with the death of Sir Walter Scott (1771—1832), both a poet and a novelist, who acquired fame and wealth with such narrative poems as *The Lady of the Lake* (1810).

This era includes the works of William Wordsworth and Samuel Coleridge, as well as William Blake, Lord Byron, John Keats, Percy Bysshe Shelley, and Jane Austen.

William Blake (1757—1827) has been called a Romantic poet. Some critics have interpreted his work, together with the poetry of Wordsworth and Coleridge, as that of a member of the first generation of the Romantics.

Lord Byron (1788—1824) would seem to be the archetypal tragic Romantic poet. Even in his lifetime, he became a legend. Byron's most important and convincing poetic works are beyond doubt *Childe Harold's Pilgrimage* and his epic satire *Don Juan*.

John Keats (1795—1821) was born in London as the son of a stable-keeper. At first he wanted to become a doctor, but in 1816 he decided to devote his life to literature. His poems were almost all written in the brief space of the five years before his death and are models of the sensuous aspect of <u>Romanticism</u>. Keats's themes were love and death, and beauty in art and nature, tinged with melancholy and heart-ache. Beauty, love, and death are also dominant themes in his finest lyrics, the "Ode to a Nightingale," the "Ode on Melancholy," and the "Ode on a Grecian Urn," all written in 1819.

Like Byron, Percy Bysshe Shelley (1792—1822) was of aristocratic origin. In 1822 he drowned in a thunderstorm while at sea. His "<u>Ode to the West Wind</u>" possesses great melodic power in the treatment of his favorite themes of freedom, beauty, and love.

Jane Austen (1775—1817) was an English novelist known primarily for her novels which interpret, critique and comment upon the life of the British landed gentry at the end of the 18th century. Austen's major novels include *Sense and Sensibility* (1811), *Pride and Prejudice* (1813), *Mansfield Park* (1814), *Emma* (1815) and the like.

> Romanticism 18世纪在欧洲兴起的文学、艺术和哲学运动，大约持续到19世纪中叶。浪漫主义强调个性、主观、非理性、想象、个人、自发、情感、空幻及玄奥等，既是启蒙运动的延续，也是对它的一种反抗。
>
> "Ode to the West Wind"《西风颂》

■ *The Victorian Period (1832—1901)*

This period is named for the reign of Queen Victoria. It was a time of great social, religious, intellectual, and economic issues.

Poets of this time include Robert and Elizabeth Barrett Browning, Christina Rossetti, Alfred, Lord Tennyson, and Matthew Arnold, among others.

Thomas Carlyle, John Ruskin, and Walter Pater were advancing the essay form.

Finally, prose fiction truly found its place and made its mark, under the auspices of Charles Dickens, Charlotte and Emily Bronte, and many others.

Charles Dickens is a famous English writer. He was born in England in 1812 and died in 1870. People all over the world love his stories. His first big success was *The Pickwick Papers*. This was in 1837, the year Victoria became Britain's Queen. Dickens lived through the Industrial Revolution. He wrote about how life was changing, especially for poor people. His other popular works include: *Oliver Twist*, *The Old Curiosity Shop*, *David Copperfield*, *Bleak House*, *Hard Times*, *A Tale of Two Cities*, and *Great Expectations*.

Charlotte Bronte (1816—1855) and her sisters Emily Bronte (1818—1848) and Anne Bronte (1820—1849) have charmed, inspired, and even shocked readers from the Victorian age to the present. Raised in Haworth, Yorkshire, the three sisters produced such classics as <u>Jane Eyre</u>, <u>Wuthering Heights</u>, and *The Tenant of Wildfell Hall*. Influenced by British Romantic poets like Wordsworth, Scott, and Byron, the Brontes produced a cast of unforgettable characters such as the devoted governess, Jane Eyre, and the lovers, Heathcliff, Cathy, and Hareton.

Jane Eyre《简·爱》,夏洛蒂·勃朗特创作的长篇小说。

Wuthering Heights《呼啸山庄》,艾米莉·勃朗特的作品,19世纪英国文学的代表作之一。

■ *The Edwardian Period (1901—1914)*

This period is named for King Edward Ⅷ and covers the period between Victoria's death and the outbreak of World War Ⅰ. Although a short period, the era includes incredible classic novelists such as Joseph Conrad, Ford Madox Ford, Rudyard Kipling, H.G. Wells, and Henry James, notable poets such as William Butler Yeats, as well as dramatists such as George Bernard Shaw.

Joseph Conrad (1857—1924) is an outstanding figure who brought a new quality into the novel. His Polish origin and his love for the sea had an impact on both his vision and his writing. Many critics agree that *Lord Jim* (1900) is Conrad's finest novel.

Ford Madox Ford (1873—1939) is a figure between traditionalists and modernists. His work has long been neglected, but there are signs that he is at last being recognized as a great novelist. Ford is remembered for his novels on Katherine Howard, such as *The Fifth Queen* (1905), and especially for *The Good Soldier* (1915).

George Bernard Shaw(1856—1950), an Irishman, he came from Dublin to London in 1876 and began his literary career with five unsuccessful novels as well as essays, theatre criticism and reviews. It was with *Widowers' Houses* (1892) and *Mrs. Warren's Profession* (1893) that he began to dominate European theatre. Shaw wrote a great many other plays that exposed illusions and false values.

Lord Jim《吉姆老爷》，英国籍波兰作家约瑟夫·康拉德于1900年创作的长篇小说。

Ford Madox Ford 福特·马多克斯·福特，代表作《好兵》《第五女王》等。

George Bernard Shaw 萧伯纳,全名乔治·伯纳德·萧,爱尔兰剧作家。作品有《鳏夫的房产》《华伦夫人的职业》等。

■ *The Georgian Period (1910—1936)*

This term usually refers to the reign of George Ⅴ (1910—1936). The themes and subject matter of this period tended to be rural or pastoral in nature, treated delicately and traditionally rather than with passion or with experimentation (as would be seen in the upcoming Modern period).

■ *The Modern Period (1914—?)*

The Modern Period traditionally applies to works written after the start of First World War. Common features include bold experimentation with subject matter, style and form, and encompasses narrative, verse, and drama.

Some of the most notable writers of this period include the novelists James Joyce, Virginia Woolf, Aldous Huxley, D. H.

Lawrence, Dorothy Richardson, Graham Greene, E. M. Forster, and Doris Lessing; the poets W. B. Yeats, T. S. Eliot, W. H. Auden, Seamus Heaney, Wilfred Owens, Dylan Thomas, and Robert Graves; and the dramatists Tom Stoppard, George Bernard Shaw, Samuel Beckett, Frank McGuinness, Harold Pinter, and Caryl Churchill.

James Joyce (1882—1941) focused on both the unconscious and language as used in the novel. Although not the first writer to use what came to be known as "stream of consciousness," Joyce was the most original of the modern novelists.

Aldous Huxley (1894—1963) also showed his satiric talent in many of his stories collected and published in 1956.

The novelist Graham Greene (1904—1991), who was also a journalist, has left vivid reports about his travels in Mexico (*The Lawless Roads*, 1939) and Africa (*Journey Without Maps*, 1936; and *In Search of a Character: Two African Journals*, 1961).

■ *The Postmodern Period (1945—?)*

This period began about the time that World War II ended. Many believe it is a direct response to Modernism. Some say the period ended about 1990, but it is likely too soon to declare this period closed. Poststructuralist literary theory and criticism developed during this time. Some notable writers of the period include Samuel Beckett, John Fowles and so on.

John Fowles (1926—2005), who is often described as the first postmodernist English novelist, seems a lesser writer because his literary effects are too laboured and because his experiments with fictional forms do not always produce the desired effects. A best-seller, *The French Lieutenant's Woman* (1969) was written by Fowles.

stream of consciousness 意识流。非戏剧性小说的一种叙事技巧,它产生无数连续不断的印象,有视觉的、听觉的、触觉的、联想的和潜意识的。意识流这个术语首先由威廉·詹姆斯在《心理学原理》(1890)一书中使用。20世纪,试图捕捉其作品中人物意识的全部流动过程的作家通常使用的内心独白的技巧,用以代表一系列的思想和感情。在乔伊斯的《尤利西斯》(1922)、福克纳的《喧哗与骚动》(1929)等小说中意识流起着重要的作用。

☐ **Understanding More about China**

1. Traditional Chinese Poetry: *Shijing* (诗经)

Traditional Chinese poetry and music are inseparably intertwined. Chinese poems are essentially lyrics. The number of words per line as well as the rhyming and the intonation of words are all strictly prescribed.

Compiled during the Zhou Dynasty, *Shijing*（诗经）, or *The Classic of Poetry*, is the earliest collection of Chinese poems. It contains 305 poems and was part of the curriculum for Confucius' students. One-hundred-and-sixty poems in the book are folk songs（风）that were collected from 15 regions in the country. One-hundred-and-five poems are in the "aesthetic" section（雅）, of which 71 were songs for entertainment at informal dinners and 34 for official banquets. The remaining 40 poems（颂）were meant for religious ceremonies and were sung at dances. All the poems were originally sung with instrumental accompaniment but the musical notes have long been lost. The poems are well-written and concise, with the economy of words being typical of old Chinese writing.

2. Tang Poetry（唐诗）

After the end of the Zhou Dynasty, Chinese poetry continued to develop over a period of more than 800 years, coming to full blossom during the Tang Dynasty.

There are two categories in classical Tang poetry: one has five words per line（五言）, and the other, seven（七言）. Each category is further divided into two patterns. One pattern is limited to four lines per poem（绝）, the other, eight（律）. There are therefore four different patterns. Apart from these stipulations, there are strict rules regarding the rhyming and intonation of words. For instance, in a seven-worded line, the second, fourth and sixth words must have a certain intonation.

Besides the rigid forms, two more liberal types of poetry were also popular during the Tang Dynasty: the "old poetry"（古诗）and the "new musical house"（新乐府）. These genres are narrative in nature and not restricted in length. The lines may have a variable number of words and the style is flowing and refreshing. The themes are mostly about specific events or persons and are often sad. For instance, famous Tang Dynasty poet Bai Juyi（白居易）wrote a long, touching poem about a grey-haired palace maid. Selected as one of the 3,000 royal concubines, she entered the palace at the age of 16. By the age of 60, she was still living in the secluded quarters and had never seen the emperor's face.

There were many excellent poets during the Tang Dynasty. Li Bai（李白）and Du Fu（杜甫）were especially outstanding. Li Bai, dubbed "The God of Poetry," was often drunk but produced the best works with flair in the intoxicated state. He drowned while trying to catch the moon in a lake. Du Fu, dubbed "The Saint of Poetry," lived an impoverished life and moved from place to place because of war. Most of his poems are sad.

3. The Song *Ci* (Verse)（宋词）

Towards the end of the Tang Dynasty, a new type of poetry called the *ci*（词）, or verse, began to develop. It entered its golden period during the Song Dynasty. It is a very restrictive form of poetry. Briefly, there are at least 150 different patterns that specify the total length of a poem, the number of words in each phrase, and the required rhyming and intonation of the words. Each pattern has a colourful name. To write a *ci*, one must first decide which pattern to use. In fact, the word "write" is not used. One is said to "fill in" the *ci*. In essence, the *ci* pattern provides the blank spaces for one to fill in the words. *Ci* is arguably the highest form of Chinese poetry. A few Song scholars known for their *ci* were Su Dongpo（苏东坡）, Li Yu（李煜）, and Li Qingzhao（李清照）.

Exercises

Ⅰ. Choose the answer that best completes the statement.
1. _____ wrote *The Canterbury Tales* in the late 14th century.
   A. Geoffrey Chaucer   B. Emily Bronte
   C. Charles Dickens   D. P. B. Shelley
2. Among the British writers, who is known as the Father of English Literature? _____
   A. William Shakespeare   B. Jane Austen
   C. Charles Dickens   D. Geoffrey Chaucer
3. Which work displayed not only the vigor and vitality of English language but also shaped the future for centuries to come? _____
   A. *The Canterbury Tales*   B. *Beowulf*
   C. *A Tale of Two Cities*   D. *Sense and Sensibility*
4. Which of the following writers is NOT from the UK? _____
   A. John Fowles   B. John Keats
   C. Jonathan Swift   D. Victor Hugo
5. Who is the author of the novel *Gulliver's Travels*? _____
   A. John Milton   B. George Eliot
   C. Daniel Defoe   D. Jonathan Swift
6. Which of the following is NOT a comedy written by William Shakespeare? _____
   A. *The Tempest*   B. *King Lear*
   C. *The Merchant of Venice*   D. *Love's Labour's Lost*
7. Daniel Defoe wrote _____ and a number of other popular adventure novels.
   A. *Robinson Crusoe*   B. *The Pilgrim's Progress*
   C. *Sense and Sensibility*   D. *Hard Times*

8. Which of the following is Jane Austen's work? _____
   A. *Jane Eyre*   B. *A Passage to India*
   C. *Great Expectations* D. *Sense and Sensibility*
9. Which of the following periods sees a huge transition in the language, culture and lifestyle of England? _____
   A. Old English Period   B. Middle English Period
   C. The Edwardian Period D. The Georgian Period

II. Read the following statements and decide whether they are true (T) or false (F).
   1. *Beowulf*, written sometime between the 18th century and the late 19th century, is the oldest surviving epic in the English language. _____
   2. The Elizabethan Age was the golden age of English drama. _____
   3. Emily Bronte is remembered for works such as *Wuthering Heights*. _____
   4. Austen's major novels include *Sense and Sensibility* (1811), *Pride and Prejudice* (1813), *Mansfield Park* (1814), *Emma* (1815) and the like. _____
   5. A great flowering of English writing took place in the late 16th century during the reign of Queen Elizabeth I. _____
   6. Charles Dickens was the most famous author in late 16th century, who portrayed the hardships of the working class while criticizing middle-class life. _____
   7. The Postmodern Period began about the time that World War II ended. _____
   8. Much of the first half of the Middle English Period was oral literature. _____

III. Short-answer questions.
   1. What are the features of the Neoclassical Period?
   2. What is the contribution made by *The Canterbury Tales* to British literature?

The United States of America
* Quick Look at USA *

Capital	Washington, D.C.
Largest city	New York City
Official language	None at the federal level; English *de facto*
Government	Federal Republic
Independence	From Great Britain
-Declared	July 4, 1776
-Recognized	September 3, 1783
Currency	United States dollar ($) (USD)
Time zone	(UTC −5 to −10)
—Summer (DST: Daylight Saving Time)	(UTC −4 to −10)
Internet TLD (top level domain)	.us .gov .edu .mil .um
Calling code	+1

Unit 5

Country Profile

❑ **In this unit you will learn about**
1. Name of the country
2. Geographic diversity
3. Major lakes
4. Climate
5. Nation of immigrants

✓参考答案
✓更多资源

Vocabulary

- abandon 抛弃, 离弃
- annex 兼并, 并吞(领土等)
- appropriate v. 拨出(尤指款项)
- assimilation 同化
- balmy (气候等)温和的
- contiguous 相邻的, 邻近的
- ferry 渡船, 渡轮
- flock 群集, 成群结队
- integration 融合, 集成, 一体化
- memorial 纪念碑, 纪念馆
- monument 纪念碑
- otter 水獭
- outlying 境界外的; 远离中心[主体]的, 边远的; 分离的
- parish 堂区(相当于其他州的县)
- permanent 永久的
- precipitation 降雨
- quota 定额, 配额
- ritual 仪式
- sacrifice 牺牲, 放弃
- tropical 热带的

Key Sentences

1. The USA is a country in North America that extends from the Atlantic Ocean to the Pacific Ocean and shares land borders with Canada and Mexico.
   美国是北美洲的一个国家, 从大西洋延伸到太平洋, 与加拿大和墨西哥接壤。

2. The 50 US states vary widely in size and population.
   美国50个州的面积和人口差别很大。

3. In 1867 Russia surprised the United States by offering Alaska for sale.
   1867年, 俄国欲将阿拉斯加出售, 令美国大吃一惊。

4. The US has an extremely varied geography, particularly in the West.
   美国的地理环境千差万别, 尤其是在西部。

5. From the west slope of the Appalachians, the Interior Plains of the Midwest are relatively flat and are the location of the Great Lakes as well as the Mississippi-Missouri River.
   从阿巴拉契亚山脉的西坡看, 中西部的内陆平原相对平坦, 是五大湖以及密西西比-密苏里河的所在地。

6. Alaska has numerous mountain ranges. The Hawaiian islands are tropical, consisting of six larger islands and another dozen smaller ones.
   阿拉斯加有许多山脉。夏威夷群岛是热带岛屿, 由六个较大的岛屿和另外十几个较小的岛屿组成。

7. The continental climate of the central portion of the country produces extreme conditions throughout the year.
   该国中部的大陆性气候全年都会产生极端的气候条件。

8. Boston, Massachusetts, is one of the country's oldest cities and holds a special place in the country's history.
   马萨诸塞州的波士顿是美国最古老的城市之一,在美国历史上占有特殊的地位。

9. They are Manhattan, the Bronx, Brooklyn, Queens, and Staten Island.
   它们是曼哈顿、布朗克斯、布鲁克林、皇后区和斯塔顿岛。

10. New York streets, sidewalks, and subways are most crowded at rush hour.
    纽约的街道、人行道和地铁在高峰时间最拥挤。

11. Los Angeles is famous for its movie industry, and many of Hollywood's movie stars and TV actors live there.
    洛杉矶以电影业闻名,好莱坞的许多电影明星和电视演员都住在那里。

12. Today, Chicago is an important financial and banking center with many tall skyscrapers.
    今天,芝加哥是一个重要的金融和银行中心,有许多摩天大楼。

13. With eighty-eight libraries and more than thirty universities, it is home to some of the best research centers in the country.
    这儿有88个图书馆和30多所大学,是国内一些最好的研究中心的所在地。

14. Houston is famous around the world for its work in space exploration.
    休斯敦因其在太空探索方面的工作而闻名于世。

15. Philadelphia was the capital city during the American War of Independence, and the Declaration of Independence was signed there.
    费城是美国独立战争期间的首都,《独立宣言》也在那里签署。

16. Massachusetts is one of the six New England states in the northeast which were so important in the country's fight for independence.
    马萨诸塞州是新英格兰东北部六个州之一,这六个州在美国争取独立的斗争中非常重要。

17. The United States has often been called a "country of immigrants," people who arrived from many distant lands in pursuit of a better life.
    美国常被称为"移民之国",人们从许多遥远的地方来到美国,追求更好的生活。

18. Native-born Americans and legal immigrants worry about the problem of illegal immigration.
    土生土长的美国人和合法移民担心非法移民的问题。

19. Many believe that illegal immigrants take jobs from citizens, especially from young

people and members of minority groups.

许多人认为非法移民会抢走公民的工作,特别是年轻人和少数族裔人员的工作。

20. The "melting pot" idea compares America to a giant soup pot. Each immigrant is an ingredient added to the pot.

"大熔炉"的概念把美国比作一个巨大的汤锅。每一个移民都是锅里的配料。

21. Immigrants also enrich American communities by bringing aspects of their native cultures with them.

移民还带来了自己的本土文化,丰富了美国社会。

22. China abounds in rivers. More than 1500 rivers each drain 1000 square kilometers or larger areas.

中国有很多河流。1 500多条河流中每一条都灌溉了1 000平方公里或更大的范围。

23. The Yangtze River is the largest river in China, and the third longest in the world, next only to the Nile in northeast Africa and the Amazon in South America.

长江是中国最长的河流,也是世界上第三长的河流,仅次于非洲东北部的尼罗河和南美洲的亚马孙河。

24. The Yellow River valley was one of the birthplaces of ancient Chinese civilization. It has lush pasture land and abundant mineral deposits.

黄河流域是中国古代文明的发祥地之一。它有郁郁葱葱的牧场和丰富的矿藏。

25. Construction work of the Grand Canal first began as early as in the fifth century BC. The Canal flows past Beijing, Tianjin, Hebei, Shandong, Jiangsu and Zhejiang and links five major rivers.

大运河的开凿早在公元前五世纪就开始了。运河流经北京、天津、河北、山东、江苏和浙江,连接了五条主要河流。

Warm-up Exercise

1. What is the name of the national capital city of USA? What does the word "Capitol" mean?

2. How many states are there in the USA? Which is the largest state and which is the smallest in area?

3. The United States of America has often been called a "country of immigrants." Make some comments on this view.

Introduce China in English

1. Describe the major rivers in China.

2. Describe the major lakes in China.

Text

The United States of America, also known as the United States, the US, the USA, the States and America, is a country in North America that extends from the Atlantic Ocean to the Pacific Ocean and shares land borders with Canada and Mexico. It consists of 48 contiguous states and the noncontiguous states of Alaska and Hawaii. In addition, the United States includes a number of outlying areas. The national capital is Washington, D.C., located along the banks of the Potomac River between the states of Maryland and Virginia.

The 50 US states vary widely in size and population. The largest states in area are Alaska at 1,717,854 km^2, followed by Texas, and California. The smallest state is Rhode Island, with an area of 4,002 km^2.

Each state is subdivided into counties, with the exception of Louisiana, where comparable political units are called parishes. Within these counties and parishes, there are communities that range in size from small villages to towns to cities.

ICT

Washington, D.C. "D.C."意思是"District of Columbia",华盛顿哥伦比亚特区。位于马里兰州和弗吉尼亚州之间,地处波托马克河航段上端,面积179平方公里。

Potomac River 波托马克河

■ The Addition of Two More States

Alaska seemed to be a useless ice box to most Americans in the nineteenth century. It was home to about 40,000 Native Americans, including the Aleut in the Aleutian Islands, the Inuit, or Eskimo, in the far north, and the Tlingit in the southeast section. About a quarter of the state lies north of the Arctic Circle, where much of the soil is permanently frozen and daylight is not visible for months at a time. Temperatures in the northern parts of Alaska can average 10 degrees Fahrenheit (−12 degrees Celsius) in the summer and colder than −60 degrees Fahrenheit (−51 degrees Celsius) in the winter!

Russia had claimed Alaska since 1741, when fur traders from that country discovered that sea otter and fur seal pelts from Alaskan waters could be sold for high profits. In 1867 Russia surprised the United States by offering Alaska for sale. William H. Seward, Secretary of State under President Andrew Johnson, drew up an agreement for the purchase.

Congress was not enthusiastic. Only a few hundred Americans, mostly miners, had ever visited Alaska. People thought Seward was foolish to even consider it, and the proposal became known as Seward's Folly. Nevertheless, the Senate voted in favor of the purchase, and on July 14, 1868, the House of Representatives appropriated $7.2 million to buy Alaska.

Like Alaska, Hawaii could only be reached by sea in the nineteenth century. But unlike Alaska, Hawaii had an organized population and a thriving economy. American businessmen had followed missionaries there after 1820 and started a profitable sugar industry. By the 1840s, five of every six ships that stopped at the islands were from the United States. In 1893 the American companies backed a revolution that overthrew Hawaii's queen. They asked the US government to annex Hawaii, and it became a US territory in 1898.

Aleutian Islands 阿留申群岛
Tlingit 特林吉特人（阿拉斯加南部等地区以航海为业的美洲印第安人）

Seward's Folly 看来愚蠢日后显示收益的行为（西沃德用巨款从俄国购买阿拉斯加，当时遭多人反对，被讥为愚蠢行动）

■ *Geographic Diversity*

The US has an extremely varied geography, particularly in the West. The eastern seaboard has a coastal plain which is widest in the south and narrows in the north. In the extreme southeast, Florida is home to the ecologically unique Everglades. Beyond the coastal plain, the rolling hills of the Piedmont region end at the Appalachian Mountains, which rise above 6,000 feet (1,830 m) in North Carolina, Tennessee, and New Hampshire.

From the west slope of the Appalachians, the Interior Plains of the Midwest are relatively flat and are the location of the Great Lakes as well as the Mississippi-Missouri River, the world's 4th longest river system. West of the Mississippi River, the Interior Plains slope uphill and blend into the vast Great Plains.

The Great Lakes include five massive inland lakes (Superior, Huron, Michigan, Erie, and Ontario), covering 244,100 km² in the upper reaches of the mid-western United States. Lake Michigan is the only one of the lakes that is located entirely in the United States. The other four lakes lie on the border between the United States and Canada.

The abrupt rise of the Rocky Mountains, at the western edge of the Great Plains, extends north to south across the continental US, reaching altitudes over 14,000 feet (4,270 m) in Colorado.

Along the Pacific coast, the Coast Ranges and the volcanic Cascade Range extend from north to south across the country. The northwestern Pacific coast shares the world's largest temperate rain forest with Canada.

Alaska has numerous mountain ranges. The Hawaiian islands are tropical, consisting of six larger islands and another dozen smaller ones.

■ *Climate*

The range of altitudes together with the sheer size of the landmass produces great variations of temperature and

---

Everglades 大沼泽地,亦译埃弗格莱兹——佛罗里达州南部亚热带锯齿草沼泽地区,面积10 000平方公里。
Piedmont 皮德蒙特高原
Appalachian Mountains 阿巴拉契亚山脉
Interior Plains of the Midwest 中西部内陆平原
Great Plains 大平原

Rocky Mountains 落基山脉

Cascade Range 喀斯喀特山脉

precipitation. In a nation that is subarctic at its highest elevations and tropical at its southernmost points, temperatures can vary from below zero in the Great Lakes region to a balmy 80 degrees in Florida. On the same day!

The continental climate of the central portion of the country produces extreme conditions throughout the year. With no high elevations to protect it, the interior lowlands are at the mercy of both the warm southern Gulf Stream and blasts of arctic air from the north. At times, these incompatible weather systems collide violently. Every year, with tragic consequences, the central plains between the Rockies and the Appalachians earn their nickname "Tornado Alley."

Tornado Alley 龙卷风巷;龙卷风胡同;龙卷风走廊

The western mountain states enjoy mild summers, but the higher elevations are blanketed in snow throughout the winter months. The low, desert areas of Arizona and New Mexico experience hot, dry air, although winters can be surprisingly cold.

The coastal areas are more temperate, blocked from extending their moderate influence inland by the Appalachian mountains in the east and the Pacific Coast ranges in the west. The Gulf Stream, a warm ocean current that flows from the Gulf of Mexico northeast across the Atlantic, produces hot, wet, energy-sapping conditions for Florida and the other Gulf Coast states.

Temperatures are moderate year-round on the Pacific Coast, although they start to dip as you venture northward into America's wettest region.

■ Washington D.C.

Where are the White House, the Capitol, and the Washington Monument? Just where they should be—in the capital of the United States. On July 16, 1790, Congress declared the city of Washington in the District of Columbia, the permanent capital of the US. Who decided how the new city should look?

the Capitol 美国国会大厦[注意与"首都"capital 一词拼写不同]

President George Washington gave French engineer Pierre-Charles L'Enfant the job of creating a plan for the city. L'Enfant designed wide avenues and open spaces so that the capital would not become a city of crowded buildings. He knew that people would need parks where they could walk and relax. Because of L'Enfant's careful planning, when you stand on the steps of the US Capitol today you can look down the National Mall and see all the way to the Washington Monument and the Lincoln Memorial.

Located on the east end of the National Mall is the US Capitol. It is built on a hill popularly called Capitol Hill and has been the home of the House of Representatives and the Senate since 1800. This is where Congress meets and conducts business. The Capitol is also a museum of American art and history. It stands as a focal point of the Government's legislative branch.

National Mall 华盛顿国家广场，位于首都华盛顿的一处开放型国家公园。该广场由数片绿地组成，一直从林肯纪念堂延伸到国会大厦，这里是美国国家庆典和仪式的首选，同时也是美国历史上重大示威游行、民权演说的重要场地。

■ *Major Cities*

The five largest cities by population in the USA are New York City, Los Angeles, Chicago, Houston, and Philadelphia. Boston, Massachusetts, is one of the country's oldest cities and holds a special place in the country's history.

■ New York

New York City is also known as "the city that never sleeps." Over forty-eight million visitors go there every year and spend over thirty billion dollars. New York is always busy day and night, with twenty-four-hour restaurants, stores, gyms, and coffee bars. This exciting city is an international financial and cultural center made up of five smaller towns, called boroughs. They are Manhattan, the Bronx, Brooklyn, Queens, and Staten Island. Manhattan, the smallest borough at twenty-two kilometers long and only three-and-a-half kilometers wide, is where most visitors go first. Manhattan has theaters on Broadway, shopping on Madison Avenue, art galleries in Soho, and museums on Museum Mile.

With the city's long history of immigration, its population has grown from less than twenty-two thousand people in 1771 to more than eight million people today. The East Side of New York became Americas first "melting pot"—an area with a large number of people from different ethnic groups all living together. Most immigrants learn to speak English, but many

melting pot 熔炉

continue to speak their own languages at home. This means that today in New York, about eight hundred languages are spoken.

■ Los Angeles

The city is one of the largest financial centers in the world today. As a cultural center, Los Angeles offers wonderful museums of art, like the Getty Museum, which has some of the world's most famous paintings. Los Angeles also has sunny weather and beautiful beaches. Angelinos, as the people are called, are proud of their ethnic diversity.

Getty Museum 盖蒂博物馆
Angelinos 洛杉矶人

Los Angeles is famous for its movie industry, and many of Hollywood's movie stars and TV actors live there. At Universal Studios, the oldest and most famous of the movie studios, visitors can see how movies are made. But Los Angeles is not just a city for movie stars. The growing difference between rich and poor people in Los Angeles is a big problem. For twenty percent of the population in Los Angeles, life can be very hard. Many of them work in low-paid jobs in restaurants, hotels, hospitals, and stores. A lot of them live in unhealthy apartment buildings; others cannot find jobs.

Universal Studios 好莱坞环球影城。位于洛杉矶市区西北郊。20世纪初,电影制片商在此发现拍片所需的理想的自然环境,便陆续集中到此,使得这儿逐渐成为世界闻名的影城。

■ Chicago

Chicago, Illinois, has a population of almost three million. The Windy City is on Lake Michigan, one of the five Great Lakes. When the Illinois and Michigan Canal was built in 1848, it gave the area a water route from the Great Lakes to the Mississippi River. When trains began moving goods across the country, Chicago became a very important center for all of the goods trains in the Midwest.

Windy City 风城(美国芝加哥市的别称)

Today, Chicago is an important financial and banking center with many tall skyscrapers. It is also an important center for education. With eighty-eight libraries and more than thirty universities, it is home to some of the best research centers in the country, including the University of Chicago, the University of Illinois at Chicago, and Northwestern University.

■ Houston

Houston, Texas, is the fourth largest city in the USA. It receives over nine million visitors every year. There is a large student population, because the city has fourteen universities and colleges and one of the country's best research centers for medicine. Houston is famous around the world for its work in space exploration.

The Johnson Space Center, built in 1961, is the center of the country's space exploration program called <u>NASA</u>(National Aeronautics and Space Administration). The center had great success when the Apollo program sent the first man to the moon on July 20, 1969.

NASA 国家航空航天局；美国航空及太空总署

Houston is very hot in summer, so the city has built eleven kilometers of tunnels under the city streets, where people can walk comfortably from stores to restaurants to businesses.

■ Philadelphia

Another city that is very important in the country's history is Philadelphia, Pennsylvania. It is the fifth largest city in the USA, with a population of about one and a half million. It was the capital city during the American War of Independence, and the Declaration of Independence was signed there. Today it is a national center of law, with seven important law schools. The first hospital in the American colonies was built there by the British, and the city is still an important research center for medicine today. The name Philadelphia comes from Greek and it means "brotherly love."

■ Boston

Massachusetts is one of the six New England states in the northeast which were so important in the country's fight for independence. Boston is also one of the country's most important centers of education, with more than one hundred colleges and universities. Harvard University, one of the country's best universities, is just across the Charles River, in Cambridge, Massachusetts.

Irish immigrants settled in Boston in large numbers, and today make up 15.8 percent of the population.

Tourists enjoy visiting Boston's historical sights like <u>Faneuil Hall</u>, where the colonists met to plan the nation's fight for independence. The city is also home to some of the country's best sports teams, including the <u>Boston Red Sox</u> baseball team.

Faneuil Hall 法尼尔厅，波士顿的一座历史建筑，靠近海滨和今天的政府中心。
Boston Red Sox 波士顿红袜队

A Nation of Immigrants

The United States has often been called a "country of immigrants," people who arrived from many distant lands in pursuit of a better life. In general, their faith in the "American dream" was rewarded with good fortune, although for some it involved a long struggle and much sacrifice.

The first European immigrants in American history came from England and the Netherlands. Attracted by reports of great economic opportunities and religious and political freedom, immigrants from many other countries flocked to the United States in increasing numbers, the flow reaching a peak in the years 1892—1924. During the late 19th century, the government operated a special port of entry on Ellis Island; it was in operation from 1892 until 1954 and is now preserved as part of the Statue of Liberty National Monument. Between 1820 and 1979, the United States admitted more than 49 million immigrants.

In 1924, the first laws were passed that set limits on how many people from specific countries would be admitted to the United States. The limits were based on the number of people from that country already living in the country. In 1965, immigration quotas were established according to who applied first; and national quotas were replaced with hemispheric ones. Preference was given to relatives of US citizens and immigrants with specific job skills. In 1978, Congress abandoned hemispheric quotas and established a worldwide ceiling. The United States accepts more immigrants than any other country.

The US Citizenship and Immigration Service (USCIS) estimates that some 5 million people are living in the United States without permission, and the number is growing by about 275,000 a year. Native-born Americans and legal immigrants worry about the problem of illegal immigration. Many believe that illegal immigrants take jobs from citizens, especially from young people and members of minority groups. Moreover, illegal immigrants can place a heavy burden on tax-supported social services.

---

country of immigrants 移民之国

American dream 美国梦

Ellis Island 埃利斯岛。美国纽约东南部上纽约湾的一个岛，位于纽约市曼哈顿岛西南。

USCIS 美国公民及移民局

■ America: A Melting Pot of Cultures

The United States is a country of immigrants. Some immigrants bring their families. Some bring a few of their favorite things. Others come alone with nothing but determination. One thing that every immigrant brings with them is their culture.

The "melting pot" idea compares America to a giant soup pot. Each immigrant is an ingredient added to the pot. Each immigrant adds their own flavor. After each immigrant comes to America, they connect to other people. People learn about each other's culture. This is the beginning of the soup pot of America melting together.

The steady stream of people coming to America's shores has had a profound effect on the American character. It takes courage to leave one's homeland and come to a new country. The American people have been noted for their willingness to take risks and try new things.

Immigrants also enrich American communities by bringing aspects of their native cultures with them. Many black Americans now celebrate both Christmas and Kwanzaa, a festival drawn from African rituals. There is large number of ethnic restaurants in many American cities. Cultural assimilation and social integration—although slower and more difficult for some than for others—has characterized the grand American experiment.

Kwanzaa 匡扎节。非洲裔美国人的节日，从12月26日到次年1月1日，仿照非洲的收获节。

◨ Understanding More about China

General Introduction of Rivers and Lakes in China

China abounds in rivers. More than 1,500 rivers each drain 1,000 square kilometers or larger areas. More than 2,700 billion cubic meters of water flow along these rivers, 5.8% of the world's total. Most of the large rivers find their source in the Qinghai-Tibet Plateau, and as a result China is rich in water power resources, leading the world in hydropower potential, with reserves of 680 million kilowatts.

China's rivers can be categorized as exterior and interior systems. The drainage area for the exterior rivers that empty into the oceans accounts for 64% of the country's total land area. The Yangtze, Yellow, Heilongjiang, Pearl, Liaohe, Haihe, Huaihe and Lancang Rivers flow east, and empty into the Pacific Ocean. The Yarlung Zangbo River in Tibet, which flows first east and then south into the Indian Ocean, boasts the Grand Yarlung Zangbo Canyon, the largest canyon in the world, 504.6 kilometers long and 6,009 meters deep. The drainage area for the interior rivers that flow into inland lakes or disappear into deserts or salt marshes makes up 36% of China's total land area. The Tarim River, 2,179 kilometers long, in southern Xinjiang, is China's longest interior river.

The Yangtze River is the largest river in China, and the third longest in the world, next only to the Nile in northeast Africa and the Amazon in South America. It has a drainage area of 1.809 million square kilometers. The middle and lower Yangtze River's warm and humid climate, plentiful rainfall and fertile soil make the area an important agricultural region. Known as the "golden waterway," the Yangtze River is a transportation artery linking west and east.

The Yellow River is the second largest river in China, 5,464 kilometers in length, with a drainage area of 752,000 square kilometers. The Yellow River valley was one of the birthplaces of ancient Chinese civilization. It has lush pasture land and abundant mineral deposits.

The Heilongjiang River is north China's largest. The Pearl River is the largest river in south China.

In addition to those endowed by nature, China has a famous man-made river—the Grand Canal, running from Beijing in the north to Hangzhou in the south. Construction work of the Grand Canal first began as early as in the fifth century BC. The Canal flows past Beijing, Tianjin, Hebei, Shandong, Jiangsu and Zhejiang and links five major rivers—the Haihe River, Yellow River, Huaihe River, Yangtze River and Qiantangjiang River. With a total length of 1,794 kilometers and a drainage area of 4,583 square meters, the Grand Canal is the longest as well as the oldest man-made waterway in the world.

Alongside of abundant rivers, China also has lots of lakes. There are more than 2,800 natural lakes, each having a surface area of over one square kilometer and over 130 lakes, each covering more than 100 square kilometers. There are also a large number of artificial lakes (reservoirs). With different salt content, the lakes are classified as saltwater and freshwater lakes. Large lakes are mainly distributed in the middle and lower reaches of the Yangtze River and on the Qinghai-Tibet Plateau. The Boyang Lake in the south of the Yangtze River is the largest freshwater lake in China while the Qinghai Lake on the Qinghai-Tibet Plateau is the largest saltwater lake.

Exercises

Ⅰ. Choose the answer that best completes the statement.
1. The largest states in area are _____, followed by Texas, and California.
   A. Alaska   B. Texas   C. Rhode Island   D. Arizona
2. Among the five lakes, Lake _____ is the only one that is located entirely in the United States.
   A. Superior   B. Huron   C. Ontario   D. Michigan
3. In the extreme southeast of the United States, _____ is home to the ecologically unique Everglades.
   A. Maine   B. New Mexico   C. Texas   D. Florida

Ⅱ. Read the following statements and decide whether they are true (T) or false (F).
1. The USA shares land borders with Canada only. _____
2. Washington, D.C. is located along the banks of the Potomac River between the states of Maryland and Virginia. _____
3. The United States consists of 48 contiguous states and two noncontiguous states of Florida and Hawaii. _____
4. The American flag has 13 stripes that represent the 13 original colonies. _____
5. The US has an extremely varied geography, particularly in the Middle. _____
6. Among the 50 states, except that one state whose political unit is called "parish," the comparable political units of all the other states are call "counties." _____

Ⅲ. Short-answer questions.
1. How diverse is the American geography?
2. How do immigrants influence American society and culture?

Unit 6

American History (1)

❑ **In this unit you will learn about**
1. History and life of native Americans
2. European colonization
3. American Revolutionary War

✓参考答案
✓更多资源

Vocabulary

- archaeologist 考古学家
- attainment 达到,到达;[*pl.*]造诣,成就;才能
- chronicle 将(某事物)载入编年史
- corridor 过道,走廊
- decimate 杀死或毁坏(某物)大部分
- immunity 免疫
- irrigation 灌溉
- marine 海的,近海的
- misnomer 错用名称;用词错误;描述失当
- outlaw 宣布(某事物)非法
- replete 充满的,充分供应的
- wake 随某事物之后到来

Key Sentences

1. It is a journey replete with mystery, adventure, and incredible good fortune. It also chronicles occasional obstacles, detours, and hardships.
   这是一个充满神秘、冒险和难以置信的好运的旅程。它也记录了偶尔遇到的障碍、绕道和困难。

2. Many questions remain unanswered in regard to the first Americans.
   关于第一批美国人,许多问题仍然没有得到回答。

3. For seven decades, archaeologists (scientists who study early peoples) believed that the Americas were settled by Asians whose pursuit of big-game animals drew them to this vast unsettled land.
   70年来,考古学家(研究早期人类的科学家)认为美洲是亚洲人首先定居的,他们对大型动物的追逐吸引了他们来到这片广袤、无人居住的土地。

4. Indian is a misnomer. First, the term comes from one of history's great geographical blunders: Columbus's belief that he had reached Southeast Asia's "East Indies."
   印第安人是用词错误。首先,这个词来自历史上的一个重大地理错误:哥伦布认为他已经到达东南亚的"东印度群岛"。

5. Many native peoples prefer to be called First Americans, Native Americans, First Nations, Amerindians, indigenous peoples, or some other more sensitive designations.
   许多原住民更喜欢被称为第一美国人、美洲土著、第一民族、美洲印第安人、土著民族或其他一些更富情感的称呼。

6. When Europeans "discovered" the "New World," they reached a land that already had been settled by the Indians thousands of years earlier.
   当欧洲人"发现"了"新大陆"时,他们到达了一块早在几千年前就已经被印第安人定居的土地。

7. Many cultures that lived near the Pacific or Arctic Ocean depended largely on marine resources for their food supply. They were skilled boat-builders and fishermen.
生活在太平洋或北冰洋附近的人们,主要依靠海洋资源提供食物。他们是熟练的造船者和渔民。

8. Through time, as European settlement and other influences spread, so did the negative impact of European diseases and other elements that severely disrupted (and often terminated) Amerindian populations and their cultures.
随着欧洲人的定居以及其他影响的蔓延,欧洲疾病和其他严重扰乱(并常常毁灭)美洲印第安人人口及其文化的因素的负面影响也在不断蔓延。

9. The destruction of Amerindian peoples and their culture is one of the saddest chapters in American history.
美国印第安人及其文化的毁灭是美国历史上最悲哀的一章。

10. Conditions were ideal for the growing of plantation crops such as cotton, indigo, tobacco, and rice. During the eighteenth century, a plantation-based economy boomed in the South.
环境条件非常利于种植棉花、木蓝属植物、烟叶和水稻等作物。18世纪,南方兴起了以种植园为基础的经济。

11. From the very beginning of settlement, however, some Europeans had brought African slaves to America.
然而,从一开始在北美定居,一些欧洲人就把非洲奴隶带到了美洲。

12. Ultimately, slavery was a key issue in the bloody conflict between the Northern and Southern states.
最终,奴隶制成为南部和北部各州之间血腥冲突的关键问题。

13. On January 24, 1848, James Marshall discovered gold at Sutter's Mill, near present-day Coloma, a small community at the western foot of the Sierra Nevada in present-day central California.
1848年1月24日,詹姆斯·马歇尔在萨姆特磨厂发现了黄金,这是一个位于现今加利福尼亚中部内华达山脉西脚的小社区,靠近今天的科洛马。

14. Later that year, the rails were extended from Sacramento westward to San Francisco, thereby spanning the continent.
那年晚些时候,铁路从萨克拉门托向西延伸到旧金山,从而横跨整个大陆。

15. In December 1773, in response to a tax on tea, colonists in Boston conducted the "Boston Tea Party" in which they raided several merchant ships and threw the tea into the harbor.
1773年12月,为回应对茶叶征税,波士顿殖民者发动了"波士顿倾茶事件",突袭了几艘商船,并将茶叶倒进港口。

Warm-up Exercise

1. How did the name "Indians" come into use?

2. On which day is the American Independence Day? Why?

3. What is "Louisiana Purchase"? What is the significance of it to the USA?

Introduce China in English

Who is Zheng He? Tell the story of Zheng He's voyages to your deskmate.

Text   ICT

American historical geography offers an amazing trip through the corridors of time. It is a journey replete with mystery, adventure, and incredible good fortune. It also chronicles occasional obstacles, detours, and hardships.

■ The First Americans

Many questions remain unanswered in regard to the first Americans. For seven decades, archaeologists (scientists who study early peoples) believed that the Americas were settled by Asians whose pursuit of big-game animals drew them to this vast unsettled land. Supposedly, they wandered across Beringia, the Bering Strait "land bridge" that linked Siberia and present-day Alaska. On entering North America, these people supposedly passed through an ice-free corridor that formed between two huge masses of glacial ice. Finally, they reached the area of

Beringia 白令陆桥
Bering Strait 白令海峡
Siberia 西伯利亚

Clovis, New Mexico, which date back about 13,000 years.

Clovis 克洛维斯

■ Early Native Cultures

Native people of the United States recognize themselves by many names. Indian is a misnomer. First, the term comes from one of history's great geographical blunders: Columbus's belief that he had reached Southeast Asia's "East Indies." Second, not all native peoples are of Indian heritage. In Alaska, there are Inuit(Eskimo) and Aleut peoples, as well as Athabascan and other native groups. Many Hawaiians are of Polynesian ancestry. Finally, many native peoples prefer to be called First Americans, Native Americans, First Nations, Amerindians, indigenous peoples, or some other more sensitive designations.

Columbus 克里斯托弗·哥伦布,意大利航海家和探险家
Inuit 因纽特人
Aleut 阿留申人
Athabascan 阿萨巴斯卡人

Unlike the lingering mysteries surrounding the arrival of the earliest residents of the United States, a number of things are quite well established in regard to them. There is no doubt, for example, that when Europeans "discovered" the "New World," they reached a land that already had been settled thousands of years earlier. Further, most native peoples showed physical features that tied them to a geographic origin somewhere in East Asia. What is known is that soon after Europeans arrived, warfare and European diseases (against which native peoples had no natural immunity) decimated native populations. Native cultures varied greatly from place to place, as did their levels of cultural attainment. In the United States alone, native peoples spoke as many as 200 different languages in 17 different linguistic families.

■ The Arrival of Europeans

Little is known about the first Europeans who set foot on what is now the United States. What is known is that, in 1492, Christopher Columbus reached a land that he believed to be the spice-rich East Indies. His discovery sparked what became a several-century search for an all-water route through or around the Americas to the Pacific Ocean and the distant riches of Asia.

The first known European to reach the shores of the United States may have been Giovanni Caboto (known in English as

John Cabot). Although this is questioned by many, some scholars believe that he reached the coast of Maine in 1497. (Seven years would pass before Columbus made landfall on the continental landmass in 1504.) In 1524, the king of France sent the Italian explorer Giovanni da Verrazzano on a voyage to the New World in search of wealth and a route to Asia. Verrazzano reached the coast of present-day North Carolina and continued northward. He is believed to have been the first European to follow the coast of present-day New England. His voyage is memorialized by the spectacular Verrazano-Narrows Bridge that spans the mouth of the Hudson River in New York City. Surprisingly, the lure of finding a water route to Asia was so strong that more than a century passed before northwest Europeans began to settle the newly found land! Not until 1607 did the first north Europeans—the British at Jamestown, Virginia—began to permanently settle the land.

American history often carries a strong north European bias. In reality, much of what is now the United States was first explored, claimed, and settled by Spaniards. In 1540, for example, long before the English or French penetrated the country's interior, Spanish explorer Francisco Coronado explored much of the southwestern United States. In his search for the fabled Seven Cities of Gold, his men explored an area that extended from Arizona eastward into Kansas. In 1565, 42 years before the Jamestown settlement was established, a Spanish foothold was built at St. Augustine (Florida). In the Southwest, the Spanish established a regional capital in Santa Fe (New Mexico) in 1610, a full decade before the Pilgrims settled at Plymouth, Massachusetts.

■ Southward Expansion

Regardless of their place of origin, Europeans came from temperate midlatitude lands in which subtropical crops could not be grown. The American South, in contrast, offered a humid subtropical climate with ample year-round moisture and a long, hot growing season. Conditions were ideal for the growing of plantation crops such as cotton, indigo, tobacco, and rice. During the eighteenth century, a plantation-based economy boomed in the South.

John Cabot 约翰·卡伯特,意大利航海家。居住在英国的布里斯托尔。后来奉英王亨利七世之命,进行找寻西北航道的探险航行。他可能是自斯堪的纳维亚人后,第一位到达北美大陆的欧洲人。

Giovanni da Verrazzano 乔瓦尼·达·韦拉扎诺,是一位在北美洲从事发现活动的意大利探险家,主要为法国国王效力。

Francisco Coronado 弗朗西斯科·科罗纳多,西班牙探险家。

Seven Cities of Gold 黄金七城

Santa Fe 圣达菲,美国新墨西哥州州府。

From the very beginning of settlement, however, some Europeans had brought African slaves to America. Sadly, for more than 150 years, the Southern plantation economy depended on and thrived because of African slave labor. Ultimately, slavery was a key issue in the bloody conflict between the Northern and Southern states—a war that sharply divided the country and took 600,000 to 700,000 lives. In the United States, the slave trade was outlawed in 1808, although the practice itself continued until 1865.

■ Westward Expansion

Like grains of sand passing through an hourglass, land-hungry frontiersmen from the eastern seaboard flowed toward narrow water gaps (east-west valleys cut through mountain ridges) and spilled across the Appalachians into the Ohio Valley and beyond. Hundreds of thousands of people sought a new life and opportunity in the fertile lands that lay in the interior valleys and plains located west of the mountains. Many Europeans, particularly those of Scandinavian and German ancestry, were skilled woodsmen. They knew how to clear land, remove stumps, and build sturdy log homes, fences, and outbuildings. Gradually, following the Ohio River, the Great Lakes, and other routes of easy access, they continued westward. In their wake, canals and railroads followed. These transportation linkages helped to maintain ties between the expanding western frontier and the rapidly expanding population and economic development along the East Coast.

The Louisiana Purchase

The westward expansion is one of the central themes of 19th-century American history. From 1803 to 1848, the size of the new nation nearly tripled as settlers pushed beyond national boundaries.

In 1803, President Thomas Jefferson purchased the territory of Louisiana from the French government for $15 million. The Louisiana Purchase stretched from the Mississippi River to the Rocky Mountains and from Canada to New Orleans, and it doubled the size of the United States.

During the mid-nineteenth century, two nearly simultaneous events served as magnets to draw fortune seekers across the country's rugged interior to the West Coast. On January 24, 1848, James Marshall discovered gold at Sutter's Mill, located on the American River near present-day Coloma, a small community at the western foot of the Sierra Nevada in present-day central California. His discovery started a rush that ultimately brought tens of thousands of gold-hungry prospectors (and others) to the "Golden State."

rush 淘金热

Golden State 金州，加利福尼亚州的别名

With the populations and economies of San Francisco, Sacramento, and nearby areas booming as a result of the gold rush, the need for safe and speedy transportation links with the East became apparent. In 1862, Congress passed the Pacific Railway Act, which authorized the Union Pacific Railroad to begin building westward from Omaha, Nebraska, and the Central Pacific Railroad to start building eastward from Sacramento, California. Nearly seven years later, on May 10, 1869, the tracks joined at Promontory Summit, in present-day Utah, and a golden spike was driven to commemorate the occasion. Later that year, the rails were extended from Sacramento westward to San Francisco, thereby spanning the continent.

Union Pacific Railroad 联合太平洋铁路公司

■ American Revolutionary War (1775—1783)

The American Revolutionary War was fought between 1775 and 1783, and was the result of increasing colonial unhappiness with British rule. During the American Revolutionary War, American forces were constantly hampered by a lack of resources, but managed to win critical victories which led to an alliance with France. With other European countries joining the fight, the conflict became increasingly global in nature forcing the British to divert resources away from North America. Following the American victory at Yorktown, fighting effectively ended and the war was concluded with the Treaty of Paris in 1783. The treaty saw Britain recognize American independence as well as determined boundaries and other rights.

American Revolutionary War 美国独立战争

Treaty of Paris《巴黎条约》

- **Causes**

With the conclusion of the French & Indian War in 1763, the British government adopted the position that its American colonies should shoulder a percentage of the cost associated with their defense. To this end, Parliament began passing a series of taxes, such as the Stamp Act, designed to raise funds to offset this expense. These were met with ire by the colonists who argued that they were unfair as the colonies had no representation in Parliament. In December 1773, in response to a tax on tea, colonists in Boston conducted the "Boston Tea Party" in which they raided several merchant ships and threw the tea into the harbor. As punishment, Parliament passed the Intolerable Acts which closed the harbor and effectively placed the city under occupation. This action further angered the colonists and led to the creation of the First Continental Congress.

Stamp Act《印花税法》

Boston Tea Party 波士顿倾茶事件
Intolerable Acts《强制法》,美国历史上英国议会针对殖民地人民的反抗,为加强英国控制而制定的一系列法律的总称。
First Continental Congress 第一届大陆会议

- **Opening Campaigns**

As British troops moved into Boston, Lt. Gen. Thomas Gage was appointed governor of Massachusetts. On April 19, 1775, Gage sent troops to seize arms from the colonial militias. Alerted by riders like Paul Revere, the militias were able to muster in time to meet the British. Confronting them in Lexington, the war began when an unknown gunman opened fire. In the resulting Battles of Lexington & Concord, the colonials were able to drive the British back to Boston. That June, the British won the costly Battle of Bunker Hill, but remained trapped in Boston. The following month, General George Washington arrived to lead the colonial army. Utilizing cannon brought from Fort Ticonderoga by Colonel Henry Knox he was able to force the British from the city in March 1776.

Lt. Gen. 中将(英文全称为 Lieutenant General)
Thomas Gage 托马斯·盖奇,1763—1774 年任北美英军总司令。

Paul Revere 保罗·瑞维尔,美国独立战争时期的一名爱国者。

Battle of Bunker Hill 邦克山战役,独立战争期间的第一场大规模战役,致约1 000名英国士兵和约400 名美国爱国者伤亡。

- **American Revolution: New York, Philadelphia, and Saratoga**

Moving south, Washington prepared to defend against a British attack on New York. Landing in September 1776, British troops led by General William Howe won the Battle of Long Island and, after a string of victories, drove Washington from the city. With his army collapsing, Washington retreated across New Jersey before finally winning victories at Trenton and Princeton. Having taken New York, Howe made plans to capture the colonial capital of Philadelphia the following year. Arriving in Pennsylvania in September 1777, he won a victory at Brandywine before occupying the city and beating Washingtone at Germantown. To the north, an American army led by <u>Maj. Gen.</u> Horatio Gates defeated and captured a British army led by Maj. Gen. John Burgoyne at Saratoga. This victory led to an American alliance with France and a widening of the war.

Maj. Gen. 少将（英文全称为 Major General）

- **American Revolution: The War Moves South**

With the loss of Philadelphia, Washington went into winter quarters at Valley Forge where his army endured extreme hardship and underwent extensive training under the guidance of Baron Friedrich von Steuben. Emerging, they won a strategic victory at the Battle of Monmouth in June 1778. Later that year, the war shifted to the South, where the British won key victories by capturing Savannah (1778) and Charleston (1780). After another British victory at Camden in August 1780, Washington dispatched Maj. Gen. Nathanael Greene to take command of American forces in the region.

- **American Revolution: Yorktown and Victory**

In August 1781, Washington learned that Cornwallis was encamped at Yorktown, Virginia where he was waiting for ships to transport his army to New York. Consulting with his French allies, Washington quietly began shifting his army south from New York with the goal defeating Cornwallis. Trapped in Yorktown after the French naval victory at the Battle of the Chesapeake, Cornwallis fortified his position. Arriving on September 28, Washington's army along with French troops under Comte de Rochambeau laid siege and won the resulting <u>Battle of Yorktown</u>. Surrendering on October 19, 1781, Cornwallis' defeat was the last major engagement of the war. The loss at Yorktown caused the British to begin the peace process which culminated in the 1783 Treaty of Paris which recognized American independence.

Battle of Yorktown 约克镇战役；约克敦战役，1781 年爆发，通常被认为是美国独立战争中最后一场陆上大型战斗。

Understanding More about China

Zheng He（郑和）

Zheng He was Emperor Zhu Di's confidant. He was said to be a huge man with an imposing appearance befitting of a military commander. He was also known as San Bao, possibly meaning "The Eunuch with Three Treasures"（三宝）. More likely, San Bao（三保）, written differently but sharing the same pronunciation as the other, was actually his childhood name.

Zhu Di began to build ocean-going ships in 1403. By 1405, the fleet was ready to set sail from Nanjing. Zheng He was appointed admiral in command of the armada with permission to issue imperial orders at sea.

The reason why Zhu Di built the ships and sent Zheng He on multiple voyages at great expense still remains a matter of conjecture. It may be that he wanted to track down his nephew, the deposed emperor, but that theory sounds far-fetched as there was no reason to look for the royal fugitive in such far-flung places as Calicut, India. Trade was another possible reason, but the amount of trade Zheng He engaged in did not justify the size of the navy or the distance the fleet sailed. Certainly, Zheng He had no intention to colonise any foreign land; he simply asked the kings he subjugated to pay tributes to the Ming court. Perhaps the elaborate voyages were intended to be a show of China's wealth and power.

Exercises

Ⅰ. Choose the answer that best completes the statement.

In _____, President Thomas Jefferson purchased the territory of Louisiana from the French government for $15 million.

A. 1803　　　　　B. 1903　　　　　C. 1776　　　　　D. 1775

Ⅱ. Read the following statements and decide whether they are true (T) or false (F).

1. When Christopher Columbus landed in the New World, he called the native people Indians because he thought he had reached India. _____
2. The first successful English settlement was at Jamestown, Virginia, in 1607. _____
3. The Louisiana Purchase stretched from the Mississippi River to the Rocky Mountains and from Canada to New Orleans, and it doubled the size of the United States. _____

Ⅲ. Short-answer question.

What are the causes, procedure and result of American Revolutionary War?

Unit 7

American History (2)

❑ **In this unit you will learn about**
1. American Civil War
2. Reconstruction
3. American Industrial Revolution
4. The US during WW Ⅰ and WW Ⅱ
5. War on terrorism

✓参考答案
✓更多资源

Vocabulary

- abolitionist 废奴主义者
- backbone 脊梁骨；脊柱；支柱；骨干
- hasten 催促，促进
- infrastructure 基础设施
- neutral 中立的
- secede 退出，脱离（组织等）
- simmer （使某物）保持在接近沸点；（指争吵、争辩等）处于即将爆发的状态
- tariff 关税
- unprecedented 前所未有的

Key Sentences

1. In the spring of 1861, decades of simmering tensions between the northern and southern United States over issues including states' rights versus federal authority, westward expansion and slavery exploded into the American Civil War.
   1861年春，美国南北之间因州权与联邦权威、西进扩张和奴隶制等问题而酝酿了数十年的紧张局势导致了美国内战。

2. In the mid-19th century, while the United States was experiencing an era of tremendous growth, a fundamental economic difference existed between the country's northern and southern regions.
   19世纪中叶，在美国经历一个巨大增长时代的同时，该国北部和南部地区之间存在着根本性的经济差异。

3. On April 12, after Lincoln ordered a fleet to resupply Sumter, Confederate artillery fired the first shots of the Civil War.
   4月12日，林肯命令一支舰队向萨姆特再补给物资后，南部邦联炮兵开了内战的第一枪。

4. By the time it ended in Confederate surrender in 1865, the Civil War proved to be the costliest war ever fought on American soil.
   到1865年南方军投降时，内战被证明是在美国土地上发生的最昂贵的战争。

5. The Industrial Revolution (1820—1870) was of great importance to the economic development of the United States.
   工业革命(1820—1870)对美国的经济发展具有重要意义。

6. The Industrial Revolution itself refers to a change from hand and home production of goods to machine and factory.
   工业革命本身指的是从手工和家庭生产商品到机器和工厂的转变。

7. In fact, the industrial revolution truly changed American society and economy into a modern urban-industrial state.
   事实上，工业革命确实把美国社会和经济变成了一个现代的城市工业化国家。

8. The Embargo Act and the War made it apparent that America needed a better

transportation system and more economic independence. Therefore, manufacturing began to expand within the new country.
《禁运法案》和战争表明,美国需要一个更好的运输系统和更多的经济独立。因此,这个新国家的制造业开始扩张。

9. The South increased its cotton supply sending raw cotton north to be used in the manufacture of cloth.
南方增加了棉花供应,把原棉运往北方用于制造布料。

10. Eli Whitney came up with the idea to use interchangeable parts in 1798 to make muskets.
惠特尼在1798年提出了用可互换零件制造步枪的想法。

11. As industries and factories arose, people moved from farms to cities. This led to other issues including overcrowding and disease.
随着工业和工厂的兴起,人们从农场搬到城市。这导致了其他问题,包括过度拥挤和疾病。

12. In 1844, Samuel F. B. Morse created the telegraph and by 1860, this network ranged throughout the eastern coast to the Mississippi.
1844年,塞缪尔·摩尔斯发明了电报,到1860年,电报网遍布东海岸,一直延伸到密西西比河。

13. During most of the 1920s, the United States enjoyed a period of unbalanced prosperity as farm prices fell and industrial profits grew. A rise in debt and an inflated stock market led to a crash in 1929, triggering the Great Depression.
在20世纪20年代的大部分时间里,随着农产品价格的下跌和工业利润的增长,美国经历了一段不平衡的繁荣时期。债务的上升和股市的膨胀导致了1929年的崩溃,引发了经济大萧条。

▣ Warm-up Exercise

1. What is the "Great Depression"? What is the "New Deal"?

2. What do you think are the roots of terrorism?

▣ Introduce China in English

Why did the US government pass the 1882 Chinese Exclusion Act?

Text

This unit introduces the following topics: the American Civil War, the Industrial Revolution, World War Ⅰ and Ⅱ, Cold War and the Civil Rights Movement, 9/11 and the War on Terrorism.

■ American Civil War

In the spring of 1861, decades of simmering tensions between the northern and southern United States over issues including states' rights versus federal authority, westward expansion and slavery exploded into the American Civil War (1861—1865). The election of the anti-slavery <u>Republican Abraham Lincoln</u> as president in 1860 caused seven southern states to secede from the Union to form the <u>Confederate States of America</u>; four more joined them after the first shots of the Civil War were fired.

In the mid-19th century, while the United States was experiencing an era of tremendous growth, a fundamental economic difference existed between the country's northern and southern regions. While in the North, manufacturing and industry were well established, and agriculture was mostly limited to small-scale farms, the South's economy was based on a system of large-scale farming that depended on the labor of black slaves to grow certain crops, especially cotton and tobacco. Growing abolitionist sentiment in the North after the 1830s and northern opposition to slavery's extension into the new western territories led many southerners to fear that the existence of slavery in America—and thus the backbone of their economy—was in danger.

Even as Lincoln took office in March 1861, Confederate forces threatened the federal-held <u>Fort Sumter</u> in Charleston, South Carolina. On April 12, after Lincoln ordered a fleet to resupply Sumter, Confederate artillery fired the first shots of the Civil War. Sumter's commander, Major Robert Anderson, surrendered after less than two days of bombardment, leaving the fort in the hands of Confederate forces under Pierre G. T. Beauregard. Four more southern states—Virginia, Arkansas,

ICT

Republican 共和党

Abraham Lincoln 亚伯拉罕·林肯,美国第 16 任总统(1861—1865)。

Confederate States of America 南部邦联,又称 Confederacy。1860—1861 年间脱离联邦的美国南方 11 个州所组成的政府。

Fort Sumter 萨姆特要塞。1861 年 4 月 12 日南方邦联军队在此打响了美国南北战争的第一枪。

North Carolina and Tennessee—joined the Confederacy after Fort Sumter. Border slave states like Missouri, Kentucky and Maryland did not secede, but there was much Confederate sympathy among their citizens.

Though on the surface the Civil War may have seemed a lopsided conflict, with the 23 states of the Union enjoying an enormous advantage in population, manufacturing (including arms production) and railroad construction, the Confederates had a strong military tradition, along with some of the best soldiers and commanders in the nation. They also had a cause they believed in: preserving their long-held traditions and institutions, chief among these being slavery. In the First Battle of Bull Run (known in the South as First Manassas) on July 21, 1861, 35,000 Confederate soldiers under the command of Thomas Jonathan "Stonewall" Jackson forced a greater number of Union forces (or Federals) to retreat towards Washington, D.C., dashing any hopes of a quick Union victory and leading Lincoln to call for 500,000 more recruits. In fact, both sides' initial call for troops had to be widened after it became clear that the war would not be a limited or short conflict.

First Manassas 第一次马纳萨斯战役，也称第一次奔牛河战役（First Battle of Bull Run），1861 年 7 月 21 日爆发，是第一场南北战争中的重要战役。

By the time it ended in Confederate surrender in 1865, the Civil War proved to be the costliest war ever fought on American soil.

While the Revolutionary War created the United States, the Civil War determined what kind of nation it would be. The war resolved two fundamental questions left unresolved by the revolution: whether the United States was to be a dissolvable confederation of sovereign states or an indivisible nation with a sovereign national government; and whether this nation, born of a declaration that all men were created with an equal right to liberty, would continue to exist as the largest slaveholding country in the world.

Northern victory in the war preserved the United States as one nation and ended the institution of slavery that had divided the country from its beginning. It was the greatest war in American history. Three million fought—600,000 died. It was the only war fought on American soil by Americans.

After the Civil War, an unprecedented arrival of immigrants, who helped to provide labor for American industry and create diverse communities in undeveloped areas—together with high tariff protections, national infrastructure building, and national banking regulations—hastened the country's rise to international power.

■ *The Industrial Revolution*

The Industrial Revolution (1820—1870) was of great importance to the economic development of the United States. The first Industrial Revolution began in Great Britain and Europe during the late eighteenth century. It then centered on the United States and Germany. The Industrial Revolution itself refers to a change from hand and home production of goods to machine and factory.

The first Industrial Revolution was important for the inventions of spinning and weaving machines operated by water power. These were eventually replaced by steam. This helped increase America's growth. In fact, the Industrial Revolution truly changed American society and economy into a modern urban-industrial state.

■ Growing Industrialization

The real impetus for America entering the Industrial Revolution was the passage of the Embargo Act of 1807 and the War of 1812. Americans were upset over an incident with the Chesapeake whereby the British opened fire on the ship when they were not allowed to search it. They seized four Americans, impressing them into service, and they hung one for desertion. This resulted in much public outrage and the passage of the Embargo Act that stopped the export of American goods and effectively ended the import of goods from other nations. Eventually, America went to war with Great Britain in 1812. The Embargo Act and the War made it apparent that America needed a better transportation system and more economic independence. Therefore, manufacturing began to expand within the new country.

Industrialization in America involved three important developments. First, transportation was expanded. Second, electricity was effectively harnessed. Third, improvements

Embargo Act of 1807 1807年的《禁运法案》由美国第十届国会通过,并由美国第三任总统托马斯·杰斐逊签署成为法律。

the War of 1812 美国第二次独立战争,也称为1812年战争,英国和美国之间的一场不分胜负的战争。

were made to industrial processes such as improving the refining process and accelerating production. The government helped protect American manufacturers by passing a protective tariff.

- **Important Inventors, Inventions, and Events of the Industrial Revolution**

    ❖ **Cotton and Cloth**

    In 1794, Eli Whitney invented the cotton gin which made the separation of cotton seeds from fiber much faster. The South increased its cotton supply sending raw cotton north to be used in the manufacture of cloth. Francis C. Lowell increased the efficiency in the manufacture of cloth by bringing spinning and weaving processes together into one factory. This led to the development of the textile industry throughout New England. In 1846, Elias Howe created the sewing machine which revolutionized the manufacture of clothing. All of a sudden, clothing began to be made in factories as opposed to at home.

    Eli Whitney 惠特尼。美国发明家、机械工程师及制造商。
    cotton gin 轧花机

    Elias Howe 伊莱亚斯·豪,发明家,缝纫机的发明者。

    ❖ **Interchangeable Parts**

    Eli Whitney came up with the idea to use interchangeable parts in 1798 to make muskets.

    If standard parts were made by machine, then they could be assembled at the end much more quickly than before. This became an important part of American industry and the Second Industrial Revolution.

    ❖ **From Agriculture to Cities**

    As industries and factories arose, people moved from farms to cities. This led to other issues including overcrowding and disease. However, advances were made in agriculture too including better machines and cultivators. For example, Cyrus McCormick created the reaper which allowed quicker and cheaper harvesting of grain. John Deere created the first steel plow in 1837 helping speed up farming across the Midwest.

    ❖ **Communication and the Industrial Revolution**

    With the increased size of the United States, better communication networks became ultra important.

    In 1844, Samuel F. B. Morse created the telegraph and by 1860, this network ranged throughout the eastern coast to the Mississippi.

    Samuel Morse 塞缪尔·摩尔斯,创立了摩尔斯电码,电报之父。

❖ **Transportation**

The Cumberland Road, the first national road, was begun in 1811. This eventually became part of the Interstate 40. Further, river transportation was made efficient through the creation of the first steamboat, the Clermont, by Robert Fulton. This was made possible by James Watt's invention of the first reliable steam engine.

The creation of the Erie Canal created a route from the Atlantic Ocean to the Great Lakes thereby helping stimulate the economy of New York and making New York City a great trading center.

Railroads were of supreme importance to the increase in trade throughout the United States. In fact, by the start of the Civil War, railroads linked the most important Midwest cities with the Atlantic coast. Railroads further opened the west and connected raw materials to factories and markets. A transcontinental railroad was completed in 1869 at Promontory, Utah.

With the great advances of the Industrial Revolution, inventors continued to work throughout the rest of the 19th and early 20th century on ways to make life easier while increasing productivity. The foundations set throughout the mid-1800's set the stage for inventions such as the light bulb (Thomas Edison), telephone (Alexander Bell), and the automobile (Karl Benz). Further, Ford's creation of the assembly line which made manufacturing more efficient just helped form America into a modern industrialized nation. The impact of these and other inventions of the time cannot be underestimated.

■ *World Wars I and II*

At the start of the World War Ⅰ in 1914, the United States remained neutral. In 1917, however, the United States joined the Allied Powers, helping to turn the tide against the Central Powers. After the war, the Senate did not ratify the Treaty of Versailles because of a fear that it would pull the United States into European affairs. Instead, the country pursued a policy of unilateralism.

During most of the 1920s, the United States enjoyed a

Interstate 40 40号州际公路。

Robert Fulton 罗伯特·富尔顿，画家。1803年制造出了由他自己设计的第一艘以蒸汽机作为动力的轮船。

Allied Powers 协约国
Central Powers 同盟国
Treaty of Versailles《凡尔赛条约》
unilateralism 单边主义

period of unbalanced prosperity as farm prices fell and industrial profits grew. A rise in debt and an inflated stock market led to a crash in 1929, triggering the Great Depression. After his election as President in 1932, Franklin Delano Roosevelt developed his plan called the New Deal, which increased government intervention in the economy in response to the Great Depression.

Great Depression 经济大萧条
New Deal 新政。美国总统罗斯福为缓解经济压力而制定的国内计划（1933—1939）。

The nation did not fully recover until 1941, when the United States was driven to join the Allies against the Axis Powers after a surprise attack on Pearl Harbor by Japan. Toward the end of World War Ⅱ, the United States dropped atomic bombs on Hiroshima and Nagasaki, Japan.

Hiroshima 广岛
Nagasaki 长崎

■ Cold War and the Civil Rights Movement

After World War Ⅱ, the United States and the Soviet Union became superpowers in an era of ideological rivalry called the Cold War. The result was a series of proxy wars, including the Korean War, the Vietnam War, the Cuban Missile Crisis, and so on.

Meanwhile, American society experienced a period of sustained economic expansion. At the same time, discrimination across the United States, especially in the South, was increasingly challenged by a growing civil-rights movement led by prominent African Americans such as Martin Luther King, Jr., which resulted in the abolition of the Jim Crow laws in the South.

Martin Luther King, Jr. 马丁·路德·金。美国民权运动领袖。
Jim Crow laws 吉姆·克劳法，泛指 1876 年至 1965 年间美国南部各州以及边境各州对有色人种实行种族隔离制度的法律。

■ September 11, 2001 and the War on Terrorism

On September 11, 2001, 19 al-Qaeda operatives hijacked four commercial airplanes and flew two planes into the World Trade Center towers, one plane into the Pentagon; the fourth plane was brought down by passengers in Shanksville, Pennsylvania. After the 9/11 attacks, the US government under President George W. Bush began a series of military operations termed the War on Terror.

al-Qaeda "基地"组织。
World Trade Center 世贸中心
the Pentagon 美国国防部；五角大楼

Understanding More about China

Passage of the 1882 Chinese Exclusion Act

Chinese immigrants began to arrive in the United States in significant numbers following the discovery of gold in California in 1848. Most came from the Pearl River delta region in Guangdong, China, and, like the majority of newcomers to California, the Chinese community was comprised mostly of male laborers. They were only a small fraction of the total immigrant population of the United States. From 1870 to 1880, a total of 138,941 Chinese immigrants entered the country, 4.3 percent of the total number of immigrants (3,199,394) who entered the country during the same decade.

Their small numbers notwithstanding, Chinese immigrants were the targets of racial hostility, discriminatory laws, and violence. This racism was grounded in an American Orientalist ideology that homogenized Asia as one indistinguishable entity and positioned and defined the West and the East in diametrically opposite terms, using those distinctions to claim American and Anglo-American superiority. Americans first learned to identify Chinese through reports from American traders, diplomats, and missionaries in China. At first seen as exotic curiosities from a distant land, Chinese immigrants came to be viewed as threats, especially as Chinese immigration increased throughout the gold rush period.

Anti-Chinese activists' charges that Chinese were unwilling and, in fact, incapable of assimilating were repeatedly used to introduce and support the idea of closing America's gates to Chinese immigration. Chinese immigrants were first set apart from both European immigrants and native-born white Americans. One witness before the 1876 California State Committee on Chinese Immigration described Chinese immigration as an unwelcome "invasion" of "new" and "different" immigrants, while the earlier classes of (European) immigrants were "welcome visitors." In this way, the country's immigrant heritage and identification as a nation of immigrants was largely preserved. Even more important, the witnesses continued to emphasize how Chinese were "permanently alien" to America, unable to ever assimilate into American life and citizenship.

Both the West's history of extending and reinforcing white supremacy in the region and its unique relationship with the federal government paved the way toward Chinese exclusion and the larger development of a gatekeeping nation. With the passage of the Chinese Exclusion Act in 1882, the exclusion of Chinese became yet one more chapter in the region's consolidation of white supremacy, but with enduring, national consequences.

Exercises

Ⅰ. Choose the answer that best completes the statement.
1. The first Industrial Revolution began in _____ and Europe during the late eighteenth century.
   A. France   B. Germany   C. Italy   D. Great Britain
2. A prominent African American civil-rights movement leader is called _____.
   A. Thomas Jefferson   B. Martin Luther
   C. Martin Luther King, Jr.   D. John Adams

Ⅱ. Read the following statements and decide whether they are true (T) or false (F).
1. After the Second World War, discrimination across the United States, especially in the North, was increasingly challenged by a growing civil-rights movement. _____
2. After the First World War, the United States and the Soviet Union became superpowers in an era of ideological rivalry called the Cold War. _____
3. At the start of the World War Ⅰ in 1914, the United States remained neutral. _____
4. The Cuban Missile Crisis is one the results of the Cold War. _____
5. After the First World War, the United States pursued a policy of unilateralism. _____

Ⅲ. Short-answer question.
What are the important developments of the American Industrial Revolution?

Unit 8

American Literature

❏ **In this unit you will learn about**
  1. Different periods of American literature
  2. Famous American writers and their representative works

✓参考答案
✓更多资源

Vocabulary

- aberrant 违反常规的；反常的
- adventure 冒险
- autobiographical 自传的，自传体的
- benevolent 好心肠的；与人为善的；助人为乐的
- corps 兵团
- credit 把某事物归功于某人
- critic 评论员，评论家（尤指对艺术、文学、音乐等作品）
- detective story 侦探小说
- elegy 挽歌；哀歌；挽诗
- embark / embark on sth 开始或从事（尤指新的或难的事）
- enlist 参军；从军
- epistolary novels 书信体小说
- essayist 散文家
- exponent （理论、信仰、事业等的）倡导者，拥护者
- fiction 小说；虚构的文学作品（包括小说、剧本等）
- frenetic 狂乱的，发狂的
- frivolous （指人、性格等）不明事理的，不严肃的，漫不经心的，轻率的，肤浅的
- masculinity 男子气质
- migrate 迁居，迁徙
- pacifist 和平主义者
- pamphlet 小册子
- pneumonia 肺炎
- prelude （行动或事件的）序幕，前奏
- prey 被捕食的动物；捕获物
- prototype 原型
- pseudonym 假名；化名；（尤指）笔名
- transience 转瞬即逝，无常
- vigorous 精力充沛的，强健的；活泼的

Key Sentences

1. American literature does not easily lend itself to classification by period.
   美国文学不容易按时期来分类。

2. This period starts from the founding of Jamestown up to the Revolutionary War. The majority of writings were historical, practical, or religious in nature.
   这一时期始于詹姆斯敦的建立，直至独立战争。大多数作品都是历史性的、实用性的或宗教性的。

3. This is arguably the richest period of political writing.
   这可以说是政治性作品最丰产的时期。

4. Washington Irving was writer called the "first American man of letters."
   华盛顿·欧文是一位被称为"美国文学第一人"的作家。

5. James Fenimore Cooper was the first major American novelist, author of the novels of frontier adventure known as the Leatherstocking Tales.
   詹姆斯·费尼莫尔·库珀是美国第一位重要的小说家，他创作了被称为"皮袜子故事"的边疆冒险小说。

6. William Cullen Bryant was the first American poet to gain international reputation.
   威廉·卡伦·布莱恩特是第一位获得国际声誉的美国诗人。

7. This relatively short period is defined by its insistence on recreating life as life really is.
   这一相对较短的时期是由它坚持重建生活的本质所决定的。

8. The book was made into a film in 1940.
   这本书在 1940 年被拍成电影。

9. Ernest Hemingway was a novelist and short-story writer, awarded the Nobel Prize in Literature in 1954.
   海明威是一位小说家和短篇小说作家,1954 年获得诺贝尔文学奖。

10. Sinclair Lewis was awarded a Nobel Prize in Literature in 1930, the first American to receive this honor.
    辛克莱·刘易斯在 1930 年被授予诺贝尔文学奖,他是第一位获此殊荣的美国人。

11. In fact, Anderson's reputation rests on his short stories, but he also wrote a remarkable novel.
    事实上,安德森的名声在于他的短篇小说,但他也写了一部了不起的小说。

12. The Beat Generation means the group of young people in the 1950s, who refused to accept the values of Western society, and showed this by refusing to work, keeping no material possessions, and wearing their own style of clothes.
    "垮掉的一代"是指 20 世纪 50 年代拒绝接受西方社会价值观的年轻人群体,他们拒绝工作,没有任何物质财富,穿着自己风格的服装。

13. Traditional Chinese drama or opera reached its peak during the Yuan Dynasty.
    中国传统戏曲在元代达到了顶峰。

14. Because of the diversity of dialect groups and the vastness of the land, Chinese opera naturally came to be divided into many branches according to dialect and geographical region.
    由于方言群的多样性和地域的辽阔性,中国戏曲自然而然地按方言和地域划分成为许多分支。

15. The Ming and Qing Dynasties were the golden age of long novels.
    明清是长篇小说的黄金时代。

16. Based on Tang Dynasty monk Xuan Zang's journey to India to bring back Buddhist scriptures, the novel is mainly fictional but highly entertaining.
    这部小说以玄奘取回佛经的印度之旅为蓝本,以虚构为主,寓教于乐。

17. Beginning from the Song Dynasty, children starting school were taught the *San Zi Jing*, or *Three-worded Jing*.

从宋代开始,开始上学的孩子们就被教导熟读《三字经》。

Warm-up Exercise

1. What is the real name of Mark Twain? What are his representative works?

2. What are the masterpieces of Ernest Hemingway?

3. What does the "Beat Generation" mean?

Introduce China in English

1. What are the "Four Great Classical Novels"(四大名著) in Chinese literature?

2. In which dynasties did "Long Novels" flourish?

American literature does not easily lend itself to classification by period. Following is a general guide to certain major periods, with examples of noted writers and works.

■ The Colonial Period (1607—1775)

This period started from the founding of Jamestown up to the Revolutionary War. The majority of writings were historical, practical, or religious in nature. One of the writers from this period is John Winthrop, who was an English Puritan lawyer and one of the leading figures in founding the Massachusetts Bay Colony. His major contributions to the literary world were *A Model of Christian Charity* (1630) and *The History of New England* (1630—1649). His writings and vision of the colony as a Puritan "city upon a hill" dominated New England colonial development, influencing the governments and religions of neighboring colonies.

Jamestown 詹姆斯敦。英国在北美洲建立的第一个永久性殖民点所在地,建于1607年5月,位于弗吉尼亚州。城市名称取自当时的英国国王詹姆斯一世。

John Winthrop 约翰·温思罗普,马萨诸塞湾殖民地首任总督,为清教徒。

■ The Revolutionary Age (1765—1790)

Beginning a decade before the Revolutionary War and ending about 25 years later, this period includes the writings of Thomas Jefferson, Thomas Paine, James Madison and Alexander Hamilton. This is arguably the richest period of political writing. Important works include the *Declaration of Independence*. Thomas Paine's *Common Sense* was the most widely read pamphlet of the American Revolution.

■ The Early National Period (1775—1828)

This era is responsible for notable first works, such as the first American comedy written for the stage (*The Contrast* by Royall Tyler, 1787) and the first American Novel (*The Power of Sympathy* by William Hill, 1789). Washington Irving, James Fenimore Cooper and Charles Brockden Brown are credited with creating distinctly American fiction, while Edgar Allan Poe and William Cullen Bryant began writing poetry that was

Royall Tyler 罗耶尔·泰勒,作品为《对比》。
William Hill 威廉·希尔,作品为《同情的力量》。

markedly different from that of the English tradition.

Washington Irving (1783—1859) was the writer called the "first American man of letters." He is best known for the short stories "The Legend of Sleepy Hollow" and "Rip Van Winkle."

James Fenimore Cooper (1789—1851) was the first major American novelist, author of the novels of frontier adventure known as "The Leatherstocking Tales", including *The Pioneers* (1823), *The Last of the Mohicans* (1826), *The Prairie* (1827), *The Pathfinder* (1840), and *The Deerslayer* (1841).

With his four novels written between 1798 and 1801 Charles Brockden Brown (1771—1810) became the pioneer for several genres of fiction and prepared the way for Cooper, Poe, and Hawthorne. In *Wieland*, *or*, *The Transformation* (1798) as well as in *Edgar Huntley* (1799), both epistolary novels, he dealt with aberrant psychology and strange adventures in American settings.

William Cullen Bryant (1794—1878) was the first American poet to gain international reputation. He was born in Massachusetts and worked as a lawyer and journalist. Death and transience of the natural world are the themes of his elegy "Thanatopsis" (1817), written in blank verse.

■ *The American Renaissance (1828—1865)*

Also known as the Romantic Period in America and the Age of Transcendentalism, this period is commonly accepted to be the greatest of American literature. Major writers include Walt Whitman, Ralph Waldo Emerson, Henry David Thoreau, Nathaniel Hawthorne, Edgar Allan Poe and Herman Melville.

Walt Whitman (1819—1892) was a poet, journalist, and essayist whose verse collection *Leaves of Grass* is a landmark in the history of American literature.

Ralph Waldo Emerson (1803—1882) was a lecturer, poet, and essayist, the leading exponent of New England Transcendentalism.

Henry David Thoreau (1817—1862) was an essayist, poet, and practical philosopher, renowned for having lived the doctrines of Transcendentalism as recorded in his masterwork, *Walden* (1854), and for having been a vigorous advocate of civil

"The Leatherstocking Tales"《皮袜子故事集》。詹姆斯·费尼莫尔·库珀是一位具有本土特色的美国作家,主要作品为长篇小说。他的代表作《皮袜子故事集》五部曲塑造了一位长年累月穿着鹿皮制成护腿的"皮袜子"纳蒂·班波(Natty Bumppo)这一形象,通过对他一生冒险经历的描写,反映了美国西部边境的真实社会。

"Thanatopsis"美国浪漫主义诗人威廉·卡伦·布莱恩特的诗作《死亡随想录》。

Transcendentalism 19世纪新英格兰哲学家与作家的运动,他们因信奉一套唯心论的思想体系而松散地结合在一起;这套思想基于以下信念:宇宙万物实质上的统一性和人类固有的善良天性,以及在揭示最深刻的真理方面,内在的洞察力优于逻辑和经验。

Walden《瓦尔登湖》,亨利·戴维·梭罗创作的散文集。

liberties, as evidenced in the essay "Civil Disobedience" (1849).

Nathaniel Hawthorne (1804—1864) was a novelist and short-story writer. He is best known for *The Scarlet Letter* (1850) and *The House of the Seven Gables* (1851).

Edgar Allan Poe (1809—1849) was a short-story writer, poet, critic, and editor. His tale *The Murders in the Rue Morgue* (1841) initiated the modern detective story. His "The Raven" (1845) numbers among the best-known poems in the national literature.

The Raven 艾伦·坡的诗《乌鸦》。

Herman Melville (1819—1891) was born in New York, the son of a wealthy businessman. He lost his father at the age of 12. Because of his father's bankruptcy, the young Herman's education was cut short, and in 1839 he went to Liverpool as a cabin boy. He was much impressed by life at sea, but returned to upstate New York for a brief period to teach school. In 1841 he embarked on the whaler Acushnet for the South Seas. At the Marquesas, he left his ship and lived for a month on those beautiful islands, escaping from the hostile natives on an Australian trading ship that took him to Tahiti. Before returning to Boston in 1844, he also visited Hawaii.

This education at sea, as it were, formed the basis for his best fiction. Combining personal experience with imagination and information from books he had read, he wrote a number of novels that, although mere preludes to *Moby-Dick*, made him famous.

■ *The Realistic Period (1865—1900)*

As a result of the American Civil War, Reconstruction and the age of Industrialism, American ideals and self-awareness changed in profound ways, and American literature responded. Certain romantic notions of the American Renaissance were replaced by realistic descriptions of American life, such as those represented in the works of William Dean Howells, Henry James and Mark Twain. This period also gave rise to regional writing.

William Dean Howells (1837—1920) put his theory into practice in a large number of short stories and novels. Of his novels, *A Modern Instance* (1882) is the one he cherished most.

It deals with a woman's marriage to and divorce from a ruthless Boston journalist.

Mark Twain, pseudonym of Samuel Langhorne Clemens (1835—1910), was a humorist, journalist, lecturer, and novelist who acquired international fame for his travel narratives, especially *The Innocents Abroad* (1869), *Roughing It* (1872), and *Life on the Mississippi* (1883), and for his adventure stories of boyhood, especially *The Adventures of Tom Sawyer* (1876) and *Adventures of Huckleberry Finn* (1885).

■ *The Naturalist Period (1900—1914)*

This relatively short period is defined by its insistence on recreating life as life really is, even more so than the realists had been doing in the decades before. American Naturalist writers such as Frank Norris, Theodore Dreiser and Jack London created some of the most powerfully raw novels in American literary history. Their characters are victims who fall prey to their own base instincts and to economic and sociological factors. Edith Wharton wrote some of her most beloved classics, such as *The Custom of the Country* (1913), *Ethan Frome* (1911) and *House of Mirth* (1905) during this time period.

■ *The Modern Period (1914—1939)*

Novelists and prose writers of the time include Willa Cather, John Dos Passos, F. Scott Fitzgerald, John Steinbeck, Ernest Hemingway, Gertrude Stein, Sinclair Lewis, Thomas Wolfe and Sherwood Anderson.

Willa Cather (1873—1947) was born in Virginia and grew up in Nebraska. She dealt with the hardships of men in a hostile environment and with the life of new settlers (e. g. *O Pioneers!*, 1913; and *My Ántonia*, 1918). Cather also wrote an outstanding historical novel on the work of the Catholic Church and of two saints in New Mexico: *Death Comes for the Archbishop* (1927).

John Dos Passos (1896—1970) studied at Harvard and in Spain and took part in World War I in a volunteer ambulance corps. He recorded his growing disillusion and the inhumanity of the military machinery in his pacifist novel *Three Soldiers* (1921). *Manhattan Transfer* (1925) was his first experiment in the novel.

F. Scott Fitzgerald (1896—1940) wrote many excellent short stories and dealt with the frenetic and frivolous youth of the post-war years in *This Side of Paradise* (1920). His masterpiece is *The Great Gatsby* (1925).

The Great Gatsby《了不起的盖茨比》

Many of John Steinbeck's (1902—1968) novels have little literary value. Outstanding are his naturalistic works emphasizing heredity and environment in the assessment of poor human "underdogs." Thus *Of Mice and Men* (1937), held mostly in dialogue, is the tragic story of the dreams and adventures of two itinerant Californian farm laborers, while *The Grapes of Wrath* (1939) traces the suffering of the Joad family in the Depression as they migrate from the Oklahoma dust bowl to California.

The Grapes of Wrath《愤怒的葡萄》

Ernest Hemingway (1899—1961) was a novelist and short-story writer, awarded the Nobel Prize in Literature in 1954. He was noted both for the intense masculinity of his writing and for his adventurous and widely publicized life. Hemingway was raised in Oak Park, Illinois. After high school, he reported for a few months for The Kansas City Star, before leaving for the Italian front to enlist with the World War Ⅰ ambulance drivers. In 1918, he was seriously wounded and returned home. His wartime experiences formed the basis for his novel *A Farewell to Arms* (1929). He published his first novel, *The Sun Also Rises*, in 1926; his other works include *For Whom the Bell Tolls* (1940) and *The Old Man and the Sea* (1952).

Because of her pervasive influence on the "Lost Generation," Gertrude Stein (1874—1946) occupies an important place in American literature.

Lost Generation "迷惘的一代"。狭义上指于第一次世界大战期间成年,并在20世纪20年代确立声誉的一批美国作家。更广义的是指在第一次世界大战后成年的一整代美国人。这个名称出自斯泰因对海明威说的一句话。这些作家之所以认为自己"迷惘",是因为他们所继承的价值观不再适合战后的世界。他们觉得在精神上与这个国家疏远起来,认为这个国家变得极端偏狭,冷漠无情。

Sinclair Lewis (1885—1951) was a journalist and novelist who travelled widely in the USA and in Europe. He refused to accept a Pulitzer Prize in 1926 and was awarded a Nobel Prize in Literature in 1930, the first American to receive this honor. Lewis died in Rome. Lewis's first major novel is *Main Street* (1920). With *Babbitt* (1922) Lewis created the prototype of the superficial and benevolent businessman who prefers to adapt to society instead of following his own inclinations.

Thomas Wolfe (1900—1938) was born in Ashville, North Carolina, studied at the University of North Carolina and at Harvard, travelled widely in Europe and died early of pneumonia. His epic and panoramic novels are autobiographical and confessional in character.

Sherwood Anderson (1876—1941) wrote sympathetic and psychologically interesting studies of small-town people. In fact, Anderson's reputation rests on his short stories, but he also wrote a remarkable novel, *Dark Laughter* (1925), which contrasts unrepressed blacks with spiritually sterile whites.

■ *The Beat Generation (1944—1962)*

The Beat Generation The means the group of young people in the 1950s, including the writers Jack Kerouac and Allen Ginsberg, who refused to accept the values of Western society, and showed this by refusing to work, keeping no material possessions, and wearing their own style of clothes. Beat writers were devoted to anti-traditional literature, in poetry and prose, and anti-establishment politics. This time period saw a rise in confessional poetry and sexuality in literature, which resulted in legal challenges and debates over censorship in America.

Beat Generation "垮掉的一代",是第二次世界大战之后出现于美国的一群松散结合在一起的年轻诗人和作家。

■ *The Contemporary Period (1939—Present)*

After World War II, American literature becomes broad and varied in terms of theme, mode, and purpose. There are a number of important writers since 1939 whose works may be considered "classic".

▫ Understanding More about China

1. Yuan Songs and Dramas

The *ci* poetry of the Tang and Song Dynasties evolved into pure musical lyrics during the Yuan Dynasty. Many songs were produced for entertainment in theatres and "green houses" (青楼). The lyrics follow the general pattern of *ci* and are bound by similar rules although certain variations are allowed. A set pattern with specifications and a fixed melody attached to it is called a "tune card"（曲牌）. There are several hundred different cards, each with its own name and specifications for the wording pattern of the lyrics and an accompanying tune. A song is created when one fits the wording into the set pattern. Thus, different songs based on the same tune card have the same melody and wording pattern but different lyrics.

Yuan songs gave rise to Yuan dramas. Traditional Chinese drama or opera reached its peak during the Yuan Dynasty. There has been no radical change from the Yuan dramas to the Chinese operas of today.

Because of the diversity of dialect groups and the vastness of the land, Chinese opera naturally came to be divided into many branches according to dialect and geographical region. In the north, Beijing opera or *jingju*（京剧）and *kunju*（昆剧）from Kunshan near Shanghai are the most refined and popular. Among the Cantonese-speaking people in the south and overseas, the Cantonese opera or *yueju*（粤剧）has many faithful fans among the older generation.

2. Chinese Literature: Ming and Qing Long Novels

While the Tang Dynasty was known for its poetry, the Song Dynasty for its *ci* and the Yuan Dynasty for its songs and drama, the Ming and Qing Dynasties were the golden age of long novels.

At the end of the Han Dynasty, the country was fragmented into three kingdoms: Wei, Wu and Shu. They fought one another incessantly for a long period before they were all finally unified as one nation under the Jin Dynasty. The events of the period were dramatised by Ming Dynasty author Luo Guanzhong（罗贯中）in the first long Chinese novel ever written, *San Guo Yan Yi*（《三国演义》）or *The Popular Story of the Three Kingdoms*. He based his story on the factual *Annals of the Three Kingdoms* by Chen Shou（陈寿）of the Jin Dynasty. The novel consists of 120 chapters, covering a period of 97 years (168—265), and describes the fascinating details of the political and military intrigues among the three kingdoms. It is a mix of fact and fiction but is so captivating and so widely read that the version of history it has generated is better known than the factual account written by the court historian.

The next most popular novel is *Shui Hu Quan Zhuan*（《水浒全传》）, or *Water Margin*, written by Shi Naian（施耐庵）, a Ming author. The story, mostly fictional, is set in the declining years of the Northern Song Dynasty, a period when corruption among government officials was widespread. It relates the tale of 108 men who fall foul of the law and take to the hills to become bandits. The men are portrayed as Chinese Robin Hoods, righteous heroes fighting against rapacious officials.

While *The Three Kingdoms* and *Shui Hu Quan Zhuan* are mainly about men's affairs, which the fairer sex may not find interesting, *Hong Lou Meng*（《红楼梦》）, or *Dream of the Red Chamber*, is mostly about women. The first 80 chapters of this romantic novel of high literary value was written by Cao Xueqin（曹雪芹）but it was not completed until 1791, almost 30 years after the author's death, when another writer named Gao E（高鹗）presented what was claimed to be the last 40 chapters of the novel, reconstructed from Cao Xueqin's notes. The story is about the rise and fall of a rich, influential family with many members. The main character is an adolescent boy who grows up in luxury among pretty girl companions and maids. He finds himself having to choose between two girls for a wife. He loves one but the family elders favor the other. The ending is tragic. The moral is Buddhist; all things in life eventually come to naught.

A novel that is popular with both adults and children is *Xi You Ji*（《西游记》）, translated as *Journey to the West* by W.J.F. Jenner. It was written by Wu Chengen（吴承恩）, a Qing scholar. Based on the Tang Dynasty monk Xuan Zang's journey to India to bring back Buddhist scriptures, the novel is mainly fictional but highly entertaining. The monk's three disciples battled numerous demons along the way to protect their master. It seems that the monk had gone through ten previous reincarnations in celibacy. All the male demons were keen to have a piece of his flesh, which would confer immortality, and all the female demons were keen to have relations with him.

Exercises

I. Choose the answer that best completes the statement.
  1. The first American comedy *The Contrast* was written by _____.
     A. Royall Tyler   B. Thomas Paine
     C. Joel Barlow   D. Philip Freneau
  2. The first American Novel *The Power of Sympathy* was written by _____.
     A. Washington Irving   B. James Fenimore Cooper
     C. Charles Brockden Brown   D. William Hill
  3. _____ is best known for the short stories "The Legend of Sleepy Hollow" and "Rip Van Winkle."
     A. James Fenimore Cooper   B. Washington Irving
     C. Thomas Jefferson   D. Thomas Paine
  4. _____ was an American poet, whose verse collection *Leaves of Grass* is a landmark in the history of American literature.
     A. Ralph Waldo Emerson   B. Henry David Thoreau
     C. Walt Whitman   D. Nathaniel Hawthorne

5. Who is the author of *Common Sense*? _____
   A. Thomas Jefferson   B. Thomas Paine
   C. James Madison   D. Alexander Hamilton
6. *The Last of the Mohicans* is one of the masterpieces of _____.
   A. James Fenimore Cooper   B. Washington Irving
   C. Royall Tyler   D. William Hill
7. *The Scarlet Letter* is the masterpiece of _____.
   A. Nathaniel Hawthorne   B. Edgar Allan Poe
   C. Henry David Thoreau   D. Ralph Waldo Emerson
8. Mark Twain was a novelist living in _____.
   A. the American Renaissance   B. the Early National Period
   C. the Naturalist Period   D. the Realistic Period
9. *The Old Man and the Sea* is written by _____.
   A. Mark Twain   B. Ernest Hemingway
   C. F. Scott Fitzgerald   D. John Steinbeck

Ⅱ. Read the following statements and decide whether they are true (T) or false (F).
1. During the Colonial Period (1607—1775), the majority of writings were historical, practical, or religious in nature. _____
2. The Colonial Period (1607—1775) is arguably the richest period of political writing. _____
3. The first American comedy written for the stage came from the Early National Period (1775—1828). _____
4. The Early National Period is also known as the Romantic Period in America. _____
5. Washington Irving was writer called the "first American man of letters." _____
6. Lost Generation, this term was coined by Gertrude Stein and popularized by Ernest Hemingway. _____

Ⅲ. Short-answer question.
What does "Beat Generation" and "Lost Generation" mean respectively?

Unit 9

Holidays and Festivals

❑ **In this unit you will learn about**
1. The meanings of holidays and festivals
2. Holidays and festivals observed in the UK
3. Holidays and festivals observed in the US

✓参考答案
✓更多资源

Vocabulary

- admirer 赞美者,羡慕者
- apostle 使徒(基督为宣传他的教导而派出的十二位门徒之一)
- armistice 休战,停战
- coincidence 巧合
- costume 服装
- crucifixion 钉死在十字架上
- crucify 把(某人)钉死在十字架上
- daffodil 水仙花
- decree 法令
- disguise 假装,假扮
- emblem 象征,标记
- excursion 短程旅行,远足
- feast 盛宴,宴会
- hostility 敌对,对抗,敌意
- infantry 步兵

- knight 骑士
- leek 韭葱(在古代的一次战争中,威尔士军队佩戴韭葱作为标志,作战胜利后,韭葱便出现于威尔士国徽的图案中)
- maiden 少女;姑娘;未婚女子
- missionary 传教士
- patriotic 爱国的
- pirate 海盗
- regalia 加冕礼中用的王权的标志(如王冠、宝球和权杖)
- regiment (英国步兵的)团队
- resurrection 复活
- scary 吓人的,可怕的
- shamrock 三叶草
- statute 成文法
- sweetheart 爱人,情人

Key Sentences

1. Festival is a day or time when people celebrate something, especially a historical or religious event.
   节日是人们庆祝某事的日子或时间,尤指历史或宗教事件。

2. Holidays and festivals can be a great way to experience the history and culture of a country. It's one way of helping maintain all the various customs and traditions we have.
   节假日是体验一个国家历史和文化的好方法。这是一种帮助我们保存各种风俗习惯的方法。

3. The Day is celebrated by the wearing of daffodils or leeks. Both plants are traditionally regarded as national symbols.
   人们戴上水仙花或韭葱来庆祝这一天。这两种植物传统上都被视为国家的象征。

4. In the United Kingdom and Ireland a bank holiday is a public holiday, when banks and many other businesses are closed for the day.
   在英国和爱尔兰,银行假日是一种公共假日,银行和许多其他业务部门在这一天都不营业。

5. Many people give their mothers a card or gift, treat them to a day out or cook a meal.
   许多人给母亲送贺卡或礼物,请她们出去玩一天或给她们做一顿饭。

6. However, each state can choose its own variation of observable holidays. It is possible for some holidays to be observed in one state and not observed in others.
   然而,每个州都可以选择自己要庆祝的节假日。有些节假日在某一个州庆祝,而在其他州并不庆祝。

7. Martin Luther King, Jr. was an African-American church leader who fought for equal rights for America's black community.
   小马丁·路德·金是一位为美国黑人群体争取平等权利的非裔美国教会领袖。

8. Labor Day is celebrated on the first Monday in September. It is the traditional end of the summer vacation season when most schools begin their new terms.
   劳动节在九月的第一个星期一庆祝。这是传统的暑假结束时刻,也是大多数学校新学期开始的时间。

9. This long weekend is usually celebrated with an excursion or a picnic. Many folks choose to stay at home to relax.
   这个漫长的周末通常是以远足或野餐的方式庆祝的。许多人选择呆在家里放松一下。

10. The traditional dish for the Thanksgiving Day dinner is a large roasted turkey. After dinner, the preferred recreation is watching football matches on the television.
    感恩节晚餐的传统菜肴是一只大大的烤火鸡。晚饭后,人们最喜欢的消遣是看电视上的美式橄榄球比赛。

11. Kwanzaa is a relatively new Afro-American holiday celebrated from December 26 through January first.
    匡扎节是一个历史较短的非裔美国人的节日,从12月26日庆祝到1月1日。

12. A family reunion dinner is usually held on Chinese New Year's Eve. All members of a family would try to attend the dinner.
    家庭团圆饭通常在除夕夜举行。一个家庭的所有成员都会想办法参加晚宴。

13. On Chinese New Year's Day, people usually wear new clothes. Children wish their parents good fortune and receive red packets containing money.
    在春节,人们通常穿新衣服。孩子们祝福他们的父母好运,并会收到红包。

14. Firecrackers are set off unless they are specifically banned.
    除非特别禁止,否则会燃放鞭炮。

15. It is customary to visit relatives and friends during the season.
    探亲访友是一种习俗。

16. Yuanxiao is the fifteenth day of the Chinese New Year. In ancient China, this was the night when the emperor would come out of the palace to celebrate the season

with the populace.

中国新年的第十五天是元宵节。在中国古代，这是一个皇帝出宫与民众共度佳节的夜晚。

17. The custom of putting up new "couplets" on either side of the door for the Chinese New Year is still practised.

    过年时在门的两边贴"对联"的习俗仍在实行。

18. The Duanwu Festival falls on the fifth day of the fifth lunar month. The festival is the Memorial Day for Qu Yuan, a well-liked high official, a patriot and an excellent poet in the Chu state during the Warring States period.

    农历五月初五是端午节。这一天是为纪念战国时期楚国著名的高官、爱国者和杰出诗人屈原。

19. That is how the custom of holding a dragon boat race on this day began. The people also threw rice dumplings into the river to feed the fishes so that they would keep away from Qu Yuan's body.

    在这一天举行龙舟比赛的习俗就是这样开始的。人们还把粽子扔进河里喂鱼，这样鱼就远离屈原的身体了。

20. The Zhongqiu Festival, or the Mid-Autumn Festival, probably originated during the Tang Dynasty.

    中秋节可能起源于唐代。

21. The celebrations for this festival are held mostly at night. Each family would have a reunion dinner. Mooncakes, confections that symbolise family togetherness, are exchanged between friends and relatives.

    这个节日的庆祝活动大多在晚上举行。每个家庭都会吃一顿团圆饭。月饼，象征着家庭团聚的甜点，在亲朋好友之间交换。

22. The Dongzhi Festival, or Winter Festival, is the only traditional festival with an origin that is not associated with a myth or a historical event although it is believed by some that it was the day when the Kitchen God went to heaven to report to the Jade Emperor the conduct of a family.

    冬至节是唯一一个与神话或历史事件无关的传统节日，尽管有些人认为这是灶神上天向玉皇大帝报告家庭情况的日子。

Warm-up Exercise

Fill the blanks with the names of holidays and festivals celebrated in each of the following countries throughout the year. Some of the blanks have been filled in, you can use them as examples.

Month \ Country	UK	USA	China
January			
February			
March			
April			
May			
June			
July		Independence Day	
August			
September			
October			National Day
November			
December			

■ Introduce China in English

1. Discuss with your partner how you and your family celebrate the Spring Festival.

   ----

2. Why do we Chinese people celebrate the Dragon Boat Festival?

Text ICT

Holiday is a day of rest when people do not go to work, school, etc. Festival is a day or time when people celebrate something, especially a historical or religious event. So, the difference is in **Festival** there is an activity or specific actions happening as a generally accepted thing but in **Holiday** just rest and no work, however, it can be a festival in a holiday as a coincidence.

Holidays and festivals can be a great way to experience the history and culture of a country. It's one way of helping maintain all the various customs and traditions we have.

The British and Americans share some of the festivals, such as Valentine's Day, Easter, April Fool's Day, Christmas, and so on, however they also have their own particular holidays and festivals to observe.

Valentine's Day 情人节
Easter 复活节

❖ **Valentine's Day**

Valentine's Day, on February 14, is a celebration of love and marriage. On that day, admirers send each other Valentine Day greeting cards. Lovers and spouses buy flowers, candy and gifts for their sweethearts. Many couples go to restaurants for intimate dinners. All stores and businesses are open. This holiday is celebrated in many countries around the world.

❖ **April Fool's Day**

It's possible that the British embrace April Fool's Day (April 1) with more enthusiasm than any other nation. Even the BBC and the national newspapers carry strange tricks disguised as straightforward reportage. All jokes are supposed to end at noon, but keep your wits about you for the rest of the day.

❖ **Halloween**

Halloween (October 31) is a day when people emphasize scary things, wear colorful costumes, and have parties. Young children wear costumes and travel around their neighborhoods to collect candy from neighbors (known as "trick-or-treating").

Halloween 万圣节

trick-or-treating 不请吃就捣蛋(指万圣节孩子们挨门逐户要糖果等礼物，如不遂愿便恶作剧一番的风俗)

■ *British Holidays and Festivals*

UK holidays include national UK holidays and UK

festivals, as well as UK festivals that are more specific to England, Scotland, Wales and Northern Ireland.

■ National Day

National Days are not celebrated in Britain in the same extent as National Days are in a number of other countries. Only in Northern Ireland (and the Republic of Ireland) is <u>St. Patrick's Day</u> taken as an official holiday. All the other national days are normal working days. Each part of the United Kingdom has its own national day:

> St. Patrick's Day——圣·帕特里克节。每年的3月17日,为了纪念爱尔兰守护神圣·帕特里克。这一节日于5世纪末期起源于爱尔兰,如今已成为爱尔兰的国庆节。

❖ **1 March, St. David's Day, is the national day of Wales.**

St. David's Day is celebrated in honor of St. David, the patron saint of Wales. He was a Celtic monk and bishop, who lived in the sixth century. He spread the word of Christianity across Wales. The Day is celebrated by the wearing of daffodils or leeks. Both plants are traditionally regarded as national symbols.

❖ **17 March, St. Patrick's Day, is the national day of Northern Ireland and Republic of Ireland.**

St. Patrick is the patron saint of Ireland. He is credited with bringing Christianity to Ireland. Born in Britain, he was carried off by pirates and spent six years in slavery before escaping and training as a missionary. The most famous story about St. Patrick is him driving the snakes from Ireland. The day is marked by the wearing of shamrocks, the national emblem of both Northern Ireland and the Republic of Ireland.

❖ **23 April, St. George's Day, is the national day of England.**

A story dating back to the 6th century tells that St. George rescued a maiden by slaying a fearsome fire-breathing dragon. The Saint's name was shouted as a battle cry by English knights who fought beneath the red-cross banner of St. George during the <u>Hundred Years War</u>(1338—1453). Some people wear a red rose on St. George's Day.

> Hundred Years War 英法百年战争

❖ **30 November, St. Andrew's Day, is the national day of Scotland.**

St. Andrew was one of Christ's twelve apostles. Some of his bones are said to have been brought to what is now St. Andrews during the 4th century. Since medieval times the

X-shaped saltire cross upon which St. Andrew was supposedly crucified has been the Scottish national symbol.

X-shaped saltire cross X 形十字

■ Bank Holidays

In the United Kingdom and Ireland a bank holiday is a public holiday, when banks and many other businesses are closed for the day, but days that banks are shut aren't always bank holidays. The dates for bank holidays are set out in statute or are proclaimed by royal decree. The term "bank holiday" was coined by Sir John Lubbock.

bank holiday 银行公共假日

Sir John Lubbock 约翰·卢伯克爵士

The following are days when most businesses are closed:
New Year's Day: January 1
Good Friday: (March or April) The anniversary of Jesus Christ's crucifixion
Easter Monday: (March or April) Commemoration of Christ's resurrection
Early May Bank Holiday: the first Monday in May
Late May Bank Holiday: the last Monday in May
Late Summer Bank Holiday: the last Monday in August
Christmas Day: December 25; Celebration of Christ's birth
Boxing Day: December 26; Boxed holiday gifts are given to mailmen, housekeepers and other service workers.

Good Friday 耶稣受难节（复活节前的星期五）

Boxing Day 节礼日，为每年的 12 月 26 日，圣诞节次日或是圣诞节后的第一个星期日。这一日传统上要向服务业从业人员赠送圣诞节礼物。

■ Other British Holidays and Festivals

British people also celebrate other holidays and festivals.

❖ Remembrance Day

Remembrance Day (on 11 November) commemorates the end of war hostilities in 1918 and 1945.

Remembrance Day 阵亡将士纪念日（纪念在两次世界大战中的死难者）

❖ Mother's Day

Mother's Day (early spring) is a day to celebrate motherhood, and to thank mothers for everything they do throughout the year. Many people give their mothers a card or gift, treat them to a day out or cook a meal.

❖ Guy Fawkes Night

Guy Fawkes Night, also known as Guy Fawkes Day, or Bonfire Night, is an annual commemoration observed on 5 November. Its history begins with the events of 5 November 1605, when Guy Fawkes, a member of the Gunpowder Plot, was arrested while guarding explosives the plotters had placed

Guy Fawkes Night 盖伊·福克斯之夜（或篝火节之夜）

Gunpowder Plot 火药阴谋

beneath the House of Lords. Celebrating the fact that King James Ⅰ had survived the attempt on his life, people lit bonfires around London, and months later the introduction of the Observance of 5th November Act enforced an annual public day of thanksgiving for the plot's failure.

❖ **Hogmanay**

Hogmanay is the Scots word for the last day of the year and is synonymous with the celebration of the New Year (Gregorian calendar) in the Scottish manner. However, it is normally only the start of a celebration that lasts through the night until the morning of New Year's Day (1 January) or, in some cases, 2 January—a Scottish Bank Holiday.

Hogmanay 元旦前夕（尤指苏格兰的）

Gregorian calendar 格列高利历, 公历

❖ **Eisteddfod**

An Eisteddfod is a Welsh festival of literature, music and performance. The tradition of such a meeting of Welsh artists dates back to at least the 12th century.

Eisteddfod 艾斯特福德：在威尔士举行的诗人与音乐家的比赛年会

❖ **The Queen's Birthday**

The Queen's Birthday, also called Trooping the Color (celebrated on the second Saturday in June) features a parade in London and plenty of horses and regalia. Among the audience are the Royal Family, invited guests, ticketholders and the general public. The colourful ceremony is broadcast live by the BBC within the UK and is telecast also in Germany and Belgium.

Trooping the Color 皇家军队阅兵仪式

Trooping the Color is a ceremony performed by regiments of the British and Commonwealth armies. It has been a tradition of British infantry regiments since the 17th century, although the roots go back much earlier.

Commonwealth 英联邦

■ *American Holidays and Festivals*

The federal holidays are specified by the government in the US. However, each state can choose its own variation of observable holidays. It is possible for some holidays to be observed in one state and not observed in others. Bank, schools, post offices, etc., are closed on legal holidays. Many businesses are closed as well.

Unlike other countries, many US holidays are celebrated on days that are more convenient and are combined with weekends, rather than being observed in the middle of the week. As most people don't work on Saturdays and Sundays, many holidays are observed on Mondays. Following are some of the holidays and festivals that are specifically celebrated by Americans.

❖ **Martin Luther King, Jr. Day**

<u>Martin Luther King, Jr. Day</u> is celebrated on the third Monday in January. It is the newest holiday, which Americans started celebrating in 1986. Martin Luther King, Jr. was an African-American church leader who fought for equal rights for America's black community. He was an inspiring leader and his "I Have a Dream" speech is widely known around the world. He was killed on April 4, 1968. King and other black leaders worked very hard to improve life for African-Americans. As a result, President Johnson, with King next to him, signed the Voting Rights Act on August 6, 1965. After that, all African-Americans had the right to vote.

Martin Luther King, Jr. Day 马丁·路德·金日,这是唯一一个纪念美国黑人的联邦假日。

❖ **Memorial Day**

<u>Memorial Day</u> is usually celebrated on the last Monday in May. It is the traditional beginning of the summer vacation season and the start of the long school break. Most people use this long weekend for picnics, excursions, short vacation trips, or just relaxation and shopping.

Memorial Day 阵亡将士纪念日

❖ **Independence Day**

<u>Independence Day</u>, the Fourth of July, is a federal holiday commemorating the adoption of the Declaration of Independence on July 4, 1776. It is a time for patriotic celebrations, picnics and relaxation. Many cities and towns across the country hold parades, musical performances and fireworks displays.

Independence Day 独立日

❖ **Labor Day**

Labor Day is celebrated on the first Monday in September. It is the traditional end of the summer vacation season when most schools begin their new terms. This long weekend is usually celebrated with an excursion, a picnic or one last mini vacation of the season. Many folks choose stay at home to relax.

Labor Day 劳动节

❖ **Columbus Day**

<u>Columbus Day</u>(second Monday in October)honors

Columbus Day 哥伦布日

Christopher Columbus, who is credited with discovering the Americas in 1492.

❖ **Thanksgiving Day**

Thanksgiving Day is celebrated on the fourth Thursday in November. It is not a religious holiday. Most people celebrate this holiday by gathering at their family home for a feast. The traditional dish for the Thanksgiving Day dinner is a large roasted turkey. After dinner, the preferred recreation is watching football matches on the television. Most business offices will close on this day. Some stores, shopping centers, restaurants and bars will remain open. The Saturday after Thanksgiving is the traditional opening of the Christmas shopping season.

Thanksgiving Day 感恩节

❖ **Veterans Day**

Veterans Day is celebrated on November 11. This holiday was originally called Armistice Day and established to honour Americans who had served in World War Ⅰ. It now honours veterans of all wars in which the US has fought. Veterans' organizations hold parades, and the president places a wreath on the Tomb of the Unknowns at Arlington National Cemetery in Virginia.

Veterans Day 退伍军人节

Armistice Day 停战日；第一次世界大战停战日；休战纪念日

Tomb of the Unknowns 无名烈士墓

Arlington National Cemetery 阿灵顿国家公墓

■ **Ethnic festivals celebrated in the US**

❖ **Kwanzaa**

Kwanzaa is a relatively new Afro-American holiday celebrated from December 26 through January 1. It has no religious affiliation but is a joyous celebration of the oneness and goodness of life with an emphasis on Afro-American heritage and culture. Together the three holidays of Christmas, Hanukah and Kwanzaa make December the most joyous and festive month in the USA.

Hanukah 光明节，献殿节(犹太教节日,于每年11月或12月举行,为期8天)

Understanding More about China

1. The Chinese New Year

The Chinese New Year is the first day of the first lunar month in the Chinese calendar and generally falls near the first day of spring. The Chinese government has long ago adopted the first day of the solar year as the New Year and renamed the traditional Chinese New Year the Spring Festival. However, old traditions are not easily forgotten and most Chinese still celebrate the Chinese New Year.

A family reunion dinner is usually held on Chinese New Year's Eve. All members of a family would try to attend the dinner. On Chinese New Year's Day, people usually wear new clothes. Children wish their parents good fortune and receive red packets containing money. In fact, any unmarried family member is entitled to receive a red packet from every married member. Firecrackers are set off unless they are specifically banned. Traditionally, the celebration would go on until the fifteenth day with a programme of things to do for every day.

Nowadays, most people still do not work for the first three days of the Chinese New Year. It is customary to visit relatives and friends during the season. On the ninth day of the New Year, a traditional offering is made to the Jade Emperor in heaven. This day is supposed to mark the deity's birthday, a belief that is related to Daoism.

A mythical tale is associated with the Chinese New Year. In ancient times, a beast called *nian* or "year" would emerge from the sea on Chinese New Year's Eve to eat people and destroy property. Hence, people used to keep themselves awake through Chinese New Year's Eve. Firecrackers were meant to frighten the beast away. On Chinese New Year's Day, people would congratulate each other on their safe passage through the "year" or *nian* hazard.

Yuanxiao is the fifteenth day of the Chinese New Year. In ancient China, this was the night when the emperor would come out of the palace to celebrate the season with the populace. Buildings were decorated with lanterns and shows were put up on streets. The festival is no longer celebrated but traditional families would still have a sumptuous family dinner on this night to mark the end of the Chinese New Year season.

The custom of putting up new "couplets" on either side of the door for the Chinese New Year is still practised. It began in the Zhou Dynasty some 2,500 years ago. Originally, a board made of peach wood with the name of a god written on it was hung on each side of the door. It was meant to chase away evil spirits. By the Ming Dynasty, the practice was superseded by the display of auspicious "couplets," which are two matching lines of script written on red paper. The two lines are equal in the number of words and must match word for word. If a word on the right is a noun, the corresponding word on the left must also be one. Similarly, an adjective is matched by an adjective and a verb by a verb. The closer the match, the better the couplet. For instance, a quantitative adjective is matched by another quantitative adjective. If the adjective refers to a colour, the corresponding word on the other side is also the name of a colour. Repetitions are regarded poor in standard.

2. The Duanwu (Dragon Boat) Festival

The Duanwu Festival falls on the fifth day of the fifth lunar month. The festival is the Memorial Day for Qu Yuan, a well-liked high official, a patriot and an excellent poet in the Chu state during the Warring States period. He was totally frustrated when he could not get the king to heed his good advice.

Upon the instigation of unscrupulous officials, the king exiled him, and he ended up drowning himself in the Miluo River. When the people heard about his suicide, they raced to the river to try to recover his body. That is how the custom of holding a dragon boat race on this day began. The people also threw rice dumplings into the river to feed the fishes so that they would keep away from Qu Yuan's body. That was the origin of the custom of making rice dumplings wrapped in bamboo leaves. The Duanwu customs are still regularly observed even after the passage of some 2,500 years. Qu Yuan's poems showing concern for the country and the people are still found in school textbooks today.

3. The Zhongqiu (Mid-Autumn) Festival

The Zhongqiu Festival, or the Mid-Autumn Festival, probably originated during the Tang Dynasty. Also known as the Moon Festival, it is observed on the fifteenth day of the eighth month in the Chinese calendar. On this day, the moon is the brightest and the fullest it will be the entire year.

The celebrations for this festival are held mostly at night. Each family would have a reunion dinner. Mooncakes, confections that symbolise family togetherness, are exchanged between friends and relatives. Children would gather and, each carrying a lantern, roam about the neighbourhood. In the old days, scholars would drink wine, gaze at the moon and compose poetry.

There are several mythological tales about the Moon Festival. One is about the goddess of the moon. A warrior in ancient times had a very beautiful wife named Chang E. The warrior was given a magical drug by the Mother Goddess of Heaven, which when consumed would enable a person to fly to heaven and become a god. The warrior was however reluctant to leave his wife and handed her the drug for safekeeping. On the night of the fifteenth of the eighth month, when the warrior was occupied elsewhere, a student of his tried to force Chang E to hand over the drug. Chang E refused to yield and swallowed the drug herself. She then rose to the sky and flew to the moon where she became the Moon Goddess. It is said one can still see her image in the full moon.

4. The Dongzhi (Winter) Festival

The Dongzhi Festival, or Winter Festival, is the only traditional festival with an origin that is not associated with a myth or a historical event although it was believed by some that it was the day when the Kitchen God went to heaven to report to the Jade

Emperor the conduct of a family.

It falls on 22 or 23 December when the sun is over the Tropic of Capricorn. In the northern hemisphere, it is the day of the year with the least amount of daylight hours, and consequently the longest night. Presumably, it marks the end of harvesting and the beginning of a rest period for farmers.

On this day, it is customary to make sweetened, multi-coloured rice balls, which signify family reunions. How this custom has come about is not clear, but children certainly enjoy eating this food prepared in conjunction with the festival.

Exercises

Ⅰ. Choose the answer that best completes the statement.
1. St. Patrick's Day is on _____.
   A. 17 March   B. 23 April   C. 30 May   D. 30 November
2. In which country is Hogmanay celebrated? _____
   A. Scotland   B. England   C. Wales   D. Northern Ireland
3. Which one is NOT involved in the Welsh festival, Eisteddfod? _____
   A. literature   B. music   C. sports   D. poems
4. Which of the following festivals means the celebration of Christ's birth? _____
   A. Easter   B. Good Friday   C. Black Friday   D. Christmas Day
5. Gunpowder Plot is associated with _____.
   A. Guy Fawkes Night   B. Remembrance Day
   C. Labour Day   D. Independence Day
6. Hogmanay is the _____ word for the last day of the year.
   A. English   B. Welsh   C. Irish   D. Scottish
7. Thanksgiving Day is celebrated on the fourth Thursday in _____.
   A. November   B. December   C. October   D. September
8. A large roasted turkey is the traditional dish for the _____ dinner.
   A. Thanksgiving Day   B. Hogmanay
   C. Easter   D. Boxing Day

Ⅱ. Read the following statements and decide whether they are true (T) or false (F).
1. National Days are not celebrated in Britain in the same extent as National Days are in a number of other countries. _____
2. The Queen's Birthday is celebrated on the second Monday in July. _____
3. St. David's Day, the national day of Wales, is observed on 1 March. _____
4. St. George's Day is marked by the wearing of shamrocks. _____
5. Some people would wear a red rose on St. David's Day. _____

6. Memorial Day in the US is the traditional beginning of the summer vacation season and the start of the long school break. _____
7. St. Patrick's Day is only celebrated in Northern Ireland. _____
8. In the United Kingdom, days that banks are shut are always bank holidays. _____
9. Boxing Day is celebrated on 26 December. On that day, boxed holiday gifts are given to mailmen, housekeepers and other service workers. _____
10. An Eisteddfod is a Welsh festival of food and drinks. _____
11. In the USA, it is possible for some holidays to be observed in one state and not observed in others. _____
12. Labor Day is celebrated on the first Monday in May in the US. _____
13. Thanksgiving Day is not a religious holiday. _____
14. Most people celebrate Thanksgiving Day by gathering at their family home for a feast. _____

Ⅲ. Short-answer questions.
1. What does "Bank holiday" mean?
2. How do the Americans celebrate "Thanksgiving Day"?

Unit 10

Food and Drink

❑ **In this unit you will learn about**
1. What food culture is
2. Typical food in the UK
3. British pub culture
4. Typical food in the USA

✓参考答案
✓更多资源

Vocabulary

- apple pie 苹果派
- bartender 酒吧招待员
- batter 接连猛击［某人（某物）］
- bean curd (doufu) 豆腐
- bland（指食物）不油腻的,无刺激性的,清淡的,无味的
- brainchild 智力结晶
- burrito 玉米卷饼
- cider 苹果酒
- clam 蛤
- cod 鳕鱼
- condiment 调味品,佐料
- Cornish pasty 康沃尔馅饼（用肉和土豆做馅的）
- cornmeal 玉米粉
- cranberry 蔓越莓
- croissant 羊角包
- crustless 无硬皮的
- cucumber 黄瓜
- cuisine 烹饪（风味）
- customary 依照习俗的；习惯上的
- descending order 降序
- deteriorate 变坏,恶化
- diet（某人、共同生活的人等）通常吃的食物；日常食物
- digestion 消化,吸收
- dim sum (dianxin) 点心
- doughnut 炸面包圈
- Duchess 公爵夫人
- encase 把……包起来
- exile 流放,放逐
- ferment 发酵
- fish and chips 鱼和炸薯条
- French fries 炸薯条
- fry-up 全英式早餐
- fusion 融合
- gravy 肉汁；调味肉汁
- haddock 黑线鳕（海鱼,用作食物）
- ham 火腿肉
- hamburger 汉堡包
- hygiene 卫生
- ingredient（烹调用的）材料,原料,成分
- inheritance 遗产
- junk 不利健康的小吃
- ketchup 番茄酱
- lager 窖藏啤酒（一种淡啤酒,酿成后通常贮藏数月,澄清后饮用）
- lettuce 生菜
- lobster 龙虾
- maize 玉蜀黍,玉米（美国、加拿大叫corn）
- maple syrup 枫糖浆
- masa 湿润粉糊
- millet 小米
- molasses 糖蜜,糖浆
- mustard 芥末
- oatmeal 燕麦片
- okra 秋葵
- pale ale ［英］淡色啤酒（白麦酒）
- panacea 治百病的药
- pancake 烙饼；薄饼
- pastry 酥皮糕点
- patty 小馅饼
- pecan 美洲山核桃
- persistent 持久的
- pint 品脱（容量名,＝1/8加仑）
- plantation 种植园,大农场
- pluck（动物的）心,肝,肺（作食物）
- processed 加工食品
- pudding 布丁（通常用面粉经烘烤或蒸煮做成的甜品）
- quahog 圆蛤（产于北美洲）

- recipe 烹饪法,食谱
- relish 开胃小菜,调味品
- round （游戏、比赛等的）一轮,一局,一场,一回合
- savory 美味的
- scatter 散布;散开
- sorghum 高粱
- stock 高汤
- stout （烈性的）黑啤酒
- succotash [美]豆煮玉米(常加有腊肉)
- suet （牛羊等腰部的）板油
- tacos 墨西哥煎玉米卷
- tamale （墨西哥的）玉米面团包馅卷
- tout 兜售（货物）；招揽（生意）
- trawl （渔船用的）拖网
- trifle 松糕点心
- watercress 水田芥[色拉用]

Key Sentences

1. Food plays an inseparable role in our daily lives. Without food we cannot survive.
   食物在我们的日常生活中起着不可分割的作用。没有食物我们就无法生存。

2. Food is much more than a tool of survival. Food is a source of pleasure, comfort and security. Food is also a symbol of hospitality, social status, and religious significance.
   食物不仅仅是生存的工具,还是快乐、舒适和安全的源泉。食物也是好客、社会地位和宗教意义的象征。

3. What we select to eat, how we prepare it, serve it, and even how we eat it are all factors profoundly touched by our individual cultural inheritance.
   我们选择吃什么,如何烹调,如何上菜,甚至如何吃,这些都深受我们文化的影响。

4. British food has traditionally been based on beef, lamb, pork, chicken and fish and generally served with potatoes and one other vegetable.
   英国食物传统上是以牛肉、羊肉、猪肉、鸡肉和鱼为主料,通常与土豆和其他蔬菜搭配一起食用。

5. The most common and typical foods eaten in Britain include sandwiches, fish and chips, pies like the Cornish pasty, trifle and roast dinners.
   在英国最常见和典型的食物包括三明治、炸鱼和薯条、康沃尔馅饼之类的馅饼、小点心和烤肉。

6. A full English breakfast is a breakfast meal, usually including bacon, sausages, eggs, and a variety of other cooked foods, with a beverage such as coffee or tea.
   一顿丰盛的英式早餐通常包含培根、香肠、鸡蛋和其他各种熟食,以及咖啡或茶等饮料。

7. The full breakfast is among the most internationally recognised British dishes, along with fish and chips and the Christmas dinner.
   丰盛的英式早餐是最受国际认可的英国菜肴之一,此外还有炸鱼薯条和圣诞晚餐。

8. It is a common take-away food.
   这是一种常见的外卖食品。

9. In 1860, the first fish and chips shop was opened in London by Joseph Malin.
   1860年,约瑟夫·马林在伦敦开了第一家炸鱼薯条店。

10. The Dutch first brought tea to Europe from China in 1610.
    荷兰人在1610年第一次从中国把茶叶带到欧洲。

11. Touted as a panacea for everything, it soon became a trend among London's high society.
    它被吹捧为包治百病的灵丹妙药,很快成为伦敦上流社会的潮流。

12. By 1725, England was importing a quarter of a million pounds of tea annually. By 1800, the figure had risen to 24 million pounds.
    到1725年,英国每年进口25万磅茶叶。到1800年,这个数字已经上升到了2 400万磅。

13. The pub is the cornerstone of British social life, and it serves many purposes.
    酒吧是英国社会生活的基石,它有很多用途。

14. Table service is rare, even where food is served.
    餐桌服务是罕见的,即使是提供食物。

15. What do ordinary Americans order when they go to restaurants on a typical day?
    普通美国人去餐馆通常点些什么呢?

16. American cuisine embraces Native American ingredients such as turkey, potatoes, corn, and squash, which have become integral parts of American culture.
    美国菜包含了土著美国人的食材,如火鸡、土豆、玉米和南瓜,它们已经成为美国文化不可分割的组成部分。

17. Fast, junk, processed—when it comes to American food, the country is best known for the stuff that's described by words better suited to greasy, grinding industrial output.
    快餐、垃圾食品、加工食品——说到美国食品,这个国家最出名的是用这些词语来描述那些油腻的、研磨出来的工业产品。

18. It is a 4-inch (10.16 cm) piece of pork sausage served on a bun.
    一块4英寸(10.16厘米)长的猪肉香肠放在面包上吃。

19. Hamburgers are made with a round beef patty, put between two pieces of a round bun. Along with the beef patty, hamburgers will have onions, lettuce, tomatoes, ketchup and mustard.
    汉堡包是把一块圆牛肉饼夹在两块圆面包中间做成的。除了牛肉饼,汉堡包还配有洋葱、生菜、西红柿、番茄酱和芥末。

20. Apple pie is sweet and is therefore mainly eaten as a dessert. It is made with a sweet pastry

crust filled with mashed apples and other sweet baking ingredients in the middle.
苹果派是甜的,因此主要作为饭后甜点。它是用甜馅饼皮制成的,中间装满苹果泥和其他甜的烘焙原料。

21. Pumpkin pie is a required Thanksgiving dessert.
南瓜派是感恩节必备的甜点。

22. There are a few things to avoid when using chopsticks. First, don't beat your bowls or plates with your chopsticks while eating, since the behaviour used to be practiced by beggars. Second, when you use them, don't stretch out your index finger, which would be regarded as a kind of accusation to others. Never use your chopsticks to point at others. Third, it is thought to be an impolite behaviour when you suck the end of a chopstick. People will think you lack family education. Fourth, don't use it to poke at every dish without knowing what you want. And last, don't insert chopsticks in a bowl upright because it is a custom exclusively used in sacrifice.
使用筷子时有几件事要避免。首先,吃饭时不要用筷子敲打碗碟,因为在过去乞丐才这么做。第二,使用筷子时不要伸出食指,这会被视为对他人的一种指责。永远不要用筷子指着别人。第三,吮吸筷头被认为是一种不礼貌的行为。人们会认为你缺乏家教。第四,不要在不知道自己想要吃什么的情况下用筷子戳每道菜。最后,不要将筷子直立插入碗中,因为这是一种专门用于祭祀的习俗。

Warm-up Exercise

1. What does a typical English breakfast look like?

2. What is "pub culture"?

3. What are the typical foods in the USA?

Introduce China in English

1. What are the typical foods in China? List as many as possible.

2. What are the taboos when we use chopsticks?

Text

In all cultural traditions, food is only one aspect but yet it is probably one of the most persistent. Food plays an inseparable role in our daily lives. Without food we cannot survive. But food is much more than a tool of survival. Food is a source of pleasure, comfort and security. Food is also a symbol of hospitality, social status, and religious significance. What we select to eat, how we prepare it, serve it, and even how we eat it are all factors profoundly touched by our individual cultural inheritance.

■ *British Food*

British food has traditionally been based on beef, lamb, pork, chicken and fish and generally served with potatoes and one other vegetable. The most common and typical foods eaten in Britain include sandwiches, fish and chips, pies like the Cornish pasty, trifle and roast dinners. Some of the main dishes have strange names like <u>Bubble & Squeak</u> and <u>Toad-in-the-Hole</u>.

❖ **Full Breakfast** *vs*. **Continental Breakfast**

A <u>full breakfast</u> is a breakfast meal, usually including bacon, sausages, eggs, and a variety of other cooked foods, with a beverage such as coffee or tea. It is especially popular in the UK and Ireland, to the extent that many cafés and pubs offer the meal at any time of day as an "all-day breakfast." It is also popular in other English-speaking countries.

In England it is usually referred to as a "full English breakfast" (often shortened to "full English") or "fry-up." Other regional names and variants include the "full Scottish," "full Welsh," "full Irish" and the "Ulster fry."

The full breakfast is among the most internationally recognised British dishes, along with fish and chips and the Christmas dinner. The full breakfast became popular in the British Isles during the Victorian era. It is often contrasted (e.g. on hotel menus) with the lighter alternative of a <u>Continental breakfast</u>, traditionally consisting of tea, milk or coffee and fruit juices with bread, croissants, or pastries.

ICT

Bubble & Squeak 蔬菜土豆饼
Toad-in-the-Hole 烤香肠
full breakfast 全英式早餐

Continental breakfast 欧洲大陆式早餐,主要食品有茶、咖啡、面包卷和果酱,以冷食为主。

❖ **Fish and chips**

"Fish and chips" is a hot dish of English origin, consisting of battered fish, commonly Atlantic cod or haddock, and chips. It is a common take-away food.

Fish and chips became a stock meal among the working classes in England as a consequence of the rapid development of trawl fishing in the North Sea, and the development of railways which connected the ports to major industrial cities during the second half of the 19th century, which meant that fresh fish could be rapidly transported to the heavily populated areas. In 1860, the first fish and chips shop was opened in London by Joseph Malin.

❖ **Haggis**

Haggis is a savory pudding containing sheep's pluck (heart, liver and lungs); minced with onion, oatmeal, suet, spices, and salt, mixed with stock, traditionally encased in the animal's stomach though now often in an artificial casing instead. It is a traditional Scottish dish.

Fish and chips 炸鱼、炸薯条

Haggis 哈吉斯。用羊的心、肺及肝制成的苏格兰食品。

■ *Tea, the National Drink*

The Dutch first brought tea to Europe from China in 1610. King Charles II, having grown up in exile at The Hague (because his father, Charles I, had been beheaded by Cromwell), brought home a taste for the leafy beverage. Touted as a panacea for everything, it soon became a trend among London's high society. By 1725, England was importing a quarter of a million pounds of tea annually. By 1800, the figure had risen to 24 million pounds.

The Hague 海牙。荷兰城市。

A Brief History of the Discovery of Tea
A popular legend about the discovery of tea as a beverage dated back to about 2700 BC in China. According to the story, Emperor Shen Nong was drinking a cup of boiled water. The Emperor, concerned about hygiene, always insisted that water be boiled before he drank it. Some leaves from a nearby tree fell into his cup, turning the water a deep shade of brown. The colour intrigued the Emperor, and he

> decided to drink the brownish water. Shen Nong was an advocate of herbal medicine, so this wasn't the first time he had tasted something made from a plant. He had been suffering from aches and pains, but after this new "brown" tea he felt refreshed, energetic, and pain-free.
>
> The tea tree, or plant, Camellia Sinensis, is indigenous to China, India, and other parts of Southeast Asia. However, little is known about the use of tea anywhere outside China until sometime in the sixth century, when legends tell of the discovery of tea in other parts of world.

Today, tea is drunk all day long, but especially in the afternoon. <u>Afternoon Tea</u> was the brainchild of Anna, the seventh Duchess of Bedford. In the late 1700s, huge breakfasts and late suppers were customary, and by 5 o'clock, the duchess suffered what she called "sinking feeling." So she ordered tea and cakes to be served. It became an aristocratic fashion and then a national habit. Today, afternoon tea might include crustless cucumber or watercress sandwiches, pastries and biscuits (cookies).

Afternoon Tea 下午茶

❖ **Pubs and Pub Culture**

The pub, short for public house, is the cornerstone of British social life, and it serves many purposes—from a place to relax after work for professionals to an extension of one's living rooms for working types. There are about 80,000 of them scattered throughout the United Kingdom; some date back to the 15th century.

Don't turn down an invitation to one just because you don't drink; you're more likely to strike up a conversation with a local here than elsewhere. And keep in mind that British beer (usually in the form of stout, bitter, mild or pale ale) is served at a cool room temperature, while lager is served chilled. Cider is an alcoholic brew of fermented apple or pear juice.

Bartenders don't expect tips, and may be slightly annoyed if you leave money on the bar; it means they have to come out from behind the bar to return it to you, thinking you left it by accident. Table service is rare, even where food is served.

Drinks are typically ordered in rounds, with drinkers taking turns buying for everyone at the table. Even if you're not drinking, don't miss an opportunity to buy (or at least offer to buy) a round. If you're not drinking, and the conversation is deteriorating (often after three or four rounds of pints), feel free to excuse yourself.

■ *American Food*

Food is a big business in America.

What does it mean to have an American meal? There is no recipe for cooking the American way. American cooking, like American life, is an individual effort in which innovation and efficiency are prized. Quite simply, American food is what Americans cook and eat. It is food appropriated from the cultures of the people who lived or came there and, in most all cases, changed to fit local circumstance, taste, and the means of mass production.

What do ordinary Americans order when they go to restaurants on a typical day? The top 10 selections for men in descending order according to one survey were a hamburger, French fries, pizza, a breakfast sandwich, a side salad, eggs, doughnuts, hash brown potatoes, Chinese food, and a main salad. Women ordered French fries, a hamburger, pizza, a side salad, a chicken sandwich, a breakfast sandwich, a main salad, Chinese food, and rice.

> hash brown potatoes 煎土豆饼

American cuisine embraces Native American ingredients such as turkey, potatoes, corn, and squash, which have become integral parts of American culture. Such popular icons as apple pie, pizza, and hamburgers are either derived from or are actual European dishes. Burritos and tacos have their origins in Mexico. Soul food, which originated among African slaves, is popular in the US as well. However, many foods now enjoyed worldwide either originated in the United States or were altered by American chefs.

> soul food 美国南方黑人的传统食物。这个词组起源于20世纪60年代中期,当时"soul"(灵魂)这个词通常用来形容黑人文化,比如：soul music。

Fast, junk, processed—when it comes to American food, the country is best known for the stuff that's described by words better suited to greasy, grinding industrial output. But Americans have an impressive appetite for good stuff, too. The most popular foods you will find in the United States are as follows:

❖ Hot dog

As one of the most popular foods eaten during a baseball game or on a hot day, this snack is an American summer-time classic. It is a 4-inch (10.16 cm) piece of pork sausage served on a bun. Usually people add other things on top of the sausage such as cheese, onions, mustard, ketchup, relish, and other condiments.

❖ Hamburger

A hamburger is an icon of any fast-food chain in the USA. Hamburgers are made with a round beef patty, put between two pieces of a round bun. Along with the beef patty, hamburgers will have onions, lettuce, tomatoes, ketchup and mustard.

❖ Apple pie

Apple pie is one of the most traditional foods in America. Apple pie is sweet and is therefore mainly eaten as a dessert. It is made with a sweet pastry crust filled with mashed apples and other sweet baking ingredients in the middle.

❖ BLT

This is one of the most popular sandwiches in America. It contains bacon, lettuce, and tomatoes, which is why it is called a BLT.

BLT指"咸肉、生菜和番茄三明治"(bacon, lettuce, tomato)。

❖ Buffalo wings

Buffalo wings are spicy chicken wings that are fried and dipped in a special sauce to make them extra hot.

Buffalo wings 布法罗鸡翅,一种辣味的烤鸡翅。

Understanding More about China

History and Culture of Chopsticks

Chopsticks play an important role in Chinese food culture. Chopsticks are called *kuaizi* in Chinese and were called *zhu* in ancient times. It is believed that chopsticks have been around for about 5,000 years and that they were first used in China.

There are a few things to avoid when using chopsticks. First, don't beat your bowls or plates with your chopsticks while eating, since the behaviour used to be practiced by beggars. Second, when you use them, don't stretch out your index finger, which would be regarded as a kind of accusation to others. Never use your chopsticks to point at others. Third, it is thought to be an impolite behaviour when you suck the end of a chopstick. People will think you lack family education. Fourth, don't use it to poke at every dish without knowing what you want. And last, don't insert chopsticks in a bowl upright because it is a custom exclusively used in sacrifice.

Nowadays, chopsticks serve many new functions besides tableware. For instance, you can buy a pair as a gift to your friends and relatives. In Chinese, it reads *kuaizi*, which means to have sons soon, so a newly-married couple will be very happy to accept them as their wedding gift. Skillful craftsmen paint beautiful sceneries on chopsticks to make them like fine artworks. Many people love to collect them as their treasure.

◆ Exercises

Ⅰ. Choose the answer that best completes the statement.
  1. The _____ first brought tea to Europe from China in 1610.
     A. English   B. French   C. German   D. Dutch
  2. _____ is sweet and is therefore mainly eaten as a dessert.
     A. BLT   B. Buffalo wings   C. Hamburger   D. Apple pie

Ⅱ. Read the following statements and decide whether they are true (T) or false (F).
  1. Bubble & Squeak and Toad-in-the-Hole are the typical names of drinks. _____
  2. The full breakfast is among the most internationally recognised British dishes, along with fish and chips and the Christmas dinner. _____
  3. A full breakfast is a breakfast meal, usually including bacon, sausages, eggs, and a variety of other cooked food, with a beverage such as coffee or tea. _____
  4. In British pubs, drinks are typically ordered in rounds. _____
  5. The "full breakfast" is only offered in the morning. _____
  6. In pubs, it's good of you to leave tips for the bartenders. _____
  7. A British will turn down an invitation to pub if s/he doesn't drink. _____
  8. In the USA, apple pie, pizza, and hamburgers are either derived from or are actual European dishes. _____
  9. Soul food, which has its origin in Mexico, is popular in the US. _____

Ⅲ. Short-answer question.
  What is food culture?

Unit 11

Sports and Films

❏ **In this unit you will learn about**
1. Popular sports played in Britain and America
2. British film industry
3. Film industry

✓参考答案
✓更多资源

Vocabulary

- amateur 业余的
- aristocracy 贵族
- ballet 芭蕾
- baseball 棒球
- batter 击球手
- biopic 传记片
- blockbuster（尤指）非常成功的书（或电影）；好莱坞大片
- box-office 票房纪录
- caber（在苏格兰人的运动中为测臂力而投掷使用的）长而重的木杆
- cachet 威望
- carry off 拿走，夺走
- cast 挑选演员扮演（影剧等中的）角色
- celebrity 名人
- clubland 俱乐部区
- colt 小马
- cricket 板球
- dismiss 解雇
- dolphin 海豚
- eccentric 古怪的
- edgy 急躁的
- fair play 公平比赛
- fierce 激烈的
- film industry 电影产业
- film noir 黑色电影
- glut 过剩
- gritty（对消极事物的描述）逼真的，真实的，活生生的
- guru（受下属崇敬的）领袖，头头；[美俚]头面人物；专家，权威
- helmet 头盔
- heyday 全盛时期
- hobnob 聚会，恳谈
- ice hockey 冰球
- inaugurate 为（组织或工程的创立或开工）举行仪式；为（建筑物、展览会等）举行落成或开幕仪式
- kilt（苏格兰男子穿的）短褶裙（羊毛织成长及膝盖，为苏格兰民族服装的一部分）
- lacrosse 长曲棍球
- lay down 规定，制定
- Mickey Mouse 米老鼠
- newsreel 新闻短片
- opponent 对手，敌手
- Oscar 奥斯卡
- pad 衬垫
- panther 黑豹
- passionate 热情的
- pastime 消遣
- pinnacle 尖峰，顶峰
- pitcher 投掷者
- ploy 策略
- puck 冰球
- quarterback 四分卫
- quirky 古怪的
- recreational 娱乐的，消遣的
- romp 嬉戏
- rugby 橄榄球
- saucy 俏皮
- slapstick 闹剧
- soccer 足球
- spawn 大批涌现，大量产生
- spearhead 带头；当……的先锋
- spectator 观看者；（尤指表演或比赛的）观众
- stadium 体育场
- star（在戏剧、电影等中）担任主角，主演
- studio 工作室
- tinge 使某事物略受影响
- toss 扔；抛；掷
- touchdown 触地得分

Key Sentences

1. declare a draw in the end 最后宣布平局

2. The game did not find international popularity until the late 19th century.
   这种运动直到 19 世纪末才在国际上流行起来。

3. Playing sports is very popular at the high school level.
   体育运动在高中阶段很受欢迎。

4. Hockey is mainly played in the northern states where winters are cold.
   曲棍球主要在冬季寒冷的北方各州进行。

5. Many of the team names come from animals.
   许多球队的名字来自动物名。

6. Traditionally, American football has been a man's sport, but in the past few years, women have started their own football teams.
   传统上，美式足球是男人的运动，但在过去的几年里，女人们已经成立了自己的球队。

7. American football can be a dangerous game, and so the players wear helmets to protect their heads, and shoulder pads to protect their necks and shoulders.
   美式足球是一项危险的运动，因此运动员要戴头盔保护头部，戴护肩保护脖子和肩膀。

8. Basketball is played in high schools and colleges across the country.
   全国各地的高中和大学都打篮球。

9. The pitcher throws the ball fast and the batter tries to hit it. When he does, he runs to first base, but if a player on the other team catches the ball and touches the base before the batter gets there, he is out.
   投球手快速将球抛出，击球手试图击球。击球后，击球手会跑到一垒，但如果另一队的球员在击球手到达之前接住球并触到垒，击球手就出局了。

10. After a decline in film output during WW Ⅱ, the British film recovery in the 1940s and 1950s was led by Ealing Studios.
    第二次世界大战期间电影产量下降，英国电影在 1940 年代和 1950 年代的复苏是由伊林工作室主导的。

11. The following year, Richard Attenborough's big-budget epic *Gandhi* carried off eight Oscars including Best Director and Best Picture.
    第二年，理查德·阿滕伯勒的史诗巨作《甘地》捧走了包括最佳导演奖和最佳影片奖在内的八项奥斯卡奖。

12. Hollywood in Los Angeles is the home of the American movie industry.
    洛杉矶的好莱坞是美国电影业的发源地。

13. The history of American cinema is sometimes divided into four main periods.
    美国电影史有时划分为四个主要时期。

14. At the end of the nineteenth century and into the early twentieth century, movies had no sound, and are known as silent movies.
    在十九世纪末二十世纪初这一时期,电影没有声音,被称为无声电影。

15. A drive-in theater is a large, open space where people can sit in their cars to watch a movie.
    汽车影院是一个很大的开放空间,人们可以坐在车里看电影。

16. The Chinese film industry should have more confidence in its cultural heritage.
    中国电影业应该对自己的文化底蕴更有信心。

17. China has become one of the largest film markets in the world, ranking second only to the United States.
    中国已经成为世界上最大的电影市场之一,仅次于美国。

18. According to a survey, China's film box office revenue surpassed 60 billion *yuan* (more than $8.7 billion) in 2018, reaching a record high, and the number of Chinese film screens increased from 50,776 to 60,079 and more than 1,000 Chinese films were produced.
    据统计,2018年中国电影票房收入突破600亿元人民币(超过87亿美元),创历史新高,中国电影银幕数量从50,776块增加到60,079块,中国电影产量超过1,000部。

19. Though accomplishing great achievements, the Chinese film industry still has a long way to go.
    中国电影业虽然取得了巨大成就,但仍有很长的路要走。

20. The Chinese film industry should focus more on its culture and spend more time raising talents to come up with creative ideas for it.
    中国电影业应该更多地关注中国文化,花更多的时间培养人才,从而提出自己的创意。

21. So the Chinese film industry should do its best to find out what the distinctive Chinese culture is and tell distinctive Chinese cultural stories to the world.
    因此,中国电影业应该尽最大努力,找出什么是中国特色文化,然后向世界讲述中国特色文化的故事。

22. The first thing is to understand the targeted countries' cultural heritage and to get these countries to understand your own cultural heritage.
    首先要了解目标国家的文化遗产,然后让这些国家了解自己的文化遗产是什么。

Warm-up Exercise

1. What are the most popular sports in the UK?

2. What are the most popular sports in the USA?

Introduce China in English

1. What are the most popular sports in China? What are your favourite sports?

2. Describe one of your favourite Chinese films to your deskmate. Do you have any suggestions on how to make Chinese films go to the world?

Text

If you want to take a shortcut into the heart of British culture, watch the British at play. They're fierce and passionate about their sports, whether participating or watching. The British invented—or at least laid down the modern rules for—many of the world's most popular spectator sports, including cricket, tennis, golf, rugby and football.

■ Sports in Britain

❖ Rugby

Rugby, when played in the South, is called Rugby Union, and many top-level players are amateurs who have daytime jobs. Played in the North, it becomes Rugby League, with mostly professional players and an entirely different set of rules aimed at making the game faster.

Rugby Union 橄榄球联赛

Rugby League 橄榄球竞赛联合会

> **Rugby Roots**
>
> Rugby traces its origins to a football match in 1823 at Rugby School, in Warwickshire in the English Midlands. A player called William Webb Ellis, frustrated at the limitations of mere kicking, reputedly picked up the ball and ran with it towards the opponents' goal. True to the British sense of fair play, rather than Ellis being dismissed from the game, a whole new sport was developed around his tactic, and the Rugby Football Union was formally inaugurated in 1871.

❖ Cricket

Cricket, with its upper-class, private-school cachet, is more popular in the South. International matches can last for five or six days, with breaks for meals, rain, tea, injuries, rest, and they're often declared a draw in the end.

❖ Golf

The origins of golf are unclear and much debated. However, it is generally accepted that modern golf developed in Scotland during the Middle Ages. The game did not find international popularity until the late 19th century, when it spread into the rest of the United Kingdom and then to the

United States and other countries.

❖ **Royal Ascot**

Royal Ascot is one of the most spectacular race-meetings in the world, it has been held since 1711 during the reign of Queen Anne. For just four days each year the aristocracy, sports celebrities and fashion gurus of England hobnob in grand style at one of the highlights of their social calendar. It is called Royal Ascot because the Royal family attends every year.

Royal Ascot 皇家爱斯科赛马会

❖ **Football and Premier League**

The Premier League is an English professional league for men's association football clubs. Seasons run from August to May, with teams playing 38 matches each totaling 380 matches in the season. Most games are played in the afternoons of Saturdays and Sundays, the other games during weekday evenings. The competition formed as the FA Premier League on 20 February 1992 following the decision of clubs in the Football League First Division to break away from the Football League, which was originally founded in 1888, and took advantage of a profitable television rights deal.

Premier League 英超

FA: Football Association（英国）足球协会

❖ **Highland Games**

The sporting tradition of Highland Games is Scottish. Some of the sports at the Games are international: the high jump and the long jump, for example. But other sports happen only at the Highland Games. One is tossing the caber. "Tossing" means throwing, and a "caber" is a long, heavy piece of wood. In tossing the caber you lift the caber (it can be five or six meters tall). Then you throw it in front of you. At the Highland Games a lot of men wear kilts. These are traditional Scottish skirts for men.

Highland Games（苏格兰）高地运动会

tossing the caber 抛杆比赛。所用的杆由杉木制成，重约40千克。抛时要让杆翻转，使杆着地时细端指向前方。

Sports in America

In the USA, sports are a national pastime, and playing sports, especially American football, baseball, and basketball, is very popular at the high school level.

Team sports, like American football, basketball, baseball, and ice hockey, also called the "Big Four" sports, are very popular in the USA. American football is different from football played in other countries, which Americans call soccer.

Big Four 美国四大职业体育联盟，由NFL（National Football League，美国国家橄榄球联盟）、MLB（Major League Baseball，美国职业棒球大联盟）、NBA（National Basketball Association，美国职业篮球联赛）和NHL（National Hockey League，国家冰球联盟）组成。

Hockey is mainly played in the northern states where winters are cold.

❖ American football

The National Football League's seventeen-week season starts in early September. Half of the NFLs thirty-two teams are in the American Football Conference (AFC) and half in the National Football Conference (NFC). Each team plays sixteen games, and, on average, over 67,000 fans go to football stadiums to watch each game. Each team wants to play on <u>Super Bowl Sunday</u>, but only the two best teams will play, and only one will win!

> **Super Bowl**
>
> A football game played in the US each year in late January on a Sunday, known as Super Bowl Sunday, that decides which team is the winning team of the year in the NFL. It was first held in 1967, and is watched on television by millions of people.

Super Bowl Sunday 超级碗是 NFL 职业橄榄球大联盟的年度冠军赛,胜者被称为"世界冠军"。超级碗一般在每年 1 月最后一个或 2 月第一个星期天举行,那一天被称为超级碗星期天。

Many of the team names come from animals in the state, such as Indianapolis Colts (a young male horse), Miami Dolphins (a sea animal), Carolina Panthers (a large wild cat), and Arizona Cardinals (a type of bird). Other names come from an important industry, such as the Pittsburgh Steelers, where the steel-making industry is very important.

Traditionally, American football has been a man's sport, but in the past few years, women have started their own football teams, such as New Hampshire Freedom, Philadelphia Firebirds, Houston Energy, and California Quake.

Football teams have a lot of players, but only eleven from each team play on the football field at one time. Making a touchdown by putting the ball past the other team's goal line is the way to score points and win the game. Every player is important, but the quarterback—the player who throws the ball to his team—must be able to throw long and fast.

Football can be a dangerous game, and so the players wear helmets to protect their heads, and shoulder pads to protect their necks and shoulders. The number on each player's shirt represents his place on the team, like quarterback.

❖ **Basketball**

Basketball is played in high schools and colleges across the country. The National Basketball Association (NBA)—the highest professional group—is internationally famous.

❖ **Baseball**

Two teams with nine players play on the playing field at one time. The pitcher throws the ball fast and the batter tries to hit it. When he does, he runs to first base, but if a player on the other team catches the ball and touches the base before the batter gets there, he is out. If the other team is still running for the ball, the batter runs to second base, and third base. When he gets back to home plate, he scores a point for his team. The team who scores the most points wins.

The World Series is the game played every year between the two best baseball teams in the country. Traditionally, the winning team visits the White House in Washington, D. C. and meets the president. The team gives the president a team T-shirt with his name on it.

❖ **Ice hockey**

A sport that is most popular in northern, colder areas of the country, like Rochester and Buffalo in New York State, is ice hockey, which Americans call hockey. In hockey there are two teams of six players on an ice rink for sixty minutes. Players use a hockey stick to push and hit the puck—a round, flat piece of rubber—across the ice. They score points by hitting the puck into the other team's net. It is a very fast game!

At the end of each season, which is from early October to the middle of May, the two best teams in the National Hockey League (NHL) compete for the Stanley Cup.

❖ **Other sports**

Other sports, including auto racing, lacrosse, soccer, golf, and tennis, have significant followings. The United States is among the most influential countries in shaping three popular board-based recreational sports: surfboarding, skateboarding, and snowboarding.

■ *British Film Industry*

In the early years of the 20th century, silent movies from

> Stanley Cup 斯坦利杯，为国家冰球联盟的最高奖项，在每个赛季季后赛后颁给联盟的冠军队伍。斯坦利杯以弗雷德里克·斯坦利之名命名，是为纪念其为冰球运动的贡献而设。斯坦利杯为职业运动中历史最悠久的冠军奖杯。

Britain gave the Americans a run for their money, and Blackmail by Alfred Hitchcock—still one of Britain's best-known film directors—launched the British film industry's era of sound production in 1929.

After a decline in film output during WW II, the British film recovery in the 1940s and 1950s was led by Ealing Studios with a series of eccentric comedies, such as *Kind Hearts and Coronets* and *The Ladykillers*, both starring Alec Guinness.

Super-spy James Bond exploded onto the big screen in 1962, with *Dr. No* starring Scotland's very own Sean Connery. Since then about 20 Bond movies have been made, and Bond has been played by other British actors including Roger Moore, Timothy Dalton and, since 2006, Daniel Craig.

By the end of the 1960s, British film production had declined again and didn't pick up until David Puttnam's *Chariots of Fire* won four Oscars in 1981.

Perhaps inspired by this success, TV company Channel 4 began financing films for the large and small screens, one of the first being *My Beautiful Laundrette*—a story of multicultural life and love in the Thatcher era. The following year, Richard Attenborough's big-budget epic *Gandhi* carried off eight Oscars including Best Director and Best Picture, while another classic of the 1980s was *Withnail and I*, staring Richard E. Grant and Paul McGann. The 1980s and early 1990s were also the pinnacle of the Merchant-Ivory production company, which turned out meticulously detailed period pieces, often set in Edwardian England or colonial India, including *Heat and Dust*, *The Remains of the Day*, and Oscar-winners *Howards End* and *Room with a View*.

Best Director 最佳导演奖
Best Picture 最佳影片奖

The 1990s saw another minor renaissance in British film-making, ushered in by *Four Weddings and a Funeral*, featuring US star Andie MacDowell and introducing Hugh Grant as a likeable and self-deprecating Englishman.

Despite the success stories of the 1990s, as we go through the first decade of the 21st century the UK film industry has returned to its customary precarious financial state. Advocates call for more government funding, as in reality most UK-made and UK-set films are paid for with US money—epitomised perhaps by the globally renowned series of Harry Potter adventures, starting with *Harry Potter and the Philosopher's Stone* in 2001.

Big British hits of recent years include *Hot Fuzz*, an offbeat cop comedy starring Simon Pegg (from *Shaun of the Dead*); *Atonement*, a masterly adaptation of Ian McEwan's novel that saw actors James McAvoy and Keira Knightley prove that they are much more than just pretty faces; and *Casino Royale* and *Quantum of Solace*, in which Daniel Craig made James Bond cool once more.

■ *American Movie Industry*

Hollywood in Los Angeles is the home of the American movie industry. Every year, millions of tourists visit the "Walk of Fame" on Hollywood Boulevard. This special sidewalk is covered in stars with the names of over 2,400 famous people, including actors, and people in television, radio, theater, and music.

Walk of Fame (好莱坞)星光大道

The history of American cinema is sometimes divided into four main periods: the silent era, Classical Hollywood cinema, New Hollywood, and the contemporary period (after 1980).

Rise of Hollywood—In early 1910, director D. W. Griffith was sent by the American Mutoscope and Biograph Company to the west coast with his acting troop. They started filming on a vacant lot near Georgia Street in downtown Los Angeles. The company decided while there to explore new territories, traveling several miles north to a little village that was friendly and enjoyed the movie company filming there. This place was called "Hollywood."

At the end of the nineteenth century and into the early twentieth century, movies had no sound, and are known as silent movies. They were often comedies. The first movie with sound was *The Jazz Singer* in 1927.

The Jazz Singer《爵士之王》

During the so-called Golden Age of Hollywood, which lasted from the virtual end of the silent era in the late 1920s to near the end of the 1940s, studios were producing films with a number of different genres: Western, slapstick comedy, film noir, musical, animated cartoon, biopic (biographical picture), and even newsreels.

"The New Hollywood" and "post-classical cinema" are terms used to describe the period following the decline of the studio system in the 1950s and 1960s and the end of the production code. It is defined by a greater tendency to dramatize such things as sexuality and violence, and by the rising importance of the blockbuster movie.

> **Oscar**
>
> Every year, movie companies compete for the largest audiences, and every February, over thirty-seven million people watch the Academy Awards in Hollywood on TV. At this event, the movie industry celebrates the success of the past year. The winners receive a small gold statue called an Oscar from the Academy of Motion Picture Arts and Sciences.

Watching a movie in a movie theater is something people all over the world enjoy. But watching a movie at a drive-in theater is a very American experience. A drive-in theater is a large, open space where people can sit in their cars to watch a movie. The first drive-in theater opened in 1933. By the 1950s, there were more than four thousand drive-ins in the USA. Today, there are fewer than four hundred.

Understanding More about China

1. Chinese film industry should have more confidence in its culture

The Chinese film industry should have more confidence in its cultural heritage, even though it has been developing rapidly in recent years, Amanda Nevill, chief executive officer of the British Film Industry (BFI), said in a recent interview with Xinhua.

China has become one of the largest film markets in the world, ranking second only to the United States. According to a survey, China's film box office revenue surpassed 60 billion *yuan* (more than $8.7 billion) in 2018, reaching a record high, and the number of Chinese film screens increased from 50,776 to 60,079 and more than 1,000 Chinese films were produced.

Nevill appreciated the enormous achievements in the Chinese film industry and its fast development in recent years, and also expressed her willingness to cooperate.

"We are very interested in China," Nevill said, adding that the Chinese film market is so huge that they have been "looking at it closely."

According to her, Britain's relationship with the Chinese film industry "has come a long way," and the BFI initiated plans to work with China as early as four years ago, of which British delegations were sent to China at least twice a year.

"We bring industrial professionals, producers, directors, casting crews to China. They spend two weeks meeting with their peers in China and we try to encourage them to start developing projects together," she said, adding that she has also been to China for several times.

Though accomplishing great achievements, the Chinese film industry still has a long way to go, said Nevill. It should focus more on its culture and spend more time raising talents to come up with creative ideas for it.

China has a long history with an extraordinary culture, she said, adding that she admired China which in its entire history has never aggressively gone to other countries. So the Chinese film industry should do its best to find out what the distinctive Chinese culture is and tell distinctive Chinese cultural stories to the world.

"The rest of the world is really interested in these stories; the rest of the world doesn't want to watch a sort of reinvented American blockbusters," she said.

On film export, Nevill said she was glad to see the Chinese film industry go overseas to make more cooperation with other countries, a way to break cultural barriers for film export.

"To facilitate exports, the greatest success you can have is to enter into cultural creative partnership," she said, adding that to appeal to overseas audience, the first thing is to understand the targeted countries' cultural heritage and to get these countries to understand your own cultural heritage.

2. *LEAP* (《夺冠》,电影名)

LEAP is a biographical sports drama about the China women's national volleyball team, with a focus on volleyball player-turned-coach Lang Ping, portrayed by Gong Li. The movie highlights three phases: in the 1980s when teenage Lang, starring Lang's daughter Bai Lang, and her volleyball teammates train vigorously despite the lack of technology; in 2008 during the Beijing Olympics volleyball game, where the US team led by Lang is pitted against the Chinese team led by Lang's former training partner and longtime friend, portrayed by Huang Bo; and finally in 2013 to 2016 when Lang returns from the States to serve as the head coach for China women's national volleyball team. Despite *Leap* being a biographical movie, its drama element has lent a hand to keep the story engaging.

Exercises

Ⅰ. Choose the answer that best completes the statement.
1. Where did the modern golf originate from? _____
   A. Northern Ireland   B. Scotland
   C. England   D. Wales
2. The "Big Four" sports in USA are American football, ice hockey, _____ and _____.
   A. baseball; basketball   B. tennis; basketball
   C. golf; cricket   D. basketball; golf
3. _____ is one of the most spectacular horse-race meetings in the world.
   A. Cricket   B. Golf   C. Rugby   D. Royal Ascot
4. Hollywood in _____ is the home of the American movie industry.
   A. New York   B. San Francisco   C. Los Angeles   D. San Diego
5. "Super Bowl" is the name of game for _____.
   A. baseball   B. ice hockey
   C. American football   D. basketball

Ⅱ. Read the following statements and decide whether they are true (T) or false (F).
1. The United States is among the most influential countries in shaping three popular board-based recreational sports: surfboarding, skateboarding, and snowboarding. _____
2. A drive-in theater is a large, open space where people can sit in their cars to watch a movie. _____
3. At the end of the nineteenth century and into the early twentieth century, movies had no sound, and are known as silent movies. They were often tragedies. _____
4. The first movie with sound was *The Jazz Singer* in 1927. _____
5. In hockey there are two teams of nine players on an ice rink for ninety minutes. _____
6. By the end of the 1960s, British film production had declined again. _____
7. *Blackmail* by Alfred Hitchcock launched the British film industry's era of sound production in 1929. _____
8. "Quarterback" is the player who catches the ball in American football. _____
9. In American football, making a touchdown by putting the ball past the other team's goal line is the way to score points and win the game. _____
10. Traditionally, American football has been a man's sport, but in the past few years, women have started their own football teams. _____
11. Many of the American football teams' names come from plants' names in the

state. _____
12. At the Highland Games a lot of men wear kilts. These are traditional Scottish skirts for men. _____
13. The sport of "tossing the caber" happens only at the Highland Games. _____
14. The Premier League is a Scottish professional league for both men's and women's association football clubs. _____
15. Royal Ascot is so called because the Royal family attends every year. _____
16. Cricket, with its upper-class, private-school cachet, is more popular in the North. _____
17. International matches of cricket can last for five or six days, and they're often declared a draw in the end. _____
18. In America, hockey is mainly played in the northern states where winters are cold. _____

Ⅲ. Short-answer questions.
1. What are the differences when rugby is played in the South and in the North in Britain?
2. How was Hollywood developed into the home of the American movie industry?

Unit 12

Houses, Arts, Museums and Architecture

❏ **In this unit you will learn about**
1. Houses
2. Arts
3. Museums, libraries
4. Architecture

✓参考答案
✓更多资源

Vocabulary

- aeronautics 航空学
- aesthetics 美学,审美学
- apartment 公寓
- arch 拱门
- artifact 人工制品
- artisan 技工;工匠
- ceramics ［用作单］陶瓷学;陶瓷工艺/［用作复］陶器;陶瓷制品
- column 柱子
- flat 公寓
- flowering 盛时
- following 一批支持者或拥护者
- garbage 垃圾
- gem 宝石(尤指经切割打磨的)
- geology 地质学
- grotto 洞穴;(尤指花园中的)人工洞室
- inclination 倾向,意愿
- installation 安装
- interior 内部,里面
- lawn 草地;草坪
- mailbox 邮箱,邮筒
- mansion 宅邸;公馆
- mausoleum (大而精致的)陵墓
- musical n. 音乐喜剧
- ornate 装饰华丽的
- pagoda (印度和东亚的)塔,宝塔
- pavilion 亭子,阁(如公园中的)
- ranch house 大农场主的住宅
- specimen 样品,标本
- spire 尖顶;(尤指)教堂塔尖
- squarish 近似方形的;方方的
- subsoil 底土(层)
- tango 探戈舞

Key Sentences

1. Houses, arts, museums, and architecture are all artifacts of human beings, which make a very important part of culture.
   房屋、艺术、博物馆和建筑都是人类的作品,是文化的重要组成部分。

2. Today more people are buying their own homes than in the past. About two thirds of the people in England and the rest of Britain either own, or are in the process of buying, their own home.
   如今,越来越多的人购买自己的房子。大约三分之二的英格兰人以及其他部分的英国人拥有或正在购买他们自己的房子。

3. Most houses are made of stone or brick from the local area where the houses are built.
   大多数房子是用当地的石头或砖头建造的。

4. The colours of the stones and bricks vary across the country.
   石头和砖块的颜色在全国各地不尽相同。

5. Anyway, the cost of housing has increased much faster than people's wages.
   不管怎样,住房成本的增长比人们工资的增长快得多。

6. American houses usually have private kitchens, a living room and sometimes separate areas for eating and watching television.
   美国人的房子通常有厨房、起居室,有时还有单独的吃饭和看电视的地方。

7. Britain's artistic output was focused on literature in the 16th and 17th centuries.
   在16世纪和17世纪,英国的艺术作品主要集中在文学上。

8. More people had the time to appreciate the arts.
   更多的人有时间欣赏艺术作品。

9. Britain is world famous for its outstanding libraries and museums, most of which are located in London.
   英国以其杰出的图书馆和博物馆而闻名于世,其中大部分位于伦敦。

10. Architecture, is both the process and the product of planning, designing, and constructing buildings.
    建筑,是规划、设计和建造建筑物的过程及其产品。

11. The greatest structures built by the Normans are the White Tower, which is part of the Tower of London.
    诺曼人建造的最伟大的建筑是白塔,它是伦敦塔的一部分。

12. Because London's subsoil is not suitable as a foundation for tall skyscrapers, many of the new buildings erected were big and boxy with geometric designs.
    由于伦敦的地基不适合修建高层摩天大楼,许多新建的建筑物都是大型的,带有几何形状的四方形建筑。

13. These arts were generally imported from or strongly influenced by Europe and were mainly appreciated by the wealthy and well educated.
    这些艺术通常是从欧洲引进的,或受到欧洲的强烈影响,主要受到富人和受过良好教育人士的追捧。

14. In the 20th century, these institutions became an important vehicle for educating the public about the past.
    在20世纪,这些机构成为教育公众了解过去的重要工具。

15. These libraries are essential for preserving America's history and for maintaining the records of individuals, families, institutions, and other groups.
    这些图书馆对于保存美国历史和保存个人、家庭、机构和其他群体的记录至关重要。

16. In 1800 Congress passed legislation founding the Library of Congress, which was initially established to serve the needs of the members of Congress. Since then, this extraordinary collection has become one of the world's great libraries.
    1800年,国会通过了建立国会图书馆的立法,该图书馆最初是为满足国会议员的需求而建立的。从那时起,这些非同寻常的藏书造就了世界上最伟大的图书馆之一。

17. Traditional Chinese architecture is based mainly on Han architecture, comprising roughly 15 types.
    中国传统建筑以汉代建筑为主,大致有 15 种类型。

18. It can be seen that each upsurge was correspondingly accompanied by the unification of the country, long-term stability, radical cultural exchanges and other social backgrounds.
    可见,每一次热潮都相应地伴随着国家统一、长治久安、文化交流大繁荣以及其他社会背景。

19. The unification of the Qin and Han Dynasties accelerated exchanges between the Central Plain culture and the Chu and Yue cultures.
    秦汉统一加速了中原文化与楚越文化的交流。

20. It can be said that unification, stability, economic prosperity, enhancement of national strength and cultural exchange are the internal opportunities for the development of architectural art.
    可以说,统一、稳定、经济繁荣、国力增强、文化交流是建筑艺术发展的内在契机。

21. China's architecture pays particular attention to the beauty of group combination, and often adopts a central-axis, symmetric compact composition method.
    中国的建筑特别注重群体组合之美,往往采用中轴线、对称紧凑的布局方法。

22. In ancient China, from the emperor down to any of the rich, they without exception all took pride in the ownership of a garden in their living space.
    在古代,从皇帝到任何一个富人,他们无一例外地都以拥有一个花园为荣。

23. The art of the Chinese garden emphasizes the portrayal of a mood, so that the hills, waters, plants, and buildings as well as their spatial relationship are not just a mere materialistic environment but also evoke a spiritual atmosphere.
    中国园林艺术强调对意境的刻画,使山、水、植物、建筑及其空间关系不仅仅是一种物质环境,更是一种精神氛围。

24. Also known as the Forbidden City, the Palace Museum is situated in the former imperial palace of the Ming and Qing Dynasties. Constructed between 1407 and 1420, the imperial palace occupies 72 hectares and has more than 9,000 halls and chambers, which is presently the largest and the best-preserved palace complex in the world.
    故宫博物院又称紫禁城,位于明清两代的故宫内。故宫建于 1407 年至 1420 年,占地 72 公顷,有 9 000 多个厅室,是目前世界上规模最大、保存最完好的宫殿建筑群。

Warm-up Exercise

1. What are the most famous museums and libraries in the UK?

2. What are the most famous museums and libraries in the USA?

Introduce China in English

1. What are the most famous museums and libraries in China?

2. What are the typical features of "Chinese Garden"(中国园林)?

Text   ICT

Houses, arts, museums, and architecture are all artifacts of human beings, which make a very important part of culture.

■ Houses in England

Today more people are buying their own homes than in the past. About two thirds of the people in England and the rest of Britain either own, or are in the process of buying, their own home. Most others live in houses or flats that they rent from a private landlord, the local council, or housing association.

housing association 房屋协会(以低价出租或出售房屋)

Most houses in England are made of stone or brick from the local area where the houses are built. The colours of the stones and bricks vary across the country.

The main types of houses in England are: Detached, Semi-detached, Bungalows, Terrace and Flats (apartments).

1) Detached Houses(a house not joined to another house)
2) Semi-Detached Houses (two houses joined together)
3) Bungalows(small house with one storey)
4) Terrace Houses (several houses joined together)
5) Flats (single room in a house, esp. a large one)

Detached Houses 独立式住宅
Semi-Detached Houses 半独立式住宅
Bungalows（带走廊的）平房
Terrace Houses 排房(设计相同的一排房屋)

In England, a big problem is the rising cost of houses. The cost of housing also varies dramatically. Anyway, the cost of housing has increased much faster than people's wages.

■ Houses in America

American houses usually have private kitchens, a living room and sometimes separate areas for eating and watching television. A house usually has its own mailbox, a yard with plants or perhaps a lawn, and a place to store garbage out of sight.

A bungalow is a small house with one or two bedrooms and usually one bathroom.

A mansion is a real big house with many bedrooms and several bathrooms.

A ranch house usually has three or four bedrooms. The "master bedroom" for the mother and father usually has its own bathroom.

An apartment is usually one living space within a building. Several apartments can be in the same building, with a shared yard, parking spaces, and garbage bins.

A <u>town house</u> is a two-floor apartment. The kitchen, living room and dining room are usually on the first floor and the bedrooms are on the second floor.

town house 联排别墅

A <u>studio</u> apartment may have a separate kitchen, but the living room is also the bedroom!

studio 单间公寓(通常有一个房间兼作起居室和卧室,另加小厨房和浴室)

A <u>condominium</u>, or "condo" for short, is an apartment that is owned by the occupant, not the building owners.

condominium (产权为居住者自有的)公寓

■ *British Arts*

The United Kingdom has a long history of excellence in the arts. Britain's artistic output was focused on literature in the 16th and 17th centuries. As a <u>Protestant</u> nation, Britain did not experience the full flowering of the <u>Baroque</u> era that followed the Renaissance in Roman Catholic countries, such as Italy and Spain, during the 17th and 18th centuries. In the 19th century, a movement called <u>Romanticism</u> sought to make art more emotional.

Protestant 新教
Baroque 巴洛克风格

Romanticism 浪漫主义

During the Victorian era Britain became the world's first urban, industrialized society, and a vast middle class developed. More people had the time, education, and inclination to appreciate the arts. The time and money spent on the arts continued to increase in the 20th century, particularly after World War Ⅱ.

Britain's worldwide impact in music in the second half of the 20th century, especially in the realm of popular music, was enormous. <u>The Beatles</u> appeared in the 1960s and were followed by other successful rock groups and singers, including names such as the <u>Rolling Stones</u>, The Who, Elton John, and Sting. Pop and rock music remain the most popular kinds of music in Britain, although jazz also has a large following.

The Beatles 甲壳虫乐队,又译披头士乐队。
Rolling Stones 滚石乐队

■ *British Museums and Libraries*

Britain is world famous for its outstanding libraries and

museums, most of which are located in London. The British Museum, one of the most spectacular museums in the world, is renowned for its extensive and diverse collections, from Egyptian mummies to important historical documents. Plant, animal, and mineral specimens from all over the world are part of the collection at the Natural History Museum. Particularly popular with tourists is Madame Tussaud's Waxworks, a unique collection of lifelike wax figures of famous people, both living and dead.

British Museum 大英博物馆

Natural History Museum 自然历史博物馆
Madame Tussaud's Waxworks 图索夫人蜡像馆

Several museums and galleries of note are located outside London. The National Gallery of Scotland in Edinburgh houses a collection of fine European paintings dating from the Renaissance, including many Scottish paintings. The National Museum of Wales in Cardiff focuses on Welsh life, history, and culture. In Belfast, the Ulster Museum has a diverse collection that mixes the arts, history, and sciences.

■ British Architecture

Architecture, is both the process and the product of planning, designing, and constructing buildings and other physical structures. Architectural works, in the material form of buildings, are often perceived as cultural symbols and as works of art.

Some of the oldest examples of British architecture include a few small, squarish Anglo-Saxon buildings. After the Norman Conquest in 1066, Norman architecture became prevalent in the British Isles. The Normans built monumental castles and churches with enormous arches and huge columns. Their style was called Romanesque on the Continent. The greatest structures built by the Normans are the White Tower, which is part of the Tower of London.

Romanesque 罗马风格
the Continent 欧洲大陆

From the 12th to the 15th century gracefully soaring spires and arches marked the development of the great Gothic cathedrals; two of these, Westminster Abbey in London and Lincoln Cathedral, still dominate the skylines of their cities.

Gothic 哥特式建筑的

The architecture of the late Italian Renaissance was introduced in England by Inigo Jones in the 17th century. Jones was the first of the great British architects to be influenced by

Inigo Jones 琼斯,英国画家、建筑师和设计师。

the ideas of Italian architects. Jones in turn influenced <u>Sir Christopher Wren</u>, Britain's greatest architect. After the devastating Great Fire of London in 1666, Wren helped in the rebuilding of the city. Saint Paul's Cathedral in London, is an example of Wren's distinctively graceful and monumental British style.

  Sir Christopher Wren 克利斯托弗·雷恩爵士,圣保罗大教堂设计师。

In the 18th century few English buildings followed the ornate patterns of the Baroque and <u>Rococo</u> architectures used in Europe. Rather, a more restrained, neoclassical style was introduced in Britain.

  Rococo 洛可可式的

Victorian architecture borrowed from a variety of styles, including classical, Gothic, and Renaissance, and was characterized by ornate decoration. The most famous Victorian neo-Gothic building is Parliament, built between 1840 and 1870.

In the early 20th century, Scottish architect <u>Charles Rennie Mackintosh</u> (1868—1928) rejected elaborate Victorian architecture styles for a more modern, functional design. His work influenced 20th-century architects and interior designers.

  Charles Rennie Mackintosh 麦金托什。苏格兰建筑家、家具设计师和画家。

After WWⅡ many new buildings were needed to replace the ones destroyed during the war. Because London's subsoil is not suitable as a foundation for tall skyscrapers, many of the new buildings erected were big and boxy with geometric designs.

■ *American Performing Arts*

The classical performing arts—music, opera, dance, and theater—were not a widespread feature of American culture in the first half of the 20th century. These arts were generally imported from or strongly influenced by Europe and were mainly appreciated by the wealthy and well educated.

During the 20th century, the American performing arts began to incorporate wider groups of people. The African American community produced great musicians who became widely known around the country. Jazz and <u>blues</u> singers such as Bessie Smith, Louis Armstrong, Duke Ellington, and Billie Holiday spread their sounds to black and white audiences. In the 1930s and 1940s, the <u>swing music</u> of Benny Goodman, Tommy Dorsey, and Glenn Miller adapted jazz to make a

  blues 布鲁斯,一种音乐形式。

  swing music 摇摆舞音乐

unique American music that was popular around the country. The American performing arts also blended Latin American influences beginning in the 20th century. Between 1900 and 1940, Latin American dances, such as tango from Argentina and the rumba from Cuba, were introduced into the United States. In the 1940s a fusion of Latin and jazz elements was stimulated first by the Afro-Cuban mambo and later on by the Brazilian bossa nova.

rumba 伦巴舞

mambo 曼波舞
bossa nova 巴西的博萨诺瓦舞曲(类似桑巴舞)

Perhaps the greatest, and certainly the most popular, American innovation was the Broadway musicals, which also became a movie staple.

Broadway 百老汇

■ American Libraries and Museums

Libraries, museums, and other collections of historical artifacts have been a primary means of organizing and preserving America's legacy. In the 20th century, these institutions became an important vehicle for educating the public about the past and for providing knowledge about the society of which all Americans are a part.

❖ Libraries

Private book collections go back to the early European settlement of the New World, beginning with the founding of the Harvard University library in 1638. In addition to Harvard's library, the libraries at Yale University, Columbia University, the University of Illinois at Urbana-Champaign in Urbana, and the University of California in Berkeley and Los Angeles are among the most prominent, both in scope and in number of holdings. These libraries are essential for preserving America's history and for maintaining the records of individuals, families, institutions, and other groups.

In addition to the numerous public libraries and university collections, the United States boasts two major libraries with worldwide reputation: the Library of Congress in Washington, D. C., and the New York Public Library. In 1800 Congress passed legislation founding the Library of Congress, which was initially established to serve the needs of the members of Congress. Since then, this extraordinary collection has become one of the world's great libraries.

Library of Congress 国会图书馆
New York Public Library 纽约公共图书馆,美国最大的市立公共图书馆。

❖ **Museums**

The earliest museums in the United States grew out of private collections, and throughout the 19th century they reflected the tastes and interests of a small group.

The largest and most varied collection in the United States is contained in the separate branches of the <u>Smithsonian Institution</u>, which has its headquarters in Washington, D. C. The Smithsonian, founded in 1846 as a research institution, developed its first museums in the 1880s. It now encompasses 16 museums devoted to various aspects of American history, as well as to artifacts of everyday life and technology, aeronautics and space, gems and geology, and natural history.

Smithsonian Institution 史密森学会,唯一由美国政府资助、半官方性质的第三部门博物馆机构。

The serious public display of art began when the <u>Metropolitan Museum of Art</u> in New York City, founded in 1870, moved to its present location in Central Park in 1880. At its installation, the keynote speaker announced that the museum's goal was education, connecting the museum to other institutions with a public mission.

Metropolitan Museum of Art 纽约大都会美术馆

Understanding More about China

1. The Palace Museum(故宫博物院)

Also known as the Forbidden City, the Palace Museum is situated in the former imperial palace of the Ming and Qing Dynasties. Constructed between 1407 and 1420, the imperial palace occupies 72 hectares and has more than 9,000 halls and chambers, which is presently the largest and the best-preserved palace complex in the world.

Twenty-four emperors of the Ming and Qing Dynasties had once lived here. In 1914, the "Institute for Antiques Exhibition" was established here and it was renamed the "Forbidden City Museum" in 1925. The Palace Museum displays more than 90,000 items of historical treasures and artifacts of various categories, including ceramics, treasures, clocks, paintings, bronze, jade objects, and Ming and Qing artifacts.

2. Three Stages of China's Architecture History

Traditional Chinese architecture is based mainly on Han architecture, comprising roughly 15 types such as city, temple, mausoleum, monastery, Buddhist pagoda, grotto, garden, government office, folk public building, landscape, tower and pavilion, imperial palace, residential house, great wall and bridge. In the long process of development, China's architecture has consistently kept intact the basic character of the system. The history of architectural development can be divided into several major stages:

The period from the Shang Dynasty (17th century—11th century BC) to the Qin and Han Dynasties was its embryonic growth stage; Qin and Western Han Dynasties (221 BC—220 AD) were the first high tide of development.

The period from the Wei and Jin through to the Sui, Tang and Song Dynasties (220—1279) were a stage of maturity. The achievements of the Tang (618—907) and Song (960—1279) Dynasties were even more brilliant, representing the second high tide, which can be regarded as the summit of Chinese architecture.

The period from the Yuan to Ming and Qing Dynasties (1271—1911) were the enrichment and summary stage and the period from the Ming (1368—1644) to the early Qing Dynasty (1644—1840) was the third high tide of development.

It can be seen that each upsurge was correspondingly accompanied by the unification of the country, long-term stability, radical cultural exchanges and other social backgrounds. For example, the unification of the Qin and Han Dynasties accelerated exchanges between the Central Plain culture and the Chu and Yue cultures. The unification of the Sui and Tang Dynasties increased the cultural exchanges between China and other Asian countries, as well as between north and south China; the unification of the Ming and Qing Dynasties strengthened exchanges among various Chinese nationalities and began the exchange of Chinese and Western architectural cultures.

It can be said that unification, stability, economic prosperity, enhancement of national strength and cultural exchange are the internal opportunities for the development of architectural art.

China's architecture pays particular attention to the beauty of group combination, and often adopts a central-axis, symmetric compact composition method.

3. Chinese Garden (中国园林)

In ancient China, from the emperor down to any of the rich, they without exception all took pride in the ownership of a garden in their living space. In the garden one could hold court, entertain guests, hunt, play games, read, play chess, drink tea, chant verses, recite poetry or paint, and over the years a rich garden culture was gradually formed. As more and more scholars and garden owners started participating in the making of gardens, theoretical books on garden building appeared. An outstanding example was the book *Craftsmanship of Gardening* by Ji Cheng (1582—?) in the Ming Dynasty, which discusses the technique of creating a garden as well as garden-related knowledge, experience with garden construction and theories on creating a garden—this book has become a key for people today for an understanding of the Chinese garden concepts.

The art of the Chinese garden emphasizes the portrayal of a mood, so that the hills, waters, plants, and buildings as well as their spatial relationship are not just a mere materialistic environment but also evoke a spiritual atmosphere. The builder of the garden, through symbolism and allegories, the search for a poetic mood, the gathering of relics from all over, and the building of temples, streets and even taverns, strives to reach a realm that is natural yet elegant, combining the art of the garden with classical Chinese literature, painting and theatre, where the true essence of traditional culture lies.

Exercises

Ⅰ. Choose the answer that best completes the statement.
1. The Library of Congress is located in _____.
   A. Washington, D. C.　　　　　　B. New York
   C. Los Angeles　　　　　　　　　D. San Francisco
2. The Harvard University library was founded in _____, signalling the beginning of private book collections by the early European settlers in the New World.
   A. 1492　　　　B. 1588　　　　C. 1638　　　　D. 1783
3. Between 1900 and 1940, Latin American dances, such as the _____ from _____, were introduced into the United States.
   A. blues; Argentina　　　　　　　B. bossa nova; Cuba
   C. mambo; Brazil　　　　　　　　D. tango; Argentina
4. Saint Paul's Cathedral in London was designed by _____.
   A. Sir Christopher Wren　　　　　B. Saint Paul
   C. Inigo Jones　　　　　　　　　　D. Charles Rennie Mackintosh
5. Great Fire of London took place in _____.
   A. 1066　　　　B. 1666　　　　C. 1607　　　　D. 1620
6. _____ in London and Lincoln Cathedral are the representative buildings of Gothic cathedrals constructed from the 12th to the 15th century.
   A. Houses of Parliament　　　　　B. Buckingham Palace
   C. St. Paul's Cathedral　　　　　　D. Westminster Abbey
7. The White Tower, part of the Tower of London, was built by the _____.
   A. Normans　　B. Scottish　　　C. Celts　　　　D. Welsh
8. The Norman style of architecture was called _____ on the continent of Europe.
   A. Romanesque　　　　　　　　　B. Gothic architecture
   C. Baroque　　　　　　　　　　　D. Rococo
9. _____ means "several houses joined together."
   A. Bungalows　　　　　　　　　　B. Terrace Houses
   C. Semi-Detached Houses　　　　　D. Detached Houses

10. A _____ may have a separate kitchen, but the living room is also the bedroom.
    A. mansion   B. town house   C. condominium   D. studio
11. The Smithsonian Institution, which has its headquarters in _____, now encompasses 16 museums devoted to various aspects of American history.
    A. Boston   B. Houston
    C. New York   D. Washington, D. C.

Ⅱ. Read the following statements and decide whether they are true (T) or false (F).
1. Libraries, museums, and other collections of historical artifacts are a primary means of organizing and preserving a nation's legacy. _____
2. The Broadway musicals was probably the greatest and the most popular American innovation in music, which also became a movie staple. _____
3. The classical performing arts, such as music, opera, dance, and theater, were a widespread feature of American culture in the first half of the 20th century. _____
4. London's subsoil is extremely suitable as a foundation for tall skyscrapers. _____
5. The architecture of the late Italian Renaissance was introduced in England by Inigo Jones in the 17th century. _____
6. In the early 20th century, English architect Charles Rennie Mackintosh welcomed elaborate Victorian architecture styles rather than a more modern, functional design. _____
7. Britain's artistic output was focused on literature in the 16th and 17th centuries. _____
8. Britain experienced the full flowering of the baroque era that followed the Renaissance in Roman Catholic countries, such as Italy and Spain, during the 17th and 18th centuries. _____
9. During the 20th century, the American performing arts began to incorporate wider groups of people. _____
10. The Beatles appeared in the 1920s. _____
11. Architecture just refers to the product of planning, designing, and constructing buildings and other physical structures. _____
12. Since 1066, Norman architecture became prevalent in the British Isles. _____

Ⅲ. Short-answer Questions.
1. What are the main types of houses in England?
2. What does a typical house look like in the USA?
3. What are the typical features of Gothic architectural style?

Unit 13

Customs and Traditions

❏ **In this unit you will learn about**
 1. British customs and traditions
 2. American customs and traditions

 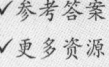

✓参考答案
✓更多资源

Vocabulary

- baggy 宽松下垂的
- bride 新娘
- chuckle 轻声地笑,暗自笑
- cleavage 分裂,分开;乳沟
- cookery 烹饪技术
- disillusion 使(某人)醒悟,理想或幻想破灭
- elaborate 精心制作的
- footwear 鞋类
- frustration 失望,沮丧;悲观情绪,失落感;挫折
- gown 女服(尤指于特殊场合穿的长服)
- groom = bridegroom 新郎
- monosyllable 单音节词
- murmur 发连续而低沉的声音
- queue 排队等候
- registrar 登记员,记录员
- sleeveless 无袖的
- tracksuit (运动练习时或作便衣穿的)宽松暖和的衣裤;运动服
- tweeds 花呢服装
- weird 非传统的,不寻常的,古怪的
- zigzag 锯齿形的线条、小径等

Key Sentences

1. If you work in an office, wear a suit. Women can wear very short skirts at work showing a lot of leg, but the shoulders must remain covered. Men must wear long trousers at work.
   如果你在办公室工作,穿西装。女性在工作时可以穿很短的裙子,露出很长的腿,但肩膀必须盖住。男人上班必须穿长裤。

2. Navy blue and grey are colours which are always right in an office for women and men. The equivalent for evening functions is black.
   海军蓝和灰色是办公室里男女皆宜的颜色。晚间活动的服装颜色以黑色为宜。

3. There are queues in front of ticket counters at railway stations, at bus stops even when there is no bus in sight, in banks, post offices and shops.
   火车站的售票柜台前,甚至在看不到公共汽车的公共汽车站,银行、邮局和商店,都排着队。

4. Never jump a queue, however much you are in a hurry.
   不要插队,不管你有多匆忙。

5. The British apologise all the time, for everything, especially for matters which are not their fault.
   英国人无时无刻不在为一切道歉,尤其是那些不是因为他们而错的事情。

6. The British avoid saying "no" for fear of disappointing, hurting or offending you.

英国人避免说"不",因为他们害怕让你失望,害怕伤害或冒犯到你。

7. There are a few subjects about which you, as a foreigner, should not talk.
作为一个外国人,你不应该谈论某些话题。

8. It is not forbidden, but the British may get very aggressive if you touch upon the subject and your opinion happens to differ from theirs.
这是不被禁止的,但是英国人可能会变得非常咄咄逼人,如果你触及某个话题或你的意见恰好与他们的不同。

9. British people rarely discuss politics except with people who are known to hold the same views.
英国人很少讨论政治问题,除非是与持相同观点的人讨论。

10. If they answer your questions in monosyllables, it means "Leave me alone!"
如果他们用单音节词回答你的问题,那就意味着"离我远点!"

11. In England and Wales there are four forms of marriage.
在英格兰和威尔士有四种婚姻形式。

12. Weddings may take place in churches or private houses.
婚礼可以在教堂或私人住宅举行。

13. Though comparatively few young people nowadays regularly attend church, most girls still dream of a white wedding, with its solemn ceremony, bridesmaids and the rest.
虽然现在经常去教堂的年轻人相对较少,但大多数女孩仍然梦想着一场白色的婚礼,有庄严的仪式、伴娘等。

14. The bridesmaids are usually the sisters, near relatives and close girl friends of the bride, and sisters of the groom. The number is purely a matter of choice but usually does not exceed six.
伴娘通常是新娘的姐妹、近亲和闺蜜,以及新郎的姐妹。人数纯粹是个人选择,但通常不超过6人。

15. In some cultures, marriage involves the formal transfer of property from parents to their marrying children or from one set of parents to the other.
在某些文化中,婚姻是指将财产从父母那里正式转移给结婚的子女,或从一对父母转移到另一对父母。

16. Once the wedding date is decided, the bride or her family sends out wedding invitations with names chosen by both families.
一旦确定了结婚日期,新娘或她的家人就会发出婚礼请柬,请柬上的名字由双方家庭选定。

17. Practiced during the Spring Festival, *shehuo* is a spontaneous traditional festive

occasion for songs and dances prevailing mainly in the countryside of North China.
在春节期间,社火是一种自发的以歌舞为主的传统节目,主要流行于中国北方农村地区。

18. *Shehuo* is also a mass entertainment that involves a great deal of performers, virtually enabling almost all the villagers to participate either in the performance or the preparation work.
社火也是一种群众性的娱乐活动,有大量的表演者参与,几乎可以让所有的村民都参与到演出或准备工作中来。

19. The lion dance is a Chinese performing art which has been perfected over a period of over a thousand years. This ancient tradition is said to bring luck and good fortune, as lions are viewed as lucky animals in Chinese culture.
舞狮是中国的一门表演艺术,经过一千多年的发展,已臻于完美。这个古老的传统据说能带来好运和福气,因为狮子在中国文化中被视为吉祥的动物。

20. Stilt walking is a popular traditional performance art for the Han ethnic people, especially in Northern China.
踩高跷是一种汉族人,特别是北方汉族人的传统表演艺术。

21. With a history dating back many centuries, the art of stilt walking has slowly developed into one of the most important folk dances in China.
踩高跷的历史可以追溯到几百年前,它已经慢慢发展成为中国最重要的民间舞蹈之一。

Warm-up Exercise

What's the taboo of wearing clothes in England?

Introduce China in English

1. What is *shehuo*(社火)? Have you ever heard of it? During the Spring Festival, what other typical performing arts are practiced in your hometown?

2. What's a typical Chinese wedding like?

📄 Text   📑 ICT

This unit introduces the customs and traditions practiced in the UK and the USA.

■ *British Customs*

■ Wearing the Right Clothes

One of the nice things about Britain is that you can wear whatever you like. You can walk down the high street or sit in the underground train wearing the weirdest clothes, and nobody will take any notice. They won't chuckle behind your back or point fingers at you.

The British are used to seeing foreign nationals in their national costumes. Even at work you can wear whatever is appropriate in your culture.

Here are some rules to follow, although they are not strict: If you work in an office, wear a suit. Women can wear very short skirts at work showing a lot of leg, but the shoulders must remain covered, and cleavage is taboo. Men must wear long trousers at work.

taboo 禁忌

For casual wear in summer, men or women can wear shorts, sandals, and sleeveless tops. In the home, many people like wearing tracksuit bottoms instead of trousers. White trainers are popular as casual footwear, especially among young people. In the evening, women can expose their shoulders and show cleavage if they wish, but men should wear long sleeves.

Navy blue and grey are colours which are always right in an office for women and men. The equivalent for evening functions is black.

Men should not wear skirts or gowns except as part of a national or regional costume, like the Scottish kilt.

In the countryside, people tend to wear old, baggy, comfortable clothes, often in tweeds or in muted colours.

■ Queuing

There's just one aspect of British life which is reflected correctly in English language textbooks abroad. The British do queue. There are queues in front of ticket counters at railway stations, at bus stops even when there is no bus in sight, in banks, post offices and shops.

queue 排队等候

Never jump a queue, however much you are in a hurry. Some understanding supermarket managers have introduced extra cash tills for "baskets with fewer than five items" which you can use if you are in a hurry (and have fewer than five items in your basket).

A special queuing system operates for multiple counters, e. g. at large post offices. There is a single queue, running zigzag across a large hall, leading to not one but a dozen or more counters. As soon as any of the counters is free, the person at the front of the queue goes there. This avoids the frustration of always being in the queue behind people with complicated time-consuming requests.

■ "So Sorry!"

The British say "please," "thank you" and "I'm sorry" all the time. They will never order someone to do something: they phrase every order as a polite request. For example, the boss will ask her secretary: "Jane, would you mind filing this pile of letters for me?" But it is an order nevertheless, and the secretary can't say "Yes, I would mind."

Protests and criticism are phrased as questions, polite and slightly apologetic. "Would you mind awfully if I asked you to move your foot? I'm afraid you are standing on my toes." If you are so inconsiderate as to block somebody's path or view, they'll say "Excuse me."

The British apologise all the time, for everything, especially for matters which are not their fault. If you bump into someone in the street because you were careless and concentrating on the shop windows, they'll say "Sorry."

If you visit someone, they'll say: "I'm so sorry about the weather. Sorry you got wet." And later "I'm so sorry I can't offer you anything special for dinner. I'm so sorry I'm not a good cook" (especially if the hostess is renowned for her cookery skills and the meal is elaborate).

■ Never Say Never

The British avoid saying "no" for fear of disappointing, hurting or offending you. For example, a group of friends discuss hiring a minibus to travel to London to see a musical. You offer to organise it. You make enquiries, find out how much the cost per person will be. "Will you come if I organise it for 2 December, and bring the money on the day?" you ask. They will all say yes, and then nobody will turn up. Some won't even bother to phone and say that they have changed their mind. You will go to London on your own and pay the huge bill for the theatre tickets and the bus hire.

If you confront your friends afterwards, they will murmur something about "had relatives to stay," "had to work late that evening," "couldn't make it," and comfort you "maybe I'll come another day when you're doing something like that again." A secure method of nailing them down is to ask for advance payment before you book, organise, or order anything for them. If they are truly interested, they won't mind. If they act offended, they never meant to pay anyway.

■ Avoiding British Taboos

There are a few subjects about which you, as a foreigner, should not talk. It is not forbidden, but the British may get very aggressive if you touch upon the subject and your opinion happens to differ from theirs. Just listen, and if asked, say "I don't have an opinion myself, as I haven't been in the country for long, but I find what you are saying very interesting."

Foxhunting—The people who are against foxhunting say it is cruel to the animals. Those in favour say that whole landscapes are preserved in their present form only because the owners use it for foxhunting. The conflict about foxhunting is sharper than about any other animal rights issue, possibly because the people who hunt foxes are perceived to be upper class and rich.

Dog mess—Should or should not dogs be permitted to lift their legs at every lamp post? Is it OK for owners to take their dogs to a children's playground, for them to use the sand pit there? Views differ, depending on whether someone has dogs or children. It may seem a harmless issue, but debates have escalated into violence. Stay clear.

Politics—The British complain about their government all the time. But they don't like foreigners doing the same! British people rarely discuss politics except with people who are known to hold the same views. If they find out that someone votes for another party, they can get hostile. If British people like you, they will automatically assume that you vote the same way they vote. Don't disillusion them. Keep quiet, even when asked which party you support and what your view is of the latest annual budget.

The underground—Don't talk to people on London underground trains. It is not done, even if you meet the same commuters day after day. The rules are a bit more relaxed on railway trains, but even there you should be careful. If they answer your questions in monosyllables, it means "Leave me alone!"

underground 地铁

■ British Weddings

In England and Wales there are four forms of marriage: by banns, by ordinary licence, by special licence and by a registrar.

banns（教堂里的）结婚预告

Marriage by Banns is the form most usually adopted. Banns must be called for three consecutive Sundays in the parish churches of both the future bride and the groom unless they both live in the same parish. They must have been resident for at least fifteen days previous to the first publication of the banns. There is a small fee for the certificate of banns.

parish 教区

Marriage by Ordinary Licence is a convenient alternative to the publications of banns. In London, application must be made by one party to the Faculty Office, where he will swear that he does not know of any impediment to the marriage such as being legally married to another or consanguineous relationship, and that one of the parties has lived for at least fifteen days in the parish of the church where the marriage is to take place.

impediment 妨碍、阻碍某事物进展或活动的人或物

consanguineous 血亲的，近亲的

Marriage by Special Licence can be obtained only for special reasons such as suddenly being sent abroad. It is never granted lightly. Application must be made in person by one of the parties at the Faculty Office. The marriage can then take place at any time and in any place, celebrated by the rites of the church, and residence qualifications are unnecessary.

rite（宗教等的）隆重的仪式或典礼

Marriage by a Registrar can be celebrated, without any religious ceremony, at a registry office. Notice must be given by one of the parties of the intended marriage, if both have resided in the district for seven days immediately preceding the notice. If one has lived in another district, notice must be given to his or her local registrar. The certificate is issued twenty-one days after the notice has been given.

■ Times of Wedding

Marriages can take place in a registered building in the presence of an authorized person between 8 a.m. and 6 p.m.

■ The Preparation

As soon as the wedding date has been decided the couple will think about the kind of wedding they want. Though comparatively few young people nowadays regularly attend church, most girls still dream of a white wedding, with its solemn ceremony, bridesmaids and the rest.

bridesmaid 伴娘

Although nowadays in Britain many young couples decide to get married in a registry office, the tradition of church weddings continues. The bridegroom may wear a smart, new suit instead of hiring or buying a morning suit and top hat, the bride may have two bridesmaids, instead of a whole fleet of maids and page-boys but their desire to make this day a real occasion full of ceremony is as strong today as it was a hundred years ago.

■ Division of Responsibilities

The rules are not absolutely hard and fast, but generally they are as follows:

The bride's parents are responsible for the press announcements, the bride's dress and trousseau, flowers in the church, the reception, cars taking the bride and her father, mother and any other close members of her family to the church and photographers' fees.

trousseau 嫁妆

The bridegroom pays for the ring and the wedding licence,

fees to the clergyman, the organist and choir, for the awning and anything else directly concerned with the service, although if there are to be orders of service, the bride's parents will have these printed at the same time as the invitations. He will pay for the bouquet for his bride and bouquets for the bridesmaids, buttonholes for his best man and ushers and any flowers worn by the bride's mother and his own mother, if they want to wear flowers—many women do not. He pays for the cars which take himself and the best man to the church and the car in which he and his bride will drive from the church to the reception. The cost of cars can, however, be divided between the parents of the bride and those of the groom, or the parents of the bride may wish to pay for it all. This is a matter for mutual arrangement.

choir 合唱队(尤指教堂做礼拜时合唱者的);唱诗班

bouquet 花束
buttonhole 钮孔,钮眼

■ The Ceremony

The parents and close relatives of the bride and groom arrive a few minutes before the bride. The bridegroom and his best man should be in their places at least ten minutes before the service starts. The bridesmaids and pages wait in the church porch with whoever is to arrange the bride's veil before she goes up the aisle.

The bride, by tradition, arrives a couple of minutes late but this should not be exaggerated. She arrives with whoever is giving her away. The verger signals to the organist to start playing, and the bride moves up the aisle with her veil over her face (although many brides do not follow this custom). She goes in on her father's right arm, and the bridesmaids follow her according to the plan at the rehearsal the day before. The bridesmaids and ushers go to their places in the front pews during the ceremony, except for the chief bridesmaid who usually stands behind the bride and holds her bouquet.

After the ceremony the couple go into the vestry to sign the register with their parents, best man, bridesmaids and perhaps a close relation such as a grandmother. The bride throws back her veil or removes the front piece (if it is removable), the verger gives a signal to the organist and the bride and groom walk down the aisle followed by their parents and those who have signed the register. The bride's mother walks down the aisle on the left arm of the bridegroom's father and the bridegroom's mother walks down on the left arm of the bride's father (or whoever has given the bride away). Guests wait until the wedding procession has passed them before leaving to go on to the reception.

■ American Wedding

In some cultures, marriage involves the formal transfer of property from parents to their marrying children or from one set of parents to the other. This formal exchange of property, known as a <u>dowry</u>, is not done in America where marriage is supposedly based on love, not wealth or possessions.

dowry 嫁妆

Weddings can be attended by just the couple or by hundreds of guests. Often the high cost of weddings might limit who attends. Once the wedding date is decided, the bride or her family sends out wedding invitations with names chosen by both families.

Unlike women in Asian, Muslim, and other countries, most women in the US adopt the last name of their husband. Today, less than eight percent do not. Some women also choose to <u>hyphenate</u> their "old" (called the maiden name) and "new" last names.

hyphenate 用连字号连接

Types of Weddings—American wedding ceremonies range from informal to formal, and religious to civil. Religious ceremonies are conducted by a clergy member in a traditional religious setting. Each of the religions has its distinctive wedding customs and ceremonies. On the other hand, some couples prefer to have a civil wedding ceremony in a commercial wedding <u>chapel</u> or reception hall, home, courthouse, or government office. These ceremonies are conducted by a judge or clerk and can be simple and less expensive than a more formal wedding.

chapel 小教堂

Formal weddings have become expensive. This includes costs for the minister, chapel or hall, the food, invitations, wedding dresses, etc. Unlike countries like China and the Middle East where the groom usually pays for the expensive wedding reception, the bride's family is often responsible for the major cost of the wedding in the US unless the couple is older and on their own. But the groom pays for the minister or the person officiating at the ceremony and for the rehearsal dinner for the parents and attendants who will be in the wedding ceremony. Some couples and parents might choose to split the costs or make other arrangements.

If a couple decides not to have a formal wedding ceremony, they might elope, a cheaper alternative where they choose to go out of town and marry, usually in a civil ceremony. Many go to the western gambling resort town of Las Vegas, Nevada, called the Wedding Capital of The World. It has 100 wedding chapels that perform over 120,000 weddings ceremonies each year, some starting at ＄100. Even celebrities like Elvis Presley and Frank Sinatra were married there.

Wedding Reception—Following the wedding ceremony, a reception is customarily held where friends and family gather to eat, drink, dance, and make toasts to the bride and groom. Sometimes the bride and groom and their parents form a reception line where they greet and thank each guest for attending their wedding as guests enter the reception room.

Sometimes buffet lines are used to serve food. Other times sit-down meals are served. Toward the end of the reception the couple cuts a wedding cake that is then shared with the guests. The cake topping is often a bride and groom figure that becomes a souvenir for the couple. Those who attend can sign a guest book that the couple keeps for a lifetime.

During the reception, an American bride may toss her floral bouquet over her shoulder to a group of single women. It is believed that the woman who catches it will be the next to marry.

The Honeymoon—After the wedding, the couple usually leaves for a vacation away from friends and family. This might last for a few days to several weeks, depending on the couple's financial and time constraints. Some parents might give the bride and groom a honeymoon as a gift. Favorite honeymoon spots are Hawaii, the Caribbean, and Mexico. Niagara Falls in New York State is a traditional honeymoon destination. Some hotels in the US have romantic honeymoon suites designed for newlyweds, but not limited to use only by them.

Understanding More about China

1. *Shehuo*(社火)

Practiced during the Spring Festival, *shehuo* is a spontaneous traditional festive occasion for songs and dances prevailing mainly in the countryside of North China. With a long history, these festive affairs are rooted in primitive sacrificial activities in which ancient people prayed for harvest and affluence with their songs and dances from "*she*," originally meaning the God of Earth, and "*huo*," literally meaning fire which ancient people believed to have the magic power of driving away evil spirits.

Scattered historical records demonstrate the existence of *shehuo* in the Spring and Autumn Period, the Warring States Period and the Song Dynasty. By the late Qing Dynasty, *shehuo* in some places had been incorporated with the Temple Fairs.

But the reasons why *shehuo* has survived and developed throughout Chinese history is not only limited to the sacrificial purposes. *Shehuo* is also a mass entertainment that involves a great deal of performers, virtually enabling almost all the villagers to participate either in the performance or the preparation work. Besides, it is also the natural outpouring of enthusiasm and love for life as well as a demonstration of talent and vitality.

2. Lion Dance(舞狮)

The lion dance is a Chinese performing art which has been perfected over a period of over a thousand years. This ancient tradition is said to bring luck and good fortune, as lions are viewed as lucky animals in Chinese culture.

In a lion dance, one or two performers wear a costume which is designed to look like a lion, although the resemblance is often quite superficial, as lion dancers were multicoloured fur and heavy masks with details in gold and other colours. The dancers move around energetically, performing a wide variety of tricks including acrobatics like jumping up onto each other's shoulders, and the dance generally follows a rough narrative, with the lion first emerging slowly and then growing bolder and capering through the streets.

Because lion dancing requires physical skills, many lion dance troupes are associated with martial arts organizations. Lion dancing has long been affiliated with kung fu, with many of the finest lion dancers coming from kung fu schools. The martial arts skills learned by these dancers allow them to engage in the strenuous demonstrations of agility required for lion dancing.

3. Stilt Walking(踩高跷)

Stilt walking, or maneuvering while on stilts, is a popular traditional performance art for the Han ethnic people, especially in Northern China. The shows are performed by stilt walkers who each have 2 long stilts tied to their feet, making them taller than everyone else around them. The spectacle is especially a delight for children and families. These performances can usually be seen during important festivals and events such as the Spring Festival and the Lantern Festival.

With a history dating back many centuries, the art of stilt walking has slowly developed into one of the most important folk dances in China. As well, it has evolved into various distinctive forms in different places in China. The most popular destinations today for viewing and experiencing stilt walking performances are the cities of Beijing, Shanxi, Shaanxi, and Shandong.

Exercises

I. **Choose the answer that best completes the statement.**
   In England and Wales, marriage _____ is the form most usually adopted.
   A. by special licence
   B. by ordinary licence
   C. by a registrar
   D. by Banns

II. **Read the following statements and decide whether they are true (T) or false (F).**
   1. One of the nice things about Britain is that you can wear whatever you like. _____
   2. The British probably are the most tolerant of all nations as far as clothing is concerned, so men can wear shorts at work. _____
   3. In the UK, you can jump a queue if you are in a hurry. _____

III. **Short-answer question.**
   What are the differences between a British wedding and an American wedding?

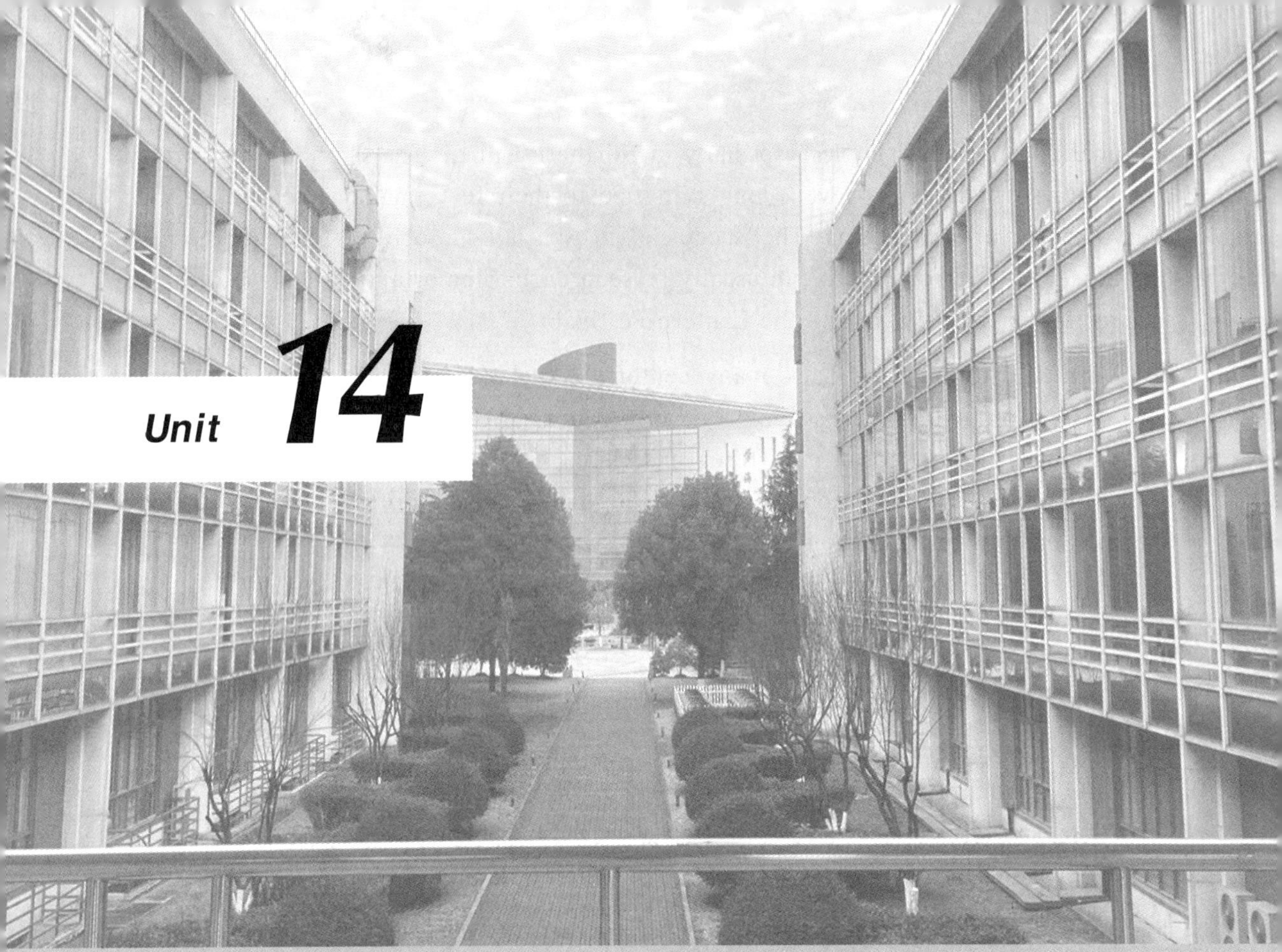

Unit 14

Educational System

❏ **In this unit you will learn about**
1. History of education in England
2. Education acts
3. Types of schools
4. Higher education
5. Life-long learning
6. American educational system

Vocabulary

- apprenticeship 学徒身份
- compulsory 强制的，义务的
- townsman 市民，镇民

Key Sentences

1. Education is an important part of British life. There are hundreds of schools, colleges and universities, including some of the most famous in the world.
   教育是英国人生活的重要组成部分。英国有数百所学校、学院和大学，其中包括一些世界上最著名的学校。

2. Education in Scotland may differ from the system used elsewhere in the United Kingdom.
   苏格兰的教育制度不同于英国其他地方的教育制度。

3. The history of education in England can be traced back to the Anglo-Saxons' settlement of England, or even back to the Roman occupation.
   英格兰教育的历史可以追溯到盎格鲁-撒克逊人在英格兰定居的时候，甚至可以追溯到罗马帝国占领时期。

4. In the 19th century the Church of England was responsible for most educations until the establishment of free, compulsory education towards the end of that century.
   在19世纪，英国教会负责大部分教育，直到该世纪末建立起了免费义务教育。

5. The theory was that "bad" schools would lose pupils to the "good" schools and either have to improve, or close.
   该理论认为，"差"学校的学生将进入"好"学校就读，因此这些"差"学校要么改进，要么关闭。

6. Most of the pupils in the UK receive free education from public funds, while the other pupils attend independent fee paying schools.
   在英国，大多数学生接受来自公共基金的免费教育，而其他学生则就读于收费学校。

7. Students normally enter university from age 18 onwards, and study for an academic degree.
   学生通常从18岁起进入大学，并为获得学位而学习。

8. The typical first degree offered at English universities is the bachelor's degree, and usually lasts for three years.
   英国大学提供的第一个学位通常是学士学位，通常为期三年。

9. Lifelong learning, also called Adult education or continuing education, is offered to students of all ages.
   终身学习,又称成人教育或继续教育,面向所有年龄段的学生。

10. Many American school children and teenagers start the day by running out the door to get on the yellow school bus.
    许多美国学校的孩子和青少年的一天从跑出门去坐黄色校车开始。

11. The school year usually starts after Labor Day in early September, and continues until the middle of June, so summer vacation is about ten weeks.
    学年通常在九月初劳动节之后开始,一直持续到六月中旬,所以暑假大约是十周。

12. In most states, teenagers must stay in school until they are sixteen years old, when they can leave early, called "dropping out," to find a job.
    在大多数州,青少年必须在学校呆到16岁。如果他们提前离开学校去找一份工作,这叫"辍学"。

13. There is no national curriculum in the USA. There can be differences not only between states, but also between towns in the same state.
    美国没有国家课程,不仅州与州之间有差异,而且同一个州不同城镇之间也有差异。

14. Private schools, which are usually organized by churches, teach religion, but public schools do not.
    通常由教会成立的私立学校教授宗教课程,但公立学校不教授。

15. The hours in the school day are broken up into periods, usually forty five or fifty minutes long.
    学校一天通常分成几节课,每节课四十五分钟或五十分钟时间。

16. Americans use the word "grade" not only for the year they are in at school, but also for the result they get for their school work and exams.
    美国人用"grade"这个词既指他们在学校就读的年级,也指他们在学业和考试中取得的成绩。

17. In American culture, most people see money as the route to success, so it is no surprise that many American teenagers work after school, on the weekends, or both.
    在美国文化中,大多数人视金钱为通往成功的路径,因此许多美国青少年在放学后和/或在周末工作也就不足为奇了。

18. June is the month for graduation ceremonies across the country.
    六月是全国举行毕业典礼的月份。

19. Many high school students who plan to go away to college need to borrow money from a bank to pay for it. College is very expensive in the USA.
    很多打算去上大学的高中生,需要从银行借钱来支付学费。在美国上大学很贵。

20. University students pursuing a Bachelor's degree are called "undergraduates," whereas students pursuing a Master's or Doctoral degree are called "graduate students."
攻读学士学位的大学生被称为"本科生",攻读硕士或博士学位的学生被称为"研究生"。

21. The Chinese Constitution requires that all Chinese children receive nine years of compulsory education, including six years of primary school and three years of junior middle school.
中国宪法要求所有中国儿童接受九年义务教育,包括小学六年和初中三年。

22. A three-tier degree system, offering bachelor's, master's, and doctorate degrees, was instituted in 1981.
1981年建立了三级学位制度,提供学士、硕士和博士学位。

Warm-up Exercise

1. What are the different types of schools in the UK?

2. What does Ivy League mean? How many universities does it constitute?

Introduce China in English

From your personal experience, make some comments on the exam system of *gaokao*(高考).

Text   ICT

Education is an important part of British life. There are hundreds of schools, colleges and universities, including some of the most famous in the world.

Education is free and compulsory for all children between the ages of 5—16. Education in Scotland may differ from the system used elsewhere in the United Kingdom. Basically, there are two systems: one covering England, Wales and Northern Ireland and one covering Scotland. The two education systems have different emphases. This unit mainly takes education in England as an example.

■ *Education in England*

The history of education in England can be traced back to the Anglo-Saxons' settlement of England, or even back to the Roman occupation. During the Middle Ages, schools were established to teach Latin grammar, whilst apprenticeship was the main way to enter practical occupations. Two universities were established: the University of Oxford, followed by the University of Cambridge. There is no clear date of foundation, but teaching existed at Oxford in some form in 1096. Founded in 1209, the University of Cambridge evolved out of an association of scholars that had escaped to the town of Cambridge from nearby Oxford after a dispute with local townsmen. The University of Cambridge and equally famous University of Oxford are often jointly referred to by the term "Oxbridge."

In the 19th century the Church of England was responsible for most educations until the establishment of free, compulsory education towards the end of that century. University College London was established, followed by King's College London; the two institutions formed the University of London. Durham University was also established in the early nineteenth century. Towards the end of the century the "redbrick" universities were founded.

■ The Education Reform Act of 1988

The 1988 Education Reform Act made considerable changes

Oxbridge（创造的名词）牛津剑桥（牛津大学和［或］剑桥大学，以别于英国其他大学）

"redbrick" universities 红砖大学。以曼彻斯特大学为首的曼彻斯特大学、布里斯托大学、伯明翰大学、谢菲尔德大学、利兹大学和利物浦大学六所著名大学。

The 1988 Education Reform Act《1988教育改革法案》

to the education system. These changes were aimed at creating a "market" in education with schools competing with each other for "customers" (pupils). The theory was that "bad" schools would lose pupils to the "good" schools and either have to improve, reduce in capacity or close.

The reforms included the following:

The National Curriculum was introduced, which made it compulsory for schools to teach certain subjects and syllabuses. Previously the choice of subjects had been up to the school.

National curriculum assessments were introduced at the Key Stages 1 to 4 (ages 7, 11, 14 and 16 respectively) through what were formerly called Standard Assessment Tests (SATS). At Key Stage 4 (age 16), the assessments were made from the GCSE exam.

League tables began showing performance statistics for each school.

The National Curriculum
英国国家课程大纲

SATS 标准评估考试。针对小学生的水平测试，共有三科，科目包括英语、数学和科学。

League tables 排名表

■ National Curriculum

The National Curriculum was introduced into England, Wales and Northern Ireland as a nationwide curriculum for primary and secondary state schools following the Education Reform Act of 1988. In spite of its name, it does not apply to independent schools, which may set their own curricula, but it ensures that state schools of all local education authorities have a common curriculum.

The purpose of the National Curriculum was to standardise the content taught across schools to enable assessment, which in turn enabled the compilation of league tables detailing the assessment statistics for each school. These league tables were intended to encourage a "free market" by allowing parents to choose schools.

■ *Types of Schools and Exams*

Education in England is compulsory, but school is not, children are not required to attend school. They could be educated at home. Most of the pupils in the UK receive free education from public funds, while the other pupils attend independent fee paying schools.

- **Categories of Schools**

The main categories of school are: local authority maintained schools (State Schools)—free to all children between the ages of 5—16; independent schools (Private/Public Schools)—parents pay for their children's education.

93% of the children in England and Wales go to "state schools." Parents are expected to make sure that their child has a pen, pencil, ruler etc., but the cost of other more specialised equipment, books, examination fees are covered by the school. 7% of the children in England go to independent schools.

- **Exams**

All children in state schools are tested in English and mathematics at the ages of 7, 11 and 14, and pupils aged 11 and 14 are also tested in science. Most young people take GCSE examinations at 16, and many take vocational qualifications, A/S and A levels (Advanced levels), at 17 and 18.

British Higher Education

Students normally enter university from age 18 onwards, and study for an academic degree. Historically, all undergraduate education outside the private Regent's University London, University of Buckingham and BPP University College was largely state-financed, with a small contribution from top-up fees, however fees of up to £9,000 each year have been charged from October 2012. There is a distinct hierarchy among universities, with the Russell Group containing most of the country's more prestigious, research-led and research-focused universities. The state does not control university syllabuses, but it does influence admission procedures through the Office for Fair Access (OfFA), which approves and monitors access agreements to safeguard and promote fair access to higher education.

- **Undergraduate Education**

The typical first degree offered at English universities is the bachelor's degree, and usually lasts for three years. Many

---

Public Schools 公学，指英国的私立精英学校。照字面理解为"公立学校"，却不表示是由政府设立的，只是表示学校可以公开招生，而不只限于特定宗教、种族或地区的学生。

GCSE 普通中等教育证书，是英国学生完成第一阶段中等教育所参加的主要会考。

A levels 英国高中课程（General Certificate of Education Advanced Level）简称 A-Level 课程，是英国普通中等教育证书考试高级水平课程，也是英国学生的大学入学考试课程。

Russell Group 罗素大学集团。成立于 1994 年，由英国一流的研究型大学组成，包含 24 所大学。该联盟被称为英国的"常春藤联盟"，代表着英国最顶尖的大学。

institutions now offer an undergraduate master's degree as a first degree, which typically lasts for four years. During a first degree students are known as undergraduates. The difference in fees between undergraduate and traditional postgraduate master's degrees makes taking an undergraduate master's degree as a first degree a more attractive option, although the novelty of undergraduate master's degrees means that the relative educational merit of the two is currently unclear.

Some universities offer a vocationally based foundation degree, typically two years in length for those students who hope to continue on to a first degree but wish to remain in employment.

■ Postgraduate Education

Students who have completed a first degree are eligible to undertake a postgraduate degree, which might be a:

1. Master's degree (typically taken in one year, though research-based master's degrees may last for two);

2. Doctorate (typically taken in three years);

3. Postgraduate education is not automatically financed by the state.

■ Lifelong Learning

Lifelong learning, also called adult education or continuing education, is offered to students of all ages. This can include the vocational qualifications, and also: one or two-year access courses, to allow adults without suitable qualifications access to university. The Open University runs undergraduate and postgraduate distance learning programmes.

■ *American Education System*

Many American school children and teenagers start the day by running out the door to get on the yellow school bus. Others walk to school, some drive themselves and their friends if they are old enough, and others are driven to school by their parents.

Open University 开放大学,是1969年成立的英国大学,学校通过广播讲座、函授与在校就读相结合的方式,致力于建立一个真正的"多媒体"大学,是世界上第一所成功的远程教育大学。开放大学提供预科、专科、本科与研究生课程。

American schools		
Age	Grade	School
5—10	K—5	Elementary
11—13	6—8	Middle (or Junior)
14—17	9—12	High

Note: grade K is Kindergarten for children under the age of 5.

The school year usually starts after Labor Day in early September, and continues until the middle of June, so summer vacation is about ten weeks. Each school year has two semesters, with the first semester from September to December, and the second from January to June. The school day is Monday to Friday, usually from about 9 am to 3 pm. In most states, teenagers must stay in school until they are sixteen years old, when they can leave early, called "dropping out," to find a job. Students are usually around seventeen or eighteen when they finish high school.

There is no national curriculum in the USA. There can be differences not only between states, but also between towns in the same state. Public and private schools usually teach the same type of courses. Private schools, which are usually organized by churches, teach religion, but public schools do not. All schools teach courses like English, math, science, history, and geography.

The hours in the school day are broken up into periods, usually forty five or fifty minutes long. When the school day ends, many students stay after school to join extra-curricular activities, which are usually sports and clubs. Some popular extra-curricular sports include basketball, baseball, tennis, and volleyball. Students who do not want to do sports may join clubs, like French or Spanish club, math club, debating club, chess club, film club, theater, student government, school newspaper, choir, photography, or ski club.

Another extra-curricular activity is working on the yearbook, which is a book of photos of every student and teacher, school life, and sport events from that year. In high schools, it is often made by a group of students as an extra-curricular activity. Everyone can buy the yearbook at the end of the school year.

When students finish middle school and begin their high school education, they are called freshmen. In their second year, they are called sophomores, in the third year juniors, and in their fourth year they are seniors. For high school students who plan to go to college, there are special courses called <u>Advanced Placement</u>. These courses let students see what college courses are like, and they can give them a good start to their college years.

Advanced Placement 美国大学预修课程

Americans use the word "grade" not only for the year they are in at school, but also for the result they get for their school work and exams. When students get good grades, they pass; when they get bad grades, they fail.

In American culture, most people see money as the route to success, so it is no surprise that many American teenagers work after school, on the weekends, or both. Some teenagers work because their parents do not have enough money, but many teenagers work to buy things they want. Some teenagers want to save money so they can buy a car or go to college. Each state has its own laws about when teenagers can start work. Without work experience, they can often get jobs in stores, hotels, and restaurants.

A very important and serious event in the school calendar is graduation. This is the ceremony at the end of the senior year, when seniors have passed all of their courses and exams, and have finished high school. June is the month for graduation ceremonies across the country. Boys and girls wear a long gown and on their heads they wear a flat hat called a <u>mortar board</u>. Parents arrive at the ceremony to watch their son or daughter receive their high school diploma. After the ceremony, parents may have a party with family and friends to celebrate.

mortar board 学位帽,方顶帽

Many high school students who plan to go away to college need to borrow money from a bank to pay for it. College is very expensive in the USA—students have to pay between \$14,500 and \$42,000 each year for four years. That does not include a room, food, books, and other expenses. But high school students with good grades, or extremely good athletes, may receive a scholarship—money given to them by an organization to pay for some or all of their college expenses. A sports scholarship has made a big difference to the lives of many young athletes by sending them to college where they can play their sport and study for free.

■ American Higher Education

Students have the option of attending a two-year community college (also known as a junior college) before applying to a four-year university. Admission to community college is easier, tuition is lower, and class sizes are often smaller than in a university. Community college students can earn an Associate's degree and transfer up to two years of course credits to a university.

Although admission policies vary from one university to the next, most determine admission based on several criteria, including a student's high school course of study, high school Grade Point Average (GPA), participation in extracurricular activities, SAT (Scholastic Aptitude Test) or ACT (American College Testing) exam scores, a written essay, and possibly a personal interview.

University students pursuing a Bachelor's degree are called "undergraduates," whereas students pursuing a Master's or Doctoral degree are called "graduate students." American undergraduate students will say they are "going to school" or "going to college," which means they are attending university. A common question one student asks another is, "What is your major?" This means, "What is your major field of study?"

■ Ivy League

The Ivy League is an athletic conference composed of sports teams from eight private institutions of higher education in the Northeastern United States. The conference name is also commonly used to refer to those eight schools as a group. The eight institutions are Brown University, Columbia University, Cornell University, Dartmouth College, Harvard University, Princeton University, the University of Pennsylvania, and Yale University.

The term became official after the formation of the NCAA Division Ⅰ athletic conference in 1954. The use of the phrase is no longer limited to athletics, and now represents an

---

community college 社区大学：主要招收学习成绩平平的学生，提供两年制的初级高等教育，程度相当于中国的大专，是美国教育体系的重要组成部分。

Associate's degree 副学士学位：一种源自美国和加拿大的学位等级。

GPA 平均成绩点数
SAT 学习能力倾向测验

Ivy League 常春藤联合会。美国东北部在学术上和社会上享有盛名的8所高等学府。

NCAA 全称为 National Collegiate Athletic Association，全国大学体育协会，由美国百所大学院校参与结盟的一个协会。

educational philosophy inherent to the nation's oldest schools, namely, academic excellence, selectivity in admissions, and social elitism. Seven of the eight schools were founded during the United States colonial period; the exception is Cornell, which was founded in 1865.

Understanding More about China

1. Education in China

The Chinese Constitution requires that all Chinese children receive nine years of compulsory education, including six years of primary school and three years of junior middle school.

Higher education has developed substantially since the founding of the People's Republic of China. A three-tier degree system, offering bachelor's, master's, and doctorate degrees, was instituted in 1981. Following a series of reforms, a diverse, multi-level system of higher education has been initiated, encompassing a full range of subjects and suited to the needs of the national economy and social development. China's institutions of higher learning include comprehensive universities and specialized universities or institutes. Most specialized programs take three years, with a small number taking two years; comprehensive programs generally take four years, with a small number taking five or six years. After completing their studies, some college graduates enter the job market, while others may pursue a second bachelor's degree or enter a master's or doctoral program. People who have received a doctorate may choose to continue their studies abroad. Students face tests at every level of China's educational system, and only those who surmount these hurdles are granted the opportunity to pursue a higher level of education. China's institutions of higher learning have produced a large amount of advanced scientific research and technical applications.

2. What's *Gaokao*(高考)?

Gaokao is the short form for the "National Higher Education Entrance Examination." This annual event may be the largest exam in the world. It is usually held across China on the same day.

Gaokao was suspended during the Cultural Revolution (1966—1976). During that decade, colleges selected students from factory workers, peasants, soldiers and other walks of life based on a recommendation system. The examination was restored in 1977, and for the past 40 years, the fierce competition has been almost the only way for candidates, especially those who are from poverty-stricken rural areas, to change their lives.

The subjects on the test vary by region. In most cases, however, they include the Chinese language, mathematics, foreign language (English by default), and one or more subjects chosen by the candidate. It could be history, politics, geography, biology, physics and chemistry.

As *gaokao* has been considered an important life-changing opportunity for the candidates, mostly the only-child of a family, parents, schools and even the whole society are making efforts to make the examination undisturbed. In some cities, there are special buses and subway routes for the candidates. Roads are blocked and constructions are suspended near schools. Medical service stands by. Hotels near examination venues are usually occupied by the candidates, as their parents want them to have a good rest during the noon break. Candidates with special needs, including those with disabilities, are given special care. The exam system, however, is not free of critics, as the fierce competition and the overemphasis on examination grades mean great pressure for the students.

Exercises

Ⅰ. Choose the answer that best completes the statement.
1. In the 19th century _____ was responsible for most educations until the establishment of free, compulsory education towards the end of that century.
   A. the Parliament   B. the Church of England
   C. the Crown   D. the Cabinet
2. In _____, the National Curriculum was introduced into the UK, which made it compulsory for schools to teach certain subjects and syllabuses.
   A. 1944   B. 1960   C. 1968   D. 1988
3. Which of the following statements concerning education in the UK is true? _____
   A. English children start school at 6 years old.
   B. State schools are non fee-paying.
   C. Most schools in England don't require children to wear a school uniform.
   D. The British academic year is split into two terms.
4. Which one is NOT a "Red Brick" university? _____
   A. University of Manchester   B. University of Bristol
   C. University of Leeds   D. University of Cardiff
5. At what age do students usually need to sit an examination called GCSE? _____
   A. 15   B. 16   C. 17   D. 18
6. Education is free and compulsory for all children between the ages of _____.
   A. 4—15   B. 5—16   C. 6—15   D. 7—18

7. The history of education in England can be traced back to the _____.
   A. Anglo-Saxon's settlement of England   B. Norman period
   C. Viking period   D. Middle Ages
8. Public school is also called _____.
   A. government-run school   B. state school
   C. private school   D. independent school
9. Which reform is NOT the reform of Education Reform Act of 1988? _____
   A. The National Curriculum
   B. Secondary education free for all publics
   C. League tables
   D. Open enrollment
10. Which statement about England's education is true? _____
    A. Children's education is normally divided into two separate stages.
    B. The history of education in England can only be tracked back to the Anglo-Saxons' settlement of England.
    C. The Education Reform Act changed the education system for secondary school in England and Wales.
    D. Most schools don't require children to wear a school uniform.

II. Read the following statements and decide whether they are true (T) or false (F).
1. During the Middle Ages, schools were established to teach Latin grammar, whilst apprenticeship was the main way to enter practical occupations. _____
2. The National Curriculum does not apply to independent schools, which may set their own curricula, but it ensures that state schools of all local education authorities have a common curriculum. _____
3. The Education Reform Act of 1988 made all schooling free for pupils. _____
4. The purpose of the National Curriculum was to standardise the content taught across schools to enable assessment, which in turn enabled the compilation of league tables detailing the assessment statistics for each school. _____
5. League tables are never shown in school. _____
6. No country-level education system or curriculum exists in the United States. _____
7. If English students want to be eligible for university, they have to take a set of exams called GCSE. _____
8. Cambridge was established earlier than Oxford. _____

III. Short-answer questions.
1. What are the purposes of the Education Reform Act of 1988?
2. What are the different types of schools in the UK?

Unit 15

Mass Media

❏ **In this unit you will learn about**
 1. Definition and role of media
 2. Government's role in British broadcasting
 3. Different types of newspaper in Britain
 4. Media in the USA

✓参考答案
✓更多资源

Vocabulary

- archive 归档
- broadsheets 大版面严肃性报纸
- circulation 发行量
- conglomerate（通过合并若干企业而组建的）大公司，企业集团
- electronic media 电子媒体
- hip-hop 嘻哈音乐
- inseparable 不可分的
- print media 平面媒体
- proceedings（讨论会、会议、大会等的）报道，记录，公报，纪要
- reap 收获，收割
- regulator 管理者
- revenue 收入
- sensationalist 耸人听闻（的报道）
- subscription 预订，预约
- tabloid 小报

Key Sentences

1. Media includes sources like print media and electronic media.
   媒体包括平面媒体和电子媒体。

2. Society is influenced by media in many ways.
   社会在许多方面受到媒体的影响。

3. It is the media for the masses that helps them to get information about a lot of things and also to form opinions and make judgments regarding various issues!
   大众媒介帮助大众获得大多数事情的信息，也帮助他们对各种问题形成意见和做出判断！

4. It is the media which keeps the people updated and informed about what is happening around them and the world.
   媒体让人们不断更新和了解在他们周遭和世界正在发生的事情。

5. The government licenses and regulates broadcasting through the Office of Communications (Ofcom).
   政府通过通信管理局发出许可并管理广播事业。

6. UK newspapers can generally be split into two distinct categories.
   英国报纸通常可以分为两大类。

7. All the major UK newspapers currently have websites, some of which provide free access.
   英国所有主要报纸目前都有网站，其中一些提供免费访问服务。

8. Media of the United States also consist of several different types: television, radio, newspapers, magazines, and Internet-based Websites.

美国的媒体也包括几种不同的类型：电视、广播、报纸、杂志和基于互联网的网站。

9. Most radio stations are commercial and profit-oriented.
大多数广播电台都是商业性的，以盈利为导向。

10. *China Daily*, established in 1981 as the national English-language newspaper, has developed into a multi-media information platform combining newspapers, websites and apps.
《中国日报》创刊于1981年，是全国性英文报纸，现已发展成为集报纸、网站、应用于一体的多媒体信息平台。

11. *China Daily* serves more than 200 million readers all over the world and is a default choice for people who read about China in English.
《中国日报》为全世界2亿多读者服务，是用英语阅读中国的人们的首选。

12. CGTN is an international media organization launched on December 31, 2016.
中国国际电视台是2016年12月31日成立的国际媒体组织。

13. CGTN aims to provide global audiences with accurate and timely news coverage as well as rich audiovisual services, promoting communication and understanding between China and the world, and enhancing cultural exchanges and mutual trust between China and other countries.
中国国际电视台旨在为全球受众提供准确及时的新闻报道和丰富的视听服务，促进中国与世界的沟通与了解，增进中国与世界各国的文化交流和互信。

14. Adhering to the principles of objectivity, rationality and balance in reporting, CGTN endeavors to present information from diverse perspectives.
秉持客观、理性、平衡的报道原则，中国国际电视台力求从多角度呈现信息。

15. *Beijing Review* is China's only national English weekly news magazine.
《北京周报》是中国唯一的全国性英文新闻周刊。

16. Launched in March 1958, *Beijing Review* reports and comments on the country's social, political, economic and cultural affairs, policy changes and latest developments.
1958年3月发行，《北京周报》对国家的社会、政治、经济和文化事务、政策变化和最新发展进行报道和评论。

17. Over the past six decades, *Beijing Review* has maintained objective and comprehensive reporting and is highly regarded both domestically and internationally for its effort to serve the needs of its readers.
六十年来，《北京周报》坚持客观、全面的报道，为满足读者的需求而努力，受到了国内外读者的高度评价。

18. *Beijing Review* is distributed throughout China and has a wide readership covering more than 150 countries on five continents. Its readers range from political and

business leaders to researchers and scholars.

《北京周报》在全国各地发行，拥有广泛的读者群，覆盖五大洲150多个国家。其读者包括政商界领袖以及研究人员和学者。

19. So far, it has established 33 branches on the Chinese mainland and set up 15 subsidiary companies or representative offices in cities such as Tokyo and New York.

到目前为止，它在中国大陆设立了33个分支机构，在东京、纽约等城市设立了15个子公司或代表处。

20. Firstly, it cultivates original content, focusing on commentaries, opinions, in-depth stories, policy analysis and policy recommendations, in order to reinforce and strengthen its content competitiveness and public opinion influence.

一是培育原创内容，聚焦评论、观点、深度报道、政策分析和政策建议，旨在增强内容的竞争力和公共舆论的影响力。

Warm-up Exercise

1. Can you name any British newspapers?

2. Do you know any American broadcasting corporations?

Introduce China in English

What media resources can be used to promote Chinese culture to the world?

Being a source of information, media includes sources like print media and electronic media. Newspapers, magazines and any other form, which is written or printed, is included in print media, while radio, television and Internet etc. are included in electronic media. Media is in charge of information, education, entertainment, advertising, and so on.

Society is influenced by media in many ways. It is the media for the masses that helps them to get information about a lot of things and also to form opinions and make judgments regarding various issues! It is the media which keeps the people updated and informed about what is happening around them and the world.

In a word, media plays a very important role in the building of a society. It is an inseparable part of our daily life. Everyone can draw something from it.

Media of the United Kingdom

Office of Communications

There are numerous satellite and cable companies, as well as independent radio stations in Britain. The government licenses and regulates broadcasting through the Office of Communications (Ofcom).

Ofcom 通信管理局

The creation of Ofcom was announced in the Queen's Speech to the UK Parliament in June 2001. Ofcom launched on 29 December 2003, formally inheriting the duties that had previously been the responsibility of five different regulators:

1. the Broadcasting Standards Commission,
2. the Independent Television Commission,
3. the Office of Telecommunications (Oftel),
4. the Radio Authority, and
5. the Radiocommunications Agency.

Ofcom has wide-ranging powers across the television, radio, telecoms and postal sectors. It has a statutory duty to represent the interests of citizens and consumers by promoting competition and protecting the public from harmful or offensive material.

Broadcasting

Television viewing is Britain's most popular pastime. The average Briton spends more than three and a half hours per day watching television, including video tapes. Historically, broadcasting in Britain has been treated as a public service responsible to the people through Parliament. In recent decades broadcasting has been opened up to market competition.

The British Broadcasting Corporation (BBC), set up in 1922, is a large public television and radio service that is primarily supported by license fees paid annually by each household. It carries no advertising and regularly transmits educational broadcasts. The proceedings of Parliament are freely broadcast on both radio and television. In 1955 Independent Television (ITV) stations were permitted and began to present some competition to the BBC.

ITV 英国独立电视台。英国第二大无线电视经营商，1955年设立。

Newspapers

UK newspapers can generally be split into two distinct categories, the more serious and intellectual newspapers, usually referred to as the broadsheets due to their large size, and sometimes known collectively as "the quality press," newspapers, generally known as tabloids, and collectively as "the popular press," which have tended to focus more on celebrity coverage and human interest stories rather than political reporting or overseas news.

The tabloids in turn have been divided into the more sensationalist mass market titles, or "red tops," such as *The Sun* and *The Mirror*, and the middle-market papers, *The Daily Express* and *The Daily Mail*.

All the major UK newspapers currently have websites, some of which provide free access. Most towns and cities in the UK have at least one local newspaper, such as the *Evening Post* in Bristol and *The Echo* in Cardiff.

red tops 红头报纸（报头用醒目的红色印刷）
middle-market papers 小报分两类，一类以《太阳报》和《镜报》为代表，面向劳工阶层的"red-tops"，另一类则是走中间路线的《每日邮报》和《每日快报》。

1. Broadsheet and former broadsheet newspapers:

Title	Published	Format	Est.	Orientation
The Daily Telegraph	Daily	Broadsheet	1855	Right, conservative
The Sunday Telegraph	Sundays	Broadsheet	1961	Centre-right, conservative
The Times	Daily	Compact since November 2004	1785	Centre-right
Financial Times	Daily	Broadsheet	1888	Economically liberal, politically centrist
The Sunday Times	Sunday	Broadsheet	1822	Right
The Guardian	Daily	Berliner since 12 September 2005	1821	Centre-left and social-liberal
The Observer	Sunday	Berliner since 8 January 2006	1791	Centre-left, social-liberal
The Independent	Daily	Compact since May 2004	1986	Economically liberal, politically centre-left
Independent on Sunday	Sunday	Compact since October 2005	1990	Centre-left, liberal views

Berliner 柏林型版式的（纸张规格为 470 mm × 315 mm）

Compact 紧凑版

2. Mass market titles, or "red tops" tabloid newspapers:

Title	Published	Format	Est.	Orientation
The Sun	Daily	Tabloid	1964	Conservative
The Sun on Sunday	Sunday	Tabloid	2012	Conservative
Daily Mirror	Daily	Tabloid	1903	Left-wing
Sunday Mirror	Sunday	Tabloid	1915	Left-wing
Daily Star	Daily	Tabloid	1978	Conservative
Daily Star Sunday	Sunday	Tabloid	2002	Conservative
The Morning Star	Daily	Tabloid	1930	Follows Britain's Road to Socialism
Sunday People	Sunday	Tabloid	1881	Left-wing

3. "Middle-market" tabloid newspapers:

Title	Published	Format	Est.	Orientation
Daily Mail	Daily	Tabloid (Broadsheet until 1971)	1896	Right
Daily Express	Daily	Compact (Broadsheet until 1977)	1900	Right
Sunday Express	Sunday	Compact (Broadsheet until 1992)	1918	Right
The Mail on Sunday	Sunday	Tabloid	1982	Right

■ *Media of the United States*

Media of the United States also consist of several different types: television, radio, newspapers, magazines, and Internet-based websites. Many of the media are controlled by large for-profit corporations who reap revenue from advertising, subscriptions, and sale of copyrighted material. American media conglomerates tend to be leading global players, generating large revenues as well as large opposition in many parts of the world.

The Telecommunications Act of 1996 was the first significantly necessary changes of telecommunications law in more than sixty years, amending the Communications Act of 1934. The Act, signed by President Bill Clinton, represented a major change in American telecommunication law. According to the Federal Communications Commission (FCC), the goal of the law was to "let anyone enter any communications business—to let any communications business compete in any market against any other."

The Telecommunications Act of 1996 美国《1996年电信法》

FCC 美国联邦通信委员会

■ Radio

American radio broadcasts in two bands: FM and AM. Some stations are only talk radio—featuring interviews and discussions—while music radio stations broadcast one particular type of music: Top 40, hip-hop, country, etc. Radio broadcast

Top 40 Casey Kasem 在1970年创立了AT40节目，所谓 AT40 就是 American Top 40, 美国的一档音乐节目。

companies have become increasingly consolidated in recent years.

National Public Radio is the nation's primary public radio network, but most radio stations are commercial and profit-oriented.

■ Television

Ninety-nine percent of American households have at least one television and the majority of households have more than one.

The four major broadcasters in the US are the National Broadcasting Company (NBC), Columbia Broadcasting System (CBS), the American Broadcasting Company (ABC) and Fox.

Public television has a far smaller role than in most other countries. However, a number of states, including West Virginia, Maryland, Kentucky, and South Carolina, among others, do have state-owned public broadcasting authorities which operate and fund all public television stations in their respective states. The income received from the government is insufficient to cover expenses and stations also rely on corporate sponsorships and viewer contributions.

DirecTV and Dish Network are the major satellite television providers. Meanwhile, the major cable television providers are Comcast with 22 million customers, Time Warner Cable with 11 million, and Cox Communications, Charter Communications, AT&T U-Verse and Verizon FiOS with 5—6 million each.

NBC 美国全国广播公司的简称
CBS 哥伦比亚广播公司
ABC 美国广播公司

■ Newspapers

Newspapers have declined in their influence and penetration into American households over the years. The US does not have a national paper. *The New York Times* and *The Wall Street Journal* are sold in most US cities.

Although *The Times*' primary audience has always been the people of New York City, *The New York Times* has gradually become the dominant national "newspaper of record." Apart from its daily nationwide distribution, the term means that back issues are archived on microfilm by every decent-sized public library in the nation, and *The Times*' articles are often cited by

The New York Times
《纽约时报》
The Wall Street Journal
《华尔街日报》

both historians and judges as evidence that a major historical event occurred on a certain date. *The Los Angeles Times* and *The Wall Street Journal* are also newspapers of record to a lesser extent. Although *USA Today* has tried to establish itself as a national paper, it has been widely treated by the academic world as the "McPaper" and is not bought by most libraries.

With very few exceptions, all the newspapers in the US are privately owned, either by large chains such as Gannett or McClatchy, which own dozens or even hundreds of newspapers; by small chains that own a handful of papers; or in a situation that is increasingly rare, by individuals or families.

Gannett 美国最大的甘尼特报业集团
McClatchy 麦克拉奇报业集团

Most general-purpose newspapers are either being printed one time a week, usually on Thursday or Friday, or are printed daily. Weekly newspapers tend to have much smaller circulation and are more prevalent in rural communities or small towns.

Understanding More about China

1. About *China Daily Group*

China Daily, established in 1981 as the national English-language newspaper, has developed into a multi-media information platform combining newspapers, websites and apps. It serves more than 200 million readers all over the world and is a default choice for people who read about China in English. The group plays an important role as a channel for information exchanges between China and the rest of the world.

Branding events conducted by *China Daily*, include the Vision China, New Era Lectures, China Watch Forum, Dongfang Fellowship, China Daily Asia Leadership Roundtable, "21st Century Cup" National English Speaking Competition, TESOL China Assembly, and inviting mainstream Asian media to China to conduct interviews, which helps improving public diplomacy and international communication.

2. China Global Television Network

China Global Television Network, or CGTN, is an international media organization launched on December 31, 2016. It aims to provide global audiences with accurate and timely news coverage as well as rich audiovisual services, promoting communication and understanding between China and the world, and enhancing cultural exchanges and mutual trust between China and other countries.

Headquartered in Beijing, CGTN has three production centers, located in Nairobi, Washington D. C. and London, all staffed with international professionals from around the world.

Adhering to the principles of objectivity, rationality and balance in reporting, CGTN endeavors to present information from diverse perspectives.

3. *Beijing Review*

Beijing Review is China's only national English weekly news magazine published in Beijing by the China International Publishing Group (CIPG).

Launched in March 1958, *Beijing Review* reports and comments on the country's social, political, economic and cultural affairs, policy changes and latest developments. It also offers in-depth analysis on major regional and international events and provides consulting and information services.

Over the past six decades, *Beijing Review* has maintained objective and comprehensive reporting and is highly regarded both domestically and internationally for its effort to serve the needs of its readers.

Beijing Review is distributed throughout China and has a wide readership covering more than 150 countries on five continents. Its readers range from political and business leaders to researchers and scholars.

4. Introduction to *People's Daily* Online

People's Daily Online, founded on January 1, 1997, is a large-scale information exchange platform established by China's largest newspaper—*People's Daily*. It is also a media and culture company with *People's Daily* at the center of its interest control.

On April 27, 2012, *People's Daily* Online went public on the Shanghai Stock Exchange, becoming China's first news website listed on the A-share market.

In addition to its Chinese version, *People's Daily* Online, as one of the largest comprehensive Internet media sources in the world, also publishes versions in seven ethnic minority languages, as well as in nine foreign languages, including English, Russian, French, Spanish and Arabic.

So far, it has established 33 branches on the Chinese mainland and set up 15 subsidiary companies or representative offices in cities such as China's Hong Kong SAR, Tokyo, New York, San Francisco, Seoul, London, Moscow, Johannesburg, Sydney, Paris, Stockholm and Bangkok.

Focusing on content as its core business, and aiming for intelligentization, *People's Daily* Online is striving to become a pioneer in the ConTech business driven by capital and technology, in a bid to enhance its influence and competitiveness.

In terms of content, *People's Daily* Online has mainly built up its business in four aspects.

Firstly, it cultivates original content, focusing on commentaries, opinions, in-depth stories, policy analysis and policy recommendations, in order to reinforce and strengthen its content competitiveness and public opinion influence.

Secondly, it has established a content operational platform that helps governmental agencies, enterprises and public institutions, universities and research institutes to manage their content and public relations, responding to the challenges brought by the all-media era.

Thirdly, it provides Internet companies with all-media, full-category content risk control services with the help of AI and generates new professions and industries, new standards and platforms via the "Risk Control Brain" platform and training services.

Finally, it has built a content aggregation and distribution platform, and aims to be a "Middle Desk" linking content creators and consumers, providing trading and technological services for the relevant parties.

Exercises

I. Choose the answer that best completes the statement.
   1. The British Broadcasting Corporation, set up in _____, is a large public television and radio service.
      A. 1912   B. 1922   C. 1932   D. 1942
   2. Which of the following is NOT published daily? _____
      A. *The Daily Telegraph*   B. *The Times*
      C. *The Observer*   D. *The Sun*
   3. Popular newspapers appeal to people wanting news of a more entertaining character. Following are popular dailies EXCEPT _____.
      A. *Daily Mirror*   B. *Daily Star*   C. *The Sun*   D. *The Times*
   4. Which of the following is NOT the feature of BBC? _____
      A. Primarily supported by license fees paid annually by each household.
      B. Carry advertising.
      C. Regularly transmits educational broadcasts.
      D. The proceedings of Parliament are freely broadcast on both radio and television.
   5. The four major broadcasters in the US are the National Broadcasting Company (NBC), _____, the American Broadcasting Company (ABC) and _____.
      A. Columbia Broadcasting System (CBS); Fox
      B. Voice of America (VOA); Broadway

    C. Columbia Broadcasting System (CBS); Voice of America (VOA)

    D. Broadway; Fox

Ⅱ. **Read the following statements and decide whether they are true (T) or false (F).**

1. Historically, broadcasting in Britain has been treated as a public service responsible to the people through Parliament. _____
2. In 1955 Independent Television (ITV) stations were permitted and began to present some competition to the BBC. _____
3. The British government licenses and regulates broadcasting through the Independent Television Commission (ITC) and the Radio Authority. _____
4. The BBC carries no advertising and regularly transmits educational broadcasts. _____
5. ITV is the competitor of BBC. _____
6. Many of the media in the US are controlled by large non-profit corporations. _____
7. The US does not have a national paper. _____
8. With very few exceptions, all the newspapers in the US are privately owned. _____

Ⅲ. **Short-answer questions.**

1. What are the types of newspapers in the UK?
2. What role is played by media in a society?

Unit 16

Economy

❏ **In this unit you will learn about**
1. The UK economy
2. The US economy

✓参考答案
✓更多资源

Vocabulary

- antique 古董;古玩
- arable 可耕的(土地)
- coal mining 采煤
- cradle 摇篮
- cutlery 刀具;餐具
- decentralize 权力下放
- denationalize 使非国有化;使私有化
- diagnosis 诊断
- epitomize 成为……的缩影
- fertilizer 肥料
- fine-tune 微调
- garment 服装;衣服
- grave 坟墓
- graze 放牧
- health care 医疗保健
- herbicide 除草剂
- impoverish 使穷困
- inflationary (通货)膨胀的;由(通货)膨胀引起的
- innovation 创新
- insure 保险;投保
- intellectual property (IP) 知识产权
- leisure industry 休闲产业
- linen 亚麻布
- livestock 家畜,牲畜(如牛羊)
- lumber 伐木业
- manufacturing 制造业
- midwife 助产士;接生员;产婆
- mixed economy 混合经济
- multiples [英]联号商店
- nationalize 公有化;国有化
- pesticide 杀虫剂
- poverty alleviation 脱贫
- poverty line 贫困线
- poverty-stricken county 贫困县
- privatize 使(某物)私有化
- protein 蛋白质
- recession (经济)衰退;不景气
- rural vitalization 乡村振兴
- sector 部门;(尤指)经济领域
- service sector 服务业
- textile 织物;纺织品
- tweed 粗花呢(常为杂色的)/Scottish tweed 苏格兰花呢
- underwrite 签名承认/担保,给……保险;签名承受,同意负担……费用/损失
- welfare system 福利制度
- woolen 毛织品的

Key Sentences

1. Like many modern developed countries, the United Kingdom has a mixed economy.
   与许多现代发达国家一样,英国的经济也是混合型的。

2. As in many modern states, the British government seeks to fine-tune the economy in order to keep economic booms from becoming too inflationary and recessions from becoming too deep.
   与许多现代国家一样,英国政府寻求对经济进行微调,以防止经济繁荣变得过于膨胀,经济衰退变得过于严重。

3. About 74 percent of Britain's land area is devoted to some type of agricultural use.
   英国约74%的土地用于某种农业用途。

4. Most farming in Britain takes place in eastern and south central England and in eastern Scotland.
   英国的大部分农业都集中在英格兰东部和中南部以及苏格兰东部地区。

5. In recent decades overfishing and conservation restrictions imposed by the European Union have caused a decline in the deep-sea industry.
   近几十年来,欧盟实施的过度捕捞和保护限制政策导致了深海工业的衰落。

6. As with agriculture, fisheries policy in Britain is largely determined by the EU through the Common Fisheries Policy (CFP).
   与农业一样,英国的渔业政策主要由欧盟通过的共同渔业政策决定。

7. Instead of being made by hand, many products were made by machine.
   许多产品不是手工制造的,而是机器制造的。

8. One sign of a highly developed nation is a large and sophisticated service sector. When a nation's economy matures, its service sector grows rapidly while its manufacturing sector stabilizes or diminishes.
   一个高度发达国家的标志之一是拥有庞大而复杂的服务产业。当一个国家的经济成熟时,它的服务业迅速增长,而制造业则保持稳定甚至减少。

9. Banking and financial services have always played an important part in London's economy.
   银行业和金融服务业一直在伦敦经济中扮演着重要角色。

10. London is the world's leading center for insurance and handles 20 percent of the world's insurance business.
    伦敦是世界领先的保险中心,处理着全球20%的保险业务。

11. The leisure industry has also been growing dynamically, commanding an increasing proportion of consumer spending.
    休闲产业也在蓬勃发展,在消费者支出中所占的比例也在不断上升。

12. Another growth area has been organizations catering to international conferences and exhibitions.
    另一个增长领域是为国际会议和展览提供服务的组织机构。

13. Ranging from advertising to architecture and fashion to film, the creative industries constitute one of the fastest-growing sectors in the UK.
    从广告到建筑、时尚到电影,创意产业是英国发展最快的行业之一。

14. At the heart of the creative economy are the cultural and creative industries that lie at the crossroads of arts, culture, business and technology.

创意经济的核心是位于艺术、文化、商业和技术十字路口的文化创意产业。

15. The economic history of the United States is a story of economic growth that began with marginally successful colonial economies and progressed to the largest industrial economy in the world in the 20th and early 21st century.
    美国的经济发展史是一个始于略显成功的殖民地经济,并在20世纪和21世纪初发展成为世界上最大的工业经济体的经济增长故事。

16. The San Francisco Bay Area and the Pacific Northwest are major centers for technology.
    旧金山湾区和美国西太平洋地区是主要的技术中心。

17. The largest sector in the United States economy is services, which employs roughly three quarters of the work force.
    美国经济中最大的部分是服务业,雇用了大约四分之三的劳动力。

18. Meanwhile, China has forged a raft of policies to prevent those who have shaken off poverty from falling back into the clutches of destitution.
    与此同时,中国制定了一系列政策,以防止那些摆脱了贫困的人再次返贫。

19. China has resolved its millennia-old issue of extreme poverty, but the Chinese people's pursuit for a better life is far from over.
    中国解决了几千年来的极端贫困问题,但中国人民对美好生活的追求远未结束。

20. The goal is to build rural areas into thriving businesses and ensure pleasant living environments, social etiquette and civility as well as effective governance and prosperity.
    目标是将农村地区建设成为繁荣的商业区,确保有宜人的生活环境、社交礼仪和文明以及有效的治理和繁荣。

21. Development is still the foundation and key to solving all challenges.
    发展仍然是解决一切挑战的基础和关键。

22. Over the past 40-plus years of reform and opening up, more than 700 million people in China have been lifted out of poverty, contributing more than 70 percent of the global poverty reduction.
    改革开放40多年来,中国共有7亿多人脱贫,占比全球减贫量七成以上。

23. China stands ready to share its experience and wisdom to contribute to the global poverty reduction efforts and build a better world that is free of poverty and enjoys common development.
    中国愿意分享经验和智慧,为全球减贫努力做出贡献,建设一个没有贫困、共同发展的更美好的世界。

Warm-up Exercise

1. What does "mixed economy" mean in the UK?

2. What role does the US government play in its economy?

3. What does service sector mean? Can you give any concrete examples?

Introduce China in English

What is China's poverty alleviation plan?

📄 Text   📄 ICT

This unit discusses two major issues: one is the UK economy, the other is the US economy.

■ *The UK Economy*

Like many modern developed countries, the United Kingdom has a mixed economy. This means that some sectors of the economy are operated by the government and some are operated by private businesses. Since World War II, Britain has worked to balance the mix of private and public enterprises in order to maximize the country's economy and ensure the economic well-being of its citizens. Historically, Britain's Conservative Party has sought a stronger private component in the mix while the Labour Party has sought to strengthen the public component. Both parties are committed to a healthy mix of both elements, however.

The public component consists of the welfare system, which includes socialized medicine, known as the National Health Service, plus government controls over business, banking, and the money supply. The welfare system provides support "from cradle to grave." The government is a major employer: public officials, the judiciary, the military, police departments, fire departments, educators, and health professionals are, for the most part, employed by the state. The government is also a major purchaser of goods, particularly military equipment.

> National Health Service 英国国民健康服务,又被称为"国家医疗保健服务"或"英国国民卫生保健"。

National Health Service (NHS)

The NHS stands for the National Health Service. It refers to the Government-funded medical and health care services that everyone living in the UK can use without being asked to pay the full cost of the service. These services include:

Visiting a doctor or a nurse at a doctor's surgery;

Getting help and treatment at a hospital if you are unwell or injured;

Seeing a midwife if you are pregnant;

> Getting urgent help from healthcare professionals working in the ambulance services if you have serious or life-threatening injuries or health problems—this might include being transported to hospital. People often refer to these health services as "free at the point of use (or delivery)." This means that any UK resident can, for example, go and see a doctor who will offer diagnosis or treatment for an illness without asking the individual to pay for this service during or after the visit. Instead, most health care services are "publicly funded," which means money has been allocated by government to pay for this visit to the doctor. Most of the money is collected through UK residents paying tax.

After World War II the government nationalized, or took over, a number of large and troubled industries. These included coal, electricity, transport, gas, oil, steel, certain car and truck manufacturing, shipbuilding, and aircraft building. Since the 1950s, the government has privatized a number of these industries, selling them to private firms. The first sales were the steel and road transportation industries. The Conservative governments between 1979 and 1996 denationalized oil companies, telecommunications, car and truck production, gas, airlines and aircraft building, electricity, water, railways, and nuclear power.

As in many modern states, the British government seeks to fine-tune the economy in order to keep economic booms from becoming too inflationary and recessions from becoming too deep.

■ Agriculture

Britain's land surface is minimal compared to many other nations, but British agriculture is very intensive and highly productive. In recent decades output has risen steadily, and agricultural labor has become more productive, due to innovations in farm machinery, biological engineering of seeds and plants, and the increased use of fertilizers, pesticides, and herbicides.

About 74 percent of Britain's land area is devoted to some type of agricultural use. Large parts of Britain, notably

Scotland and Wales, are suitable only for grazing.

More than half of the full-time farms are devoted to livestock farming—raising cattle for dairy products or beef, or raising sheep for wool and meat. Arable farming refers to farming in which land is plowed and planted for crops. Most farming in Britain takes place in eastern and south central England and in eastern Scotland.

■ Fishing

At one time the fishing industry not only provided a cheap source of protein for Britons, but it was also the training ground for the Royal Navy. In recent decades overfishing and conservation restrictions imposed by the European Union have caused a decline in the deep-sea industry. Fishing remains an important source of employment in many ports in Scotland and southwestern England. As with agriculture, fisheries policy in Britain is largely determined by the EU through the Common Fisheries Policy (CFP). It aims to protect the remaining fish stocks in European waters so that they can recover from severe overfishing. The CFP has caused some hardship to the British fishing fleet, especially through restrictions on the number of days that ships are permitted to fish.

European Union 欧盟

Common Fisheries Policy (CFP) 欧盟共同渔业政策：以资源养护为根本目标。基本内容主要包括：平等入渔原则；渔业配额制度；统一渔业执照制度；渔业资源的保护措施；减船计划。

■ Manufacturing

The history of manufacturing in Britain is unique because of Britain's role as the birthplace of the Industrial Revolution. During the Middle Ages the production of woolen textiles was a key industry in Britain. In the 16th and 17th centuries, new industries developed. These included silk weaving, garment making, and the manufacturing of hats, pottery, and cutlery. All of these operations were generally conducted in small craft shops and were labor-intensive.

In the 18th century a number of changes in British society prepared the way for the Industrial Revolution. During the Industrial Revolution new methods of manufacturing products were developed. Instead of being made by hand, many products were made by machine.

The structure of industry changed substantially in the last half of the 20th century. The coal mining and cotton textile industries declined. As coal production declined, oil production replaced it as a major industry. Motor-vehicle production became a significant part of the industrial base but was subject to severe foreign competition.

Scotland is a major producer of computers. The so-called Silicon Glen between Glasgow and Edinburgh employs about 40,000 people in the electronics industry and is the site of many overseas computer firms. Scotland and Northern Ireland are still noted for their production of whiskey and textiles, especially linen from Northern Ireland and tweed from Scotland.

Silicon Glen 苏格兰高科技区，位于英国苏格兰中部地区，被称为英国硅谷，甚至被称为欧洲硅谷，包括格拉斯哥、爱丁堡、斯特林、邓迪等地理带。

- ## The Service Sector

One sign of a highly developed nation is a large and sophisticated service sector. When a nation's economy matures, its service sector grows rapidly while its manufacturing sector stabilizes or diminishes. This was the case with Britain.

Britain developed sophisticated banking, financial, insurance, and shipping operations as early as the 17th century to support its expanding international ocean trade. Lloyd's of London, an early insurance house, began when a number of people willing to underwrite, or insure, the success of voyages gathered regularly at Lloyd's Coffee House in London to share shipping news. Lloyd's now insures approximately half of the world's shipping and cargoes as well as much of the aircraft industry.

Lloyd's, also Lloyd's of London（伦敦经营海上保险及船舶检查注册的）劳埃德商船协会

Lloyd's

An organization based in London, provides all types of insurance, including insurance for ships and aircraft. People with a lot of money can become members of Lloyd's (who are called "names"), and can make more money by sharing in its profits. But they can also lose a lot of money if Lloyd's loses money.

Banking and financial services have always played an important part in London's economy, and levels of specialization and expertise have been high. London is the world's leading center for insurance and handles 20 percent of the world's insurance business. It is also the world's largest center for foreign exchange, or currency, trading.

Several significant developments in the service sector have taken place since the latter part of the 20th century. Telecommunications has become a dynamic growth industry. Independent retailing has declined sharply as large chain stores, called multiples in Britain, have brought the advantages of size to bear on purchasing.

The leisure industry has also been growing dynamically, commanding an increasing proportion of consumer spending. In the past most Britons took vacations, or holidays, at the seashore, but overseas holidays have become more affordable and thus more common for middle- and working-class people. Another growth area has been organizations catering to international conferences and exhibitions. These organizations have been particularly successful because Britain is one of the world's top locations for business meetings and shows.

■ Banking and Financial Services

Britain is one of the world's leading financial centers.

The Bank of England, chartered in 1694, was nationalized in 1946 and is the only bank that issues banknotes in England and Wales. Several banks in Scotland and Northern Ireland issue currencies in limited amounts. There are more than a dozen major commercial banks in Britain, including Lloyds TSB, Barclays, National Westminster, and HSBC. The postal system, savings banks, and cooperative and building societies also provide some banking services.

The London Stock Exchange, one of the largest exchanges in the world, has always been a focus of international trade.

■ *British Creative Industries*

The creative industries, the term refers to the socio-economic potential of activities that trade with creativity, knowledge and information. Ranging from advertising to architecture and fashion to film, the creative industries constitute one of the fastest-growing sectors in the UK. Governments and creative sectors across the world are increasingly recognizing its importance as a generator of jobs, wealth and cultural engagement. At the heart of the creative

---

TSB 英国的信托储蓄银行。Trust(信托); Saving(储蓄); Bank(银行)。

London Stock Exchange (LSE) 伦敦证券交易所, 成立于1773年, 世界四大证券交易所之一。

economy are the cultural and creative industries that lie at the crossroads of arts, culture, business and technology. What unifies these activities is the fact that they all trade with creative assets in the form of intellectual property (IP); the framework through which creativity translates into economic value.

▪ *The US Economy*

The economic history of the United States is a story of economic growth that began with marginally successful colonial economies and progressed to the largest industrial economy in the world in the 20th and early 21st century.

Economic activity varies greatly across the country. For example, New York City is the center of the American financial, publishing, broadcasting, and advertising industries, while Los Angeles is the most important center for film and television production. The San Francisco Bay Area and the Pacific Northwest are major centers for technology. The Midwest is known for its reliance on manufacturing and heavy industry, with Detroit serving as the historic center of the American automotive industry, and Chicago serving as the business and financial capital of the region. The Southeast is a major area for agriculture, tourism, and the lumber industry, and, because of wages and costs below the national average, it continues to attract manufacturing. The largest sector in the United States economy is services, which employs roughly three quarters of the work force.

The American economy is fueled by an abundance in natural resources such as coal, petroleum, and precious metals. However, the country still depends for much of its energy on foreign countries. In agriculture, the country is a top producer of corn, soy beans, rice, and wheat, with the Great Plains labeled as the "breadbasket of the world" for its tremendous agricultural output. The US has a large tourist industry, and is also a major exporter in goods such as airplanes, steel, weapons, and electronics.

▪ Government and the Economy

Although the market system in the United States relies on

San Francisco Bay Area
旧金山湾区

private ownership and decentralized decision-making by households and privately owned businesses, the government does perform important economic functions. The government passes and enforces laws that protect the property rights of individuals and businesses. It restricts economic activities that are considered unfair or socially unacceptable. In addition, government programs regulate safety in products and in the workplace, provide national defense, and provide public assistance to some members of society coping with economic hardship.

■ Innovation

The United States is an influential country in scientific and technological research and the production of innovative technological products. During World War II, the US was the first to develop the atomic bomb, ushering in the atomic age. Beginning early the Cold War, the US achieved successes in space science and technology, leading to a space race which led to rapid advances in rocketry, weaponry, material science, computers, and many other areas. This technological progress was epitomized by the first visit of a man to the moon, when Neil Armstrong stepped off of Apollo 11 in July 1969. The US was also the most instrumental nation in the development of the Internet, developing its predecessor, Arpanet. The US also controls most of its infrastructure.

In the sciences, Americans have a large share of Nobel Prizes, especially in the fields of physiology and medicine. The National Institutes of Health, a focal point for biomedical research in the United States, has contributed to the completion of the Human Genome Project. The main governmental organization for aviation and space research is the National Aeronautics and Space Administration (NASA). Major corporations, such as Boeing and Lockheed Martin, also play an important role.

Neil Armstrong 尼尔·阿姆斯特朗,第一个踏上月球的宇航员。
Arpanet 阿帕网,是全球互联网的始祖。
Human Genome Project 人类基因组计划
NASA 美国航空航天局
Lockheed Martin 洛克希德·马丁公司,创建于1912年,是一家美国航空航天设备制造商。

Understanding More about China

China's Poverty Alleviation, a Success but not Full Stop

China has removed all remaining impoverished counties from the poverty list, marking a new starting point on the road to modernization as the country gears up to ensure the hard-won feat stands the test of time and people.

After delisting all the 832 poverty-stricken counties, the Chinese government will conduct inspections and assessments to ensure the standardization of the delisting process, the accuracy of the criteria and the authenticity of the achievement. Only after careful verification will the Communist Party of China Central Committee announce the final victory of the tough battle against poverty.

Meanwhile, the country has forged a raft of policies to prevent those who have shaken off poverty from falling back into the clutches of destitution. For instance, a poverty-relief supervision and aid mechanism was established earlier this year, focusing on those with unstable income or hovering just above the poverty line.

China has resolved its millennia-old issue of extreme poverty, but the Chinese people's pursuit for a better life is far from over. Therefore, the country has pledged to advance rural vitalization in the new development stage.

The strategy will help improve the quality, efficiency and competitiveness of agriculture, put rural construction in an important position in socialist modernization, deepen rural reforms and enhance the integrated urban-rural development mechanism.

The goal is to build rural areas into thriving businesses and ensure pleasant living environments, social etiquette and civility as well as effective governance and prosperity.

Despite the achievement in poverty alleviation, China remains the biggest developing country globally, with its per capita GDP topping 10,000 US dollars. Development is still the foundation and key to solving all challenges, including the middle-income trap facing the country.

Over the past 40-plus years of reform and opening up, more than 700 million people in China have been lifted out of poverty, contributing more than 70 percent of the global poverty reduction.

China's practice has proved that if a country can follow a people-first approach, proceed from its realities for development, and seek a targeted and practical solution, it will successfully find a poverty reduction path suiting its own conditions and needs.

China will continue to strive for innovative approaches to poverty eradication. In pursuit of this goal, a workshop on digital technology-driven poverty alleviation is scheduled next year, and many similar strategies are in the offing.

The country is also willing to play its role in the global context of poverty elimination. China stands ready to share its experience and wisdom to contribute to the global poverty reduction efforts and build a better world that is free of poverty and enjoys common development.

Exercises

Ⅰ. Choose the answer that best completes the statement.
1. _____ is the center of the American financial, publishing, broadcasting, and advertising industries.
   A. New York City   B. Washington, D. C.
   C. Los Angeles   D. San Francisco
2. In the USA, _____ is the most important center for film and television production.
   A. Los Angeles   B. New York   C. San Francisco   D. Florida
3. _____ is known for its reliance on manufacturing and heavy industry in the USA.
   A. The West   B. The East   C. The South   D. The Midwest
4. _____ serves as the historic center of the American automotive industry.
   A. Chicago   B. Boston   C. Detroit   D. Huston
5. The largest sector in the United States economy is _____, which employs roughly three quarters of the work force.
   A. First Industry   B. services
   C. Second Industry   D. agriculture
6. _____ is labeled as the "breadbasket of the world" for its tremendous agricultural output.
   A. The Great Plains   B. The Pacific coastal regions
   C. The West   D. The Northeastern

Ⅱ. Read the following statements and decide whether they are true (T) or false (F).
1. A mixed economy means that some sectors of the economy are operated by the government and some are operated by private businesses. _____
2. Historically, Britain's Conservative Party has sought a stronger public component in the mix while the Labour Party has sought to strengthen the private component. _____
3. The creative industries—ranging from advertising to architecture and fashion to film—constitute one of the fastest-growing sectors in the UK. _____
4. At the heart of the creative economy are the cultural and creative industries. _____

Ⅲ. Short-answer question.
What roles does the British government seek to play in the UK economy?

Unit 17

Social Kaleidoscope

❑ **In this unit you will learn about**
1. History of the EU
2. The UK and the EU
3. Gun violence in the USA

✓参考答案
✓更多资源

Vocabulary

- ambivalent 对某物、某人或某境况具有或显示矛盾情感的
- ban 明令禁止
- gangster 匪徒，歹徒
- lobby 游说
- outset 开始
- plague 瘟疫
- referendum 全民投票
- Silk Road 丝绸之路
- veto 否决

Key Sentences

1. Gun violence in the United States is a major national concern that results in tens of thousands of deaths and injuries annually.
   枪支暴力在美国是一个主要的全国性问题，每年造成数以万计的伤亡。

2. No official figure exists but there are thought to be about 300 million guns in the US, held by about a third of the population.
   目前还没有官方数据，但据信美国约有 3 亿支枪支，由约占总人口三分之一的人持有。

3. "I was told 'guns don't kill people, people with guns kill people.' They should not ban guns for everyone, just for those who use them wrongly."
   "有人告诉我'枪不杀人，有枪的人杀人'。他们不应该禁止所有人使用枪支，只应该禁止那些错误使用枪支的人使用枪支。"

4. The diplomatic foreign relations of the UK are implemented by the Foreign and Commonwealth Office, while the Prime Minister and other agencies play a role in setting policy, and many institutions and businesses have a voice and a role.
   英国的对外关系由外交和联邦事务部执行，而首相和其他机构在制定政策方面也发挥一定的作用，许多机构和企业在对外政策制定中都有发言权并发挥作用。

5. The European Union is set up with the aim of ending the frequent and bloody wars between neighbours.
   建立欧盟的目的是结束邻国之间频繁而血腥的战争。

6. The six founding countries are Belgium, France, Germany, Italy, Luxembourg and the Netherlands.
   六个创始国是比利时、法国、德国、意大利、卢森堡和荷兰。

7. The 1960s is a good period for the economy, helped by the fact that EU countries stop charging custom duties when they trade with each other.
   20 世纪 60 年代对经济来说是一个好时期，这得益于欧盟国家在相互贸易时停止征收关税。

8. The Silk Road was not a single road but a general name for all the passages between China and countries to the south and west.
丝绸之路不是一条单独的道路,而是中国与南部和西部国家之间所有通道的总称。

9. The Silk Road was so named because silk, which originated in China, was exported in large quantities via this route to the West. In actual fact, the Silk Road also served other functions apart from trade; it facilitated cultural and technological exchanges between the East and the West and the spread of Buddhism and Islam into China.
丝绸之路之所以得名,是因为起源于中国的丝绸通过丝绸之路大量出口到西方。事实上,丝绸之路除了贸易之外,还有其他功能:促进了东西方的文化和技术交流,促进了佛教和伊斯兰教传入中国。

10. Located at the northern foot of Lishan Mountain, 35 kilometers northeast of Xi'an, Shaanxi Province, Qinshihuang Mausoleum is the tomb of Emperor Qinshihuang, founder of the first unified empire in Chinese history during the 3rd century BCE.
秦始皇陵位于陕西省西安市东北方向35公里的骊山北麓,是公元前3世纪中国历史上第一位统一帝国的奠基人秦始皇的陵墓。

11. This tomb was found in 1983, and is known as the largest stone chamber tomb with painted sarcophagus of Han Dynasty found south of the Five Ridges of China now. Then it was officially open to the public in 1988.
该座墓葬发现于1983年,被称为中国目前在岭南地区发现的最大的汉画石棺石室墓。1988年正式对外开放。

12. For thousands of years, the Silk Road Spirit—"peace and cooperation, openness and inclusiveness, mutual learning and mutual benefit"—has been passed from generation to generation, promoted the progress of human civilization, and contributed greatly to the prosperity and development of the countries along the Silk Road.
几千年来,"和平合作、开放包容、互学互利"的丝绸之路精神代代相传,推动了人类文明的进步,为丝绸之路沿线国家的繁荣发展做出了巨大贡献。

13. Symbolizing communication and cooperation between the East and the West, the Silk Road Spirit is a historic and cultural heritage shared by all countries around the world.
丝绸之路精神象征着东西方的交流与合作,是世界各国共有的历史文化遗产。

14. When Chinese President Xi Jinping visited Central Asia and Southeast Asia in September and October of 2013, he raised the initiative of jointly building the Silk Road Economic Belt and the 21st-Century Maritime Silk Road (hereinafter referred to as the Belt and Road), which have attracted close attention from all over the world.
2013年9月和10月,习近平主席在中亚和东南亚访问时,提出了建设丝绸之路经济带和21世纪海上丝绸之路(以下简称"一带一路")的倡议,引起了世界各国的密切关注。

Warm-up Exercise

1. How many member countries does the European Union have? What are they?

2. What is the initial aim of the EU? What are the six founding countries of the EU?

3. In which year did the UK join the European Union?

4. What do you think are the roots of American gun violence?

Introduce China in English

1. What is the "Silk Road"?

2. How much do you know about the Belt and Road Initiative?

3. Which scenic spots have you been in China?

Both the United Kingdom and the United States have many social problems, such as racial discrimination, inequality of the society, and gun violence particularly in the USA. Getting to know their social problems is a way to know these two countries deeply.

■ Gun Violence in the USA

Gun violence in the United States is a major national concern that results in tens of thousands of deaths and injuries annually. No official figure exists but there are thought to be about 300 million guns in the US, held by about a third of the population. That is nearly enough guns for every man, woman and child in the country.

The right to own guns is regarded by many as enshrined in the <u>Second Amendment</u> to the US Constitution, and fiercely defended by lobby groups such as the National Rifle Association (<u>NRA</u>), which boasted that its membership surged to around five million in the aftermath of the Sandy Hook Elementary School shooting occurred on December 14, 2012, in Newtown, Connecticut.

> Second Amendment 美国宪法第二条修正案
> NRA 美国步枪协会

In the second amendment it states: "A well regulated Militia, being necessary to the security of a free State, the right of the people to keep and bear Arms, shall not be infringed." Should guns be banned or not? Let's hear what some of the Americans say about it.

"I think that banning guns would make my community safer because then the criminals would have to turn them in and the gangsters would have nothing to shoot each other with."

"Guns are a plague in the USA, I believe that they are completely wrong."

"In my opinion guns should be banned, or have very strict laws placed on them."

"... guns should not be banned because hardened criminals will still have access to them and you feel that you need to protect yourselves."

"We have a right to bear arms and defend ourselves. People who are law abiding citizens will be left defenseless, while criminals would still be armed."

"I was told 'guns don't kill people, people with guns kill people.' They should not ban guns for everyone, just for those who use them wrongly."

What are your opinions about American gun violence?

■ *Foreign Relations of the UK*

The diplomatic foreign relations of the UK are implemented by the Foreign and Commonwealth Office, while the Prime Minister and other agencies play a role in setting policy, and many institutions and businesses have a voice and a role.

Foreign and Commonwealth Office 外交与联邦事务部

■ Foreign and Commonwealth Office

Created in 1968 by merging the Foreign Office and the Commonwealth Office, the Foreign and Commonwealth Office (FCO), commonly called the Foreign Office, is responsible for protecting and promoting British interests worldwide. FCO is a ministerial department, supported by 10 agencies and public bodies. The head of the FCO is the Secretary of State for Foreign and Commonwealth Affairs, commonly abbreviated to "Foreign Secretary." The FCO is managed from day-to-day by a civil servant, the Permanent Under-Secretary of State for Foreign Affairs, who also acts as the Head of the Her Majesty's Diplomatic Service.

Foreign Secretary 外交大臣

■ The EU and the United Kingdom

The European Union is a unique economic and political union between 27 European countries that together cover much of the continent.

European Union 欧盟

❖ **History of the EU**

1. **1945—1959: A peaceful Europe, the beginnings of cooperation**

The European Union was set up with the aim of ending the frequent and bloody wars between neighbours. As of 1950, the European Coal and Steel Community began to unite European countries economically and politically in order to secure lasting peace.

European Coal and Steel Community 欧洲煤钢共同体(英文简称 ECSC)

The six founding countries are Belgium, France, Germany, Italy, Luxembourg and the Netherlands. In 1957, the Treaty of Rome created the European Economic Community (EEC), or "Common Market."

Treaty of Rome《罗马条约》

2. 1960—1969: A period of economic growth

The 1960s was a good period for the economy, helped by the fact that EU countries stopped charging custom duties when they traded with each other. They also agreed joint control over food production, so that everybody now has enough to eat—and soon there is even surplus agricultural produce.

3. 1970—1979: A growing Community, the first enlargement

Denmark, Ireland and the United Kingdom joined the European Union on 1 January 1973, raising the number of Member States to nine.

enlargement 欧盟的扩大

4. 1980—1989: The changing face of Europe, the fall of the Berlin Wall

In 1981, Greece became the 10th member of the EU, and Spain and Portugal followed five years later in 1986.

In 1986 the Single European Act was signed. This was a treaty which provided the basis for a vast six-year programme aimed at sorting out the problems with the free flow of trade across EU borders and thus created the "Single Market."

Single European Act《单一欧洲法案》

On 9 November 1989, the Berlin Wall was pulled down and the border between East and West Germany was opened for the first time in 28 years. This led to the reunification of Germany, when both East and West Germany were united in October 1990.

Berlin Wall 柏林墙

5. 1990—1999: A Europe without frontiers

In 1993 the Single Market was completed with the "four freedoms" of: movement of goods, services, people and money.

The 1990s was also the decade of two treaties: the Maastricht Treaty on European Union in 1993 and the Treaty of Amsterdam in 1999. People were concerned about how to protect the environment and also how Europeans could act together when it came to security and defence matters.

Maastricht Treaty《马斯特里赫特条约》

Treaty of Amsterdam《阿姆斯特丹条约》：对《马斯特里赫特条约》与《罗马条约》的一项修正案。

In 1995 the EU gained three more new members: Austria, Finland and Sweden. A small village in Luxembourg gave its name to the Schengen Agreements that gradually allowed people to travel without having their passports checked at the borders. Millions of young people studied in other countries with EU support.

Schengen Agreements《申根协定》

6. 2000—2009: Further expansion

In 2004, 10 new countries—Cyprus, the Czech Republic,

Estonia, Hungary, Latvia, Lithuania, Malta, Poland, Slovakia, and Slovenia, join the EU, followed by Bulgaria and Romania in 2007.

A financial crisis hit the global economy in September 2008. The Treaty of Lisbon was ratified by all EU countries before entering into force in 2009. It provided the EU with modern institutions and more efficient working methods.

Treaty of Lisbon《里斯本条约》

7. 2010—today: A challenging decade

Croatia became the 28th member of the EU in 2013.

The EU is not only faced with the dilemma of how to take care of them, but also finds itself the target of several terrorist attacks.

❖ **The UK and the EU**

From the outset, the UK's attitude to the emerging institutions of the European Community has been ambivalent. Winston Churchill considered that the UK was "with" but not "of" Europe, "associated, but not absorbed."

Twice in the 1960s, first under the Conservative Harold Macmillan in 1963 and next under the socialist Harold Wilson in 1967, the government's application to join the Community was vetoed by President Charles de Gaulle.

Charles de Gaulle 戴高乐

In 1973, Britain joined the European Community. Tory Prime Minister Edward Heath took Britain in.

In 1975, Labour Prime Minister Harold Wilson had a referendum on Britain's membership. 66% voted "yes"—to stay in the European Community.

❖ **Brexit**

Brexit is an abbreviation for "British exit," which refers to the June 23, 2016, referendum whereby British citizens voted to exit the European Union. "Leave" won by 52% to 48%. The referendum turnout was 71.8%, with more than 30 million people voting.

Brexit 英国脱欧

As of 11 pm on 31 December 2020, the transitional period for the UK's departure from the EU ended.

■ *Tourist Attractions in the UK*

■ Lake District

The Lake District is one of the nicest National Parks in England. It has some of the best mountain scenery, and as the

Lake District 英国湖区国家公园

name suggests, contains a plethora of lakes of various sizes within its boundaries. In July 2017, the outstanding natural beauty of the Lake District was acknowledged internationally by <u>UNESCO</u>, who awarded the Lake District National Park world heritage status.

UNESCO 联合国教科文组织

- **Giant's Causeway and Causeway Coast**

The <u>Giant's Causeway</u> lies at the foot of the basalt cliffs along the sea coast on the edge of the Antrim plateau in Northern Ireland. It is made up of some 40,000 massive black basalt columns sticking out of the sea. The dramatic sight has inspired legends of giants striding over the sea to Scotland. Geological studies of these formations over the last 300 years have greatly contributed to the development of the earth sciences.

Giant's Causeway 巨人堤道,位于北爱尔兰贝尔法斯特西北约80公里处大西洋海岸。由约4万根六角形石柱组成,总计8公里的海岸。

- **Loch Ness**

<u>Loch Ness</u>, lake, lies in the Highland council area, Scotland. With a depth of 788 feet (240 metres) and a length of about 23 miles (36 km), Loch Ness has the largest volume of fresh water in Great Britain. It lies in the <u>Glen Mor</u>—or Great Glen, which bisects the Highlands—and forms part of the system of waterways across Scotland that civil engineer Thomas Telford linked by means of the Caledonian Canal (opened 1822).

Loch Ness 尼斯湖

Glen Mor 莫尔峡谷或大峡谷(Great Glen)。苏格兰中北部高地议会区河谷。

Like some other very deep lochs in Scotland and Scandinavia, Loch Ness is said to be inhabited by an aquatic monster. Many sightings of the so-called Loch Ness monster have been reported, and the possibility of its existence—perhaps in the form of a solitary survivor of the long-extinct plesiosaurs—continues to intrigue many.

- *Tourist Attractions in the USA*

- **Yellowstone National Park**

<u>Yellowstone National Park</u> is the flagship of the National Park Service and a favourite to millions of visitors each year. The main attractions are all located on the grand loop road and here are some of the top reasons to visit the park.

Yellowstone National Park 黄石国家公园

　　* World's First National Park

* 2,219,789 acres (Larger than Rhode Island and Delaware combined)

* Wildlife—7 species of ungulates (bison, moose, elk, pronghorn), 2 species of bear and 67 other mammals, 322 species of birds, 16 species of fish and of course the gray wolf.

* Plants—Over 1,100 species of native plants, and more than 200 species of exotic plants.

* Geology—The park is home to one of the world's largest calderas with over 10,000 thermal features and more than 300 geysers.

* Yellowstone Lake is the largest (132 sq. mi.) high altitude lake in north America.

* 9 visitor centers

* 12 campgrounds (over 2,000 campsites)

■ Grand Canyon National Park

Grand Canyon National Park is located entirely in northern Arizona, the park encompasses 277 miles of the Colorado River and adjacent uplands. One of the most spectacular examples of erosion anywhere in the world, the Grand Canyon is unmatched in the incomparable vistas it offers to visitors on the rim. The Grand Canyon became a National Park on February 26, 1919 and was made a World Heritage Site in 1979.

Grand Canyon National Park 大峡谷国家公园,位于美国亚利桑那州北部的凯巴布高原,成立于1919年。

Understanding More about China

1. The Silk Road

The Silk Road began in Xi'an, known as Chang'an(长安) in the old days. It was not a single road but a general name for all the passages between China and countries to the south and west. There were three important passages, the oldest of which was the Southern Route passing between the Kunlun Mountain Ranges and the Taklimakan Desert of Xinjiang to reach Pakistan, Afghanistan and Iran. The other two were the Northern Route (renamed the Central Route) passing south of the Tianshan Mountains, and the New Northern Route passing north of the Tianshan Mountains. These two routes led to the shores of the Caspian Sea and the Mediterranean Sea. The two greatest empires in the world in those days, China in Asia and Rome in Europe, came to know each other through the Silk Road.

The Silk Road was so named because silk, which originated in China, was exported in large quantities via this route to the West. In actual fact, the Silk Road also served other functions apart from trade; it facilitated cultural and technological exchanges between the East and the West and the spread of Buddhism and Islam into China.

2. Belt and Road Initiative

More than two millennia ago the diligent and courageous people of Eurasia explored and opened up several routes of trade and cultural exchanges that linked the major civilizations of Asia, Europe and Africa, collectively called the Silk Road by later generations. For thousands of years, the Silk Road Spirit—"peace and cooperation, openness and inclusiveness, mutual learning and mutual benefit"—has been passed from generation to generation, promoted the progress of human civilization, and contributed greatly to the prosperity and development of the countries along the Silk Road. Symbolizing communication and cooperation between the East and the West, the Silk Road Spirit is a historic and cultural heritage shared by all countries around the world.

In the 21st century, a new era marked by the theme of peace, development, cooperation and mutual benefit, it is all the more important for us to carry on the Silk Road Spirit in face of the weak recovery of the global economy, and complex international and regional situations.

When Chinese President Xi Jinping visited Central Asia and Southeast Asia in September and October of 2013, he raised the initiative of jointly building the Silk Road Economic Belt and the 21st-Century Maritime Silk Road (hereinafter referred to as the Belt and Road), which have attracted close attention from all over the world.

3. Mausoleum of the First Qin Emperor

Located at the northern foot of Lishan Mountain, 35 kilometers northeast of Xi'an, Shaanxi Province, Qinshihuang Mausoleum is the tomb of Emperor Qinshihuang, founder of the first unified empire in Chinese history during the 3rd century BCE. Begun in 246 BCE the grave mound survives to a height of 51.3 meters within a rectangular, double-walled enclosure oriented north-south. Nearly 200 accompanying pits containing thousands of life-size terra cotta soldiers, terra cotta horses and bronze chariots and weapons—a world-renowned discovery—together with burial tombs and architectural remains total over 600 sites within the property area of 56.25 square kilometers. According to the historian Sima Qian (c. 145—95 BCE), workers from every province of the Empire toiled unceasingly until the death of the Emperor in 210 in order to construct a subterranean city within a gigantic mound.

As the tomb of the first emperor who unified the country, it is the largest in Chinese history, with a unique standard and layout, and a large number of exquisite funeral objects. It testifies to the founding of the first unified empire—the Qin Dynasty, which during the 3rd BCE, wielded unprecedented political, military and economic power and advanced the social, cultural and artistic level of the empire.

4. Western Han Nanyue King's Tomb Museum

Western Han Nanyue King's Tomb Museum houses the 2,000-year-old tomb of the Nanyue King—Zhao Mo, in Guangzhou of China. Zhao Mo was the second King of Nanyue, ruled from 137 BC to 122 BC. And this tomb was discovered in downtown Guangzhou in 1983. As the witness of change and development of Guangzhou City, the Western Han Nanyue King's Tomb Museum has a history more than 2,100 years. This tomb was found in 1983, and is known as the largest stone chamber tomb with painted sarcophagus of Han Dynasty found south of the Five Ridges of China now. Then it was officially open to the public in 1988.

Exercises

Ⅰ. Choose the answer that best completes the statement.
1. In 2013, _____ became the 28th member of the EU.
   A. Belgium   B. Croatia   C. Austria   D. the Netherlands
2. Which of the following statements is NOT true? _____
   A. The European Community was established in 1967.
   B. Britain joined the European Community in 1973.
   C. The British voted to stay in the European Community in 1975.
   D. The European Union was formed in 1999.
3. When did Britain join the European Community? _____
   A. In 1973   B. In 1974   C. In 1975   D. In 1976
4. Which Prime Minister took Britain in European Community? _____
   A. Edward Heath   B. Charles de Gaulle
   C. Harold Macmillan   D. Harold Wilson

Ⅱ. Read the following statements and decide whether they are true (T) or false (F).
1. British government's application to join the Community was vetoed twice by President Charles de Gaulle in 1960s. _____
2. The European Union was set up with the aim of securing lasting peace in Europe. _____
3. The six founding countries of the European Union are Belgium, France, Germany, Italy, Luxembourg and the United Kingdom. _____
4. The first enlargement of the European Union took place in 1960s. _____

Ⅲ. Short-answer questions.
1. What is the historical development of the EU?
2. What are the roots of American gun violence?

References

[1] Collins, A. (2001). *British Life*. London: Penguin Readers.
[2] Degnan-Veness, C. Chantal Veness. (2013). *The United States of America*. Oxford: Macmillan Education.
[3] Diniejko, A. (2011). *English-Speaking Countries: An Introduction to The United Kingdom of Great Britain and Northern Ireland and The Republic of Ireland*. Wydawnictwa Szkolne i Pedagogiczne.
[4] Dubrin, B. (2010). *Tea Culture*. MA: Charlesbridge.
[5] Else, D., et al. (2011). *Discover Great Britain: Experience the best of Great Britain*. Melbourne: Lonely Planet.
[6] Ember, M. and Carol R. Ember (Ed.). (2001). *Countries and Their Cultures*. New York: Macmillan Reference USA.
[7] Eyewitness Travel. (2011). *Great Britain*. London: Dorling Kindersley Limited.
[8] Gall, T. L. (2004). *Worldmark Encyclopedia of the States (Sixth Edition)*. New York: Thomson Gale.
[9] Gritzner, C. F. (2008). *The United States of America*. New York: Chelsea House Publishers.
[10] Hall, C. (2001). *Living & Working in Britain: How to study, work and settle in the UK (2nd edition)*. Oxford: How To Books Ltd.
[11] Johnson, L. (2012). *What Foreigners Need to Know about America from A to Z: How to understand crazy American culture, people, government, business, language and more*. Los Angeles: A to Z Publishing.
[12] Li, Y. X. (2005). Culture and Language. *US-China Foreign Language*, Volume 3.
[13] Ong, S. C. (2008). *China Condensed: 5000 years of history and culture*. Singapore: Marshall Cavendish Editions.
[14] Praill, A. (1998). *United Kingdom: 100 questions answered*. London: Foreign & Commonwealth Office.
[15] Rabley, S. (1996). *Customs and Traditions in Britain*. London: Addison Wesley Longman Limited.
[16] Rabley, S. (1996). *Customs and Traditions in Britain*. London: Longman Structural Readers.
[17] Roberts, J. (2010). *Chinese Mythology A to Z (Second Edition)*. New York: Chelsea House.
[18] Roberts, J. A. G. (2002). *China to Chinatown: Chinese food in the west*. London: Reaktion Books Ltd.
[19] Saxon, M. (2007). *An American's Guide to Doing Business in China*. Massachusetts: Adams Media.
[20] Shearer, B. F. (2008). *Culture and Customs of the United States*. London: Greenwood Press.
[21] Shearer, B. F. (2008). *Culture and Customs of the United States (Volume 1 Customs and Society)*. Connecticut: Greenwood Press.

[22] Tsuei, W. (1989). *Roots of Chinese Culture and Medicine*. CA: Chinese Culture Books Co.
[23] Walshe, I. Khimunina, and N. Konon. (2005). *Great Britain: Customs and traditions*. St.-Petersburg: Anthology Publishers.
[24] Yang, L. H., An Deming, Jessica Anderson Turner. (2005). *Handbook of Chinese Mythology*. California: ABC-CLIO, Inc.
[25] Yu, L. (2002). *Cooking the Chinese Way*. Minneapolis: Lerner Publications Company.
[26] 胡文仲. 文化与交际. 北京: 外语教学与研究出版社, 1994.
[27] 楼庆西. 中国园林. 张蕾, 于红译. 北京: 五洲传播出版社, 2003.
[28] 沈光煜, 浩瀚用英语说中国: 文明史迹(Introduce China in English: History). 北京: 科学技术文献出版社, 2008.